Research for Policy

Studies by the Netherlands Council for Government Policy

Series Editors
J. E. J. (Corien) Prins, WRR, Scientific Council for Government Policy
The Hague, Zuid-Holland, The Netherlands
F. W. A. (Frans) Brom, WRR, Scientific Council for Government Policy
The Hague, Zuid-Holland, The Netherlands

The Netherlands Scientific Council for Government Policy (WRR) is an independent strategic advisory body for government policy in the Netherlands. It advises the Dutch government and Parliament on long-term strategic issues that are of great importance for society. The WRR provides science-based advice aimed at: opening up new perspectives and directions, changing problem definitions, setting new policy goals, investigating new resources for problem-solving and enriching the public debate.

The studies of the WRR do not focus on one particular policy area, but on cross-cutting issues that affect future policymaking in multiple domains. A long-term perspective complements the day-to-day policymaking, which often concentrates on issues that dominate today's policy agenda.

The WRR consists of a Council and an academic staff who work closely together in multidisciplinary project teams. Council members are appointed by the King, and hold academic chairs at universities, currently in fields as diverse as economics, sociology, law, public administration and governance, health and water management. The WRR determines its own work programme, as well as the content of its publications. All its work is externally reviewed before publication.

The Research for Policy Series

In this series, we publish internationally relevant studies of the Netherlands Scientific Council for Government Policy. Many of the cross-cutting issues that affect Dutch policymaking, also challenge other Western countries or international bodies. By publishing these studies in this international open access scientific series, we hope that our analyses and insights can contribute to the policy debate in other countries.

About the Editors

Corien Prins is Chair of the WRR and Professor of Law and Information Technology at Tilburg Law School (Tilburg University).

Frans Brom is Council secretary and director of the WRR office. He also is Professor of Normativity of Scientific Policy Advice at the Ethics Institute of Utrecht University.

More information about this series at http://www.springer.com/series/16390

Monique Kremer • Robert Went
Godfried Engbersen

Better Work

The Impact of Automation, Flexibilization and Intensification of Work

Monique Kremer
Netherlands Scientific Council for
Government Policy (WRR)
The Hague, The Netherlands

Robert Went
Netherlands Scientific Council for
Government Policy (WRR)
The Hague, The Netherlands

Godfried Engbersen
Netherlands Scientific Council for
Government Policy (WRR)
The Hague, The Netherlands

ISSN 2662-3684   ISSN 2662-3692   (electronic)
Research for Policy
ISBN 978-3-030-78681-6   ISBN 978-3-030-78682-3   (eBook)
https://doi.org/10.1007/978-3-030-78682-3

This Springer imprint is published by the registered company Springer Nature Switzerland AG
The registered company address is: Gewerbestrasse 11, 6330 Cham, Switzerland

Foreword

This book is an adapted translation of a report on the quality of work published by the Netherlands Scientific Council for Government Policy (WRR). In addition to its three named authors, Arnoud Boot, Djurre Das, Patricia van Echtelt, André Knottnerus and trainees Sam van Dijck, Willem van den Hoogen, Youssra Ouahabi, Anne van der Put, Janneke Rooijakkers and Robin Simonse contributed to the text.

The work draws on scientific research, reviews and evaluations, policy reports, working visits, and conversations with academics, policymakers and stakeholders including employers, employees and the self-employed. It further draws on the presentations, expert meetings and discussions around the WRR publications *Mastering the Robot* and *For the Sake of Security*.

The professional portraits in this book make use of pseudonyms but are based on real people and their working days. They were compiled by Jelle van der Meer, Djurre Das, Patricia van Echtelt, Monique Kremer and Robin Simonse.

The authors wish to thank Paul de Beer, Bernard ter Haar, Peter van Lieshout, Janneke Plantenga, Frank Pot and Rob Witjes for critically reviewing and commenting on draft texts.

The Hague, The Netherlands   Monique Kremer
                                                                Robert Went
                                                          Godfried Engbersen

Contents

Chapter 1
Introduction

Max is a truck driver. He climbs into the cab of his truck between 5 and 6 am each day. When he arrives at a glass factory in Limburg at around 11 am, he must first wait for another truck to unload. Pausing the meter above his head, Max uses this time to work off half an hour of his break. Drivers must take a 45-min break for each 4.5 h they spend behind the wheel; they otherwise risk being fined. But for Max there is no rest. He uses this time to clean the truck's tires, to loosen the tarpaulin and to fill in forms. While the much-touted self-driving truck may be safer, Max does not fear for his job in the short term. The individual loads and routes, combined with loading, unloading and other essential tasks, will make automating everything difficult. "Even if it comes to that, you'll still need someone to check the machine."

Bouchra is a homecare worker. She begins her daily rounds at 7.30 am. She can see on her phone who her next clients are and how much time she has with each: 15 min, support stockings for Mrs. A; 35 min, showering Mr. C. But you must never let clients notice that you are watching the clock, she says. No one likes that. Bouchra must deal with people with all kinds of health issues, mental as well as physical. "You shouldn't do it for the money", she says. "It's for the heart." Bouchra is delighted that she recently received a permanent contract, which has finally given her a sense of "stability and security". "Maybe I can buy a house now."

Max and Bouchra's working days provide us with windows on two common professions. They also highlight three major developments in the world of work with repercussions for workers, businesses and institutions in the Netherlands and beyond:

- *Automation*: new possibilities created by robots and artificial intelligence have far-reaching consequences for the nature and amount of work people do.
- *Flexibilization*: although the rise of flexible contracts in the labour market has created employment, it also means job and income insecurity for workers and their families.

© The Author(s) 2021
M. Kremer et al., *Better Work*, Research for Policy,
https://doi.org/10.1007/978-3-030-78682-3_1

– *Intensification*: having to work more intensively, faster or under greater emotional stress places heavier demands on workers, in the workplace as well as at home.

The central question of this book is how the automation, flexibilization and intensification of labour are affecting the quality of our working lives. *Good work for everyone who can and wants to work*, we argue, is of urgent concern for governments, public institutions, businesses and organizations representing workers and employers. *Good work* is important for both individuals and for overall prosperity – for the economy to take full advantage of the possibilities offered by new technologies, and for society so that everyone can participate.

1.1   Three Major Developments: Automation, Flexibilization and Intensification

While the future of work has received ample attention from academics, governments, citizens and civil society organizations,[1] most studies focus on two developments: the emergence and application of new technologies and the rise of the flexible labour market. This book covers these two developments as well, and adds a third: the intensification of work. We introduce them in turn below.

1.1.1   Automation: Robots, Cobots and Algorithms

The first development is the emergence of technologies that allow the digitization and robotization of labour, with far-reaching consequences for the scope and nature of work. Erik Brynjolfsson and Andrew McAfee[2] argue that we have entered the "Second Machine Age" in which it is possible to automate not only physical but also intellectual tasks.[3] This is due to growing computing power, improved sensors, big data, the use of algorithms (artificial intelligence), output technology such as 3D printers, robots and "cobots" – collaborative robots that work together with people. New technologies also enable platforms such as Uber and Airbnb to act as online intermediaries between the providers of work and individuals willing to carry it out.

---

[1] The German government's white paper *Future of Work 4.0: Reimagining Work* (Federal Ministry of Labour and Social Affairs, 2017), the UK government's *The Future of Work: Jobs and Skills in 2030* (UKCES, 2014) and the Nordic Council of Ministers' *The Nordic Future of Work* (Nordic Council of Ministers, 2018) are but a few examples.

[2] Brynjolfsson and McAfee (2014).

[3] See also Baldwin (2019).

Although the gig economy[4] remains in its infancy in the Netherlands – involving 34,000 people or just 0.4% of the working population[5] – it is already posing fundamental questions about the position of workers and the quality of work. What does it mean to have an algorithm as your boss? Who is responsible for Uber drivers or Deliveroo riders who become incapacitated?

Discussion about these new technologies has evolved in recent years, with wild speculation about millions of evaporating jobs giving way to more nuanced and realistic appraisals. Fears of a robot apocalypse in the foreseeable future have proven unfounded, with some reports even predicting a shortage of human workers able to do all the new work created by new technology. For the most part, people look set to share their workspaces with robots and algorithms. Still, many jobs will change under their influence – as will the demands placed upon workers.

It may be a cliché, but new technological possibilities create both opportunities and threats (see Fig. 1.1). Will robots in the workplace leave humans side-lined and disempowered? Or will new technologies lead to more interesting tasks for humans? How we apply new technology is not a given. Technology does not just happen to us; there is room for human agency and decision-making.

1.1.2 Flexibilization of Work

The second development changing the world of work is the decline of permanent contracts and the rise of flexible work. While employment levels in the Netherlands were rising before the Covid-19 pandemic, the country is a European leader in the use of temporary contracts. The proportion of the self-employed – freelances and sole traders, officially classified as "self-employed persons without staff" – is high, twice that of Germany. Although the United Kingdom also has high rates of self-employment, fewer workers are on temporary contracts (see Figs. 1.2 and 1.3). The Organization for Economic Cooperation and Development in a 2019 report voiced its concerns about the extent of labour flexibilization in the Netherlands. On average, the OECD claims, "job quality tends to be lower among non-standard workers… and non-standard work results in significant inequalities between workers".[6]

While there were "only" one million flexible workers in the Netherlands 15 years ago, their numbers surpassed two million in 2018 when Statistics Netherlands (CBS) recorded 985,000 temporary employment contracts, 556,000 on-call and casual workers, 308,000 agency workers and 149,000 "unspecified hours" contracts. An additional 1.1 million people were self-employed. Adding these categories together, 36% of the active workforce in 2018 no longer had a permanent contract (see Chap.

---

[4] "In the gig economy, people are hired and paid per individual job (taxi ride, meal delivery, cleaning session, repair). The platform then charges a commission for each agreed job it has mediated" (Frenken & Van Slageren, 2018).

[5] SEO (2018).

[6] OECD (2019a: 35).

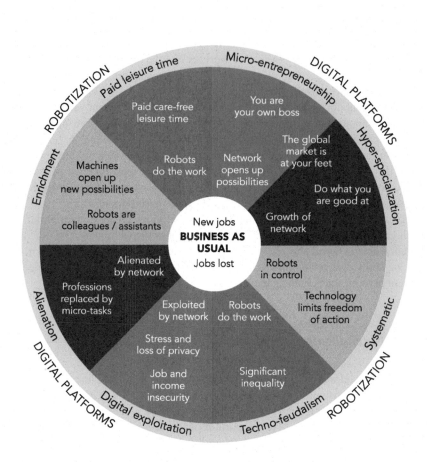

Fig. 1.1 Robots and platforms: opportunities and threats
Source: Kool & Van, Est, 2015

3, Fig. 3.1). Almost everyone in the Netherlands is now familiar with the uncertainty of flexible work, either personally or through a colleague, partner, neighbour or child.

This uncertainty often means that people cannot or dare not start a family or find a home of their own. Almost no one chooses a temporary job if a permanent position is available. On the other hand, many self-employed individuals – this is the positive side of labour flexibilization – are happy with their work and are less at risk of burn-out.[7] It has also become easier for people to switch between positions over the course of their careers, moving for instance from a temporary job into a full-time position and then reverting to part-time to take on freelance assignments. This "hybridization" of work means that people can simultaneously occupy several

---

[7] TNO (2019).

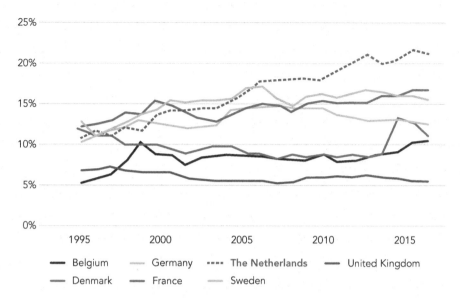

Fig. 1.2 Temporary employees as a percentage of all employees in the Netherlands and other European countries, 1998–2018
Source: Eurostat (Labour Force Survey)

different positions in the labour market or change course over their careers to accommodate their family lives and care-giving responsibilities.

Attitudes towards flexible labour are changing in the Netherlands. When the self-employed are discussed in policy texts, ornithological metaphors abound.[8] A few years ago, the freelance worker was a "free bird" or – due to their supposed prowess at innovation – "the goose that lays the golden eggs". But more recently, they have become the "cuckoo in the nest", exerting unfair competitive pressure. No bird represents them all; the self-employed flock is diverse in its plumage. But although most self-employed individuals claim to be satisfied with their work,[9] only some can spread their wings financially. Many are scratching out a living near the poverty line.

Criticism of temporary work is mounting. The Netherlands Bureau for Economic Policy Analysis points to unfair competition and increasing inequalities caused by labour market flexibilization[10] while the OECD has called on the Netherlands to rein in tax incentives for flexible work.[11] Critics argue that flexible work should no

---

[8] See, for example, the introduction to the Dutch interdepartmental policy study on "self-employed persons without staff" (Rijksoverheid, 2015).

[9] Eighty-one percent of self-employed individuals are satisfied with their work, compared with 79% of people with permanent employment contracts (CBS, 2017b).

[10] CPB (2015).

[11] OECD (2018a).

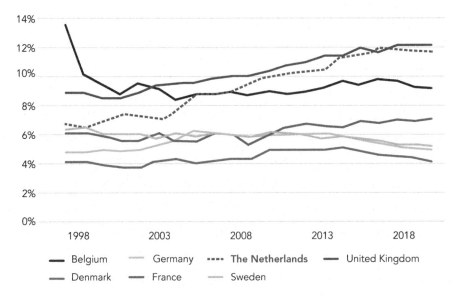

Fig. 1.3 Self-employed individuals as a percentage of all employees in the Netherlands and other European countries, 1998–2018
Source: Eurostat (Labour Force Survey)

longer be seen as inherent to business operations but as a means to cope with peaks and sickness – and only when it suits the nature of the work.[12]

The OECD concludes that the flexibilization of the labour market alongside declining trade union membership has undermined the bargaining power of workers.[13] While employees on personalized contracts can still cause collective embarrassment – and new forms of solidarity and action are emerging in the platform economy and among freelance workers[14] – individualized work is not conducive to collective bargaining. If all workers strive for individualized contracts, there will be little collective action. With platform companies, flexible jobs and self-employment, the traditional relationship of mutual responsibility binding employer and employee is no longer self-evident. It necessitates a thorough review of who is responsible for the risks and necessary investments in the new world of work.

---

[12] See also Kremer et al. (2017b).

[13] OECD (2018a); see also AWVN (2018).

[14] See van der Meer (2017), Vandaele (2018).

1.1.3 Intensification of Work

The third trend is the intensification of work – the change in its pace and nature. Consider home care workers who have less time with each client although many have complex problems, IT system administrators who must complete all their reports as a matter of urgency, and primary school teachers who now have many additional non-teaching tasks such as administration and catering to children with specific needs, not to mention their increasingly vocal parents.[15] In recent decades, both men and women in the Netherlands have been working longer and longer hours (Chap. 5). And their work has become more intensive.

What does the intensification of work look like in practice? We distinguish between two forms. In its narrow, quantitative definition, the intensification of work means that people have to do more work in the same allotted time.[16] The Netherlands Organization for Applied Scientific Research finds that it creeps in slowly and insidiously: in 2008, some 34% of the workforce said they "often" or "always" had to work fast to complete their allotted tasks in time; by 2018, it was 38% (see Fig. 1.4).[17] While excessive workloads have recently become a focal point of dissatisfaction in the Dutch public sector, the problem does not end there. The latest collective agreement for the security industry also includes reduced working hours to ease the burden on security guards. Many employers now see combating excessive pressure from work as their number one priority.[18] More and more people are taking work home or putting in overtime because they cannot finish their tasks during normal working hours.[19]

The intensification of work is a broader issue than time alone. The *nature* of work has changed as well, with more workers having to more often deal with clients, customers and colleagues. A growing number of people thus experience work as more emotionally demanding (10.7% in 2018 versus 9.4% in 2007; Fig. 1.4). While professionals in education and healthcare suffer the most, a broad spectrum of workers report greater emotional strain – from the ICT systems administrator who has to juggle conflicting demands to the security guard facing an increasingly aggressive public.[20]

Working intensively is not necessarily a problem; it can make jobs more varied and challenging.[21] But if it goes too far or lasts for too long, it can threaten the well-being of workers and their families.[22] Whether workers are able to cope largely

---

[15] van den Groenendaal et al. (2020).

[16] Korunka and Kubicek (2017).

[17] Houtman et al. (2020).

[18] van Echtelt et al. (2019b).

[19] Not in table. van Echtelt et al. (2016), see Chap. 5.

[20] van den Groenendaal et al. (2020). This working paper was commissioned by the WRR for the report underlying this book.

[21] See, for example, Johnson et al. (2018).

[22] See also Fried and Heinemeier Hansson (2018).

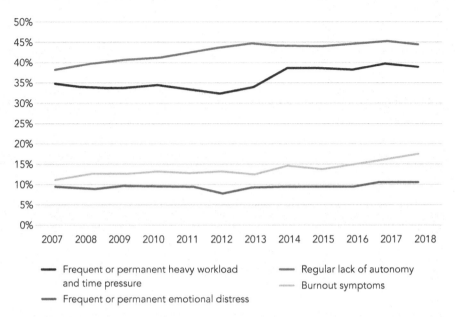

Fig. 1.4 Trends in the intensification of work, autonomy and burnout symptoms, 2007–2018
Source: NEA 2007–2018 (TNO/CBS), Houtman et al. (2020)

depends on the support they receive from managers and colleagues, including the extent to which they are able to organize their own tasks. Although more and more people in the Netherlands are educated to higher levels, autonomy at work is declining (Fig. 1.4) – a contributing factor to the rising incidence of burnout. Although the intensity of work has long been a focus of Dutch labour policy, it now seems to be taking a higher toll than ever before.

While new technologies can intensify work – in for example just-in-time manufacturing[23] – it is also a product of the shift towards the service economy, which puts a premium on social skills and teamwork.[24] In the words of Amy Edmondson: "few individuals simply do their work and then hand the output over to other people who do their work, in a linear, sequential fashion. Instead most work requires people to talk to each other to sort out shifting interdependencies. Nearly everything we value in the modern economy is the result of decisions and actions that are interdependent and therefore benefit from effective teamwork."[25] As individual employees have more and varied tasks, cooperation in the workplace becomes necessary. While this

---

[23] For example, the parcel service DHL in Bergen op Zoom has been experimenting with "smart glasses" that project the employee's assignments onto the lens. Productivity has increased by 10%, meaning that staff must move more items in the same time. The staff council has stipulated that working in this way must be limited to no more than 6 h a day (Heuts 2017).

[24] van den Berg et al. (2018).

[25] Edmondson (2019).

can make work more interesting,[26] it also demands much from the working person as a colleague.

Technological developments are also blurring the boundaries between work and private life. More and more people are reporting that they can be called in at any moment, including on weekends and holidays; others feel compelled to check e-mail outside of their formal working hours. We will examine the causes and consequences of this intensification of work and what can be done to counter it.

1.2 Better Work as a Societal Mission

The automation, flexibilization and intensification of work have consequences for the amount of work people do and *who* participates in the paid workforce. Paid work for all has been a central Dutch policy goal since the 1990s.[27] The European Commission has likewise sought to increase employment levels across the European Union, with the Lisbon Strategy in 2000 proclaiming a target employment rate of 75% by 2020. This target has long been achieved in the Netherlands, which now has one of the highest levels of employment in Europe. In the fourth quarter of 2019, some 316,000 people in the Netherlands were registered as unemployed, amounting to 3.4% of the workforce (seasonally adjusted).

Although the Netherlands has created many new jobs in recent decades, there is still not work for everyone. Many remain side-lined in the labour market, including 1.6 million people on benefits; while not all can work, one million would like to work or work more. This group includes people with occupational disabilities, whose participation in the workforce actually fell between 2003 and 2017, from 45.6% to 38.2% (Chap. 6). This is in part a side-effect of the Netherlands' intensive, high-productivity economy, which excludes less productive workers. That many people are side-lined in this way has major repercussions. A job is not only a set of tasks; employment provides people with income, self-esteem and the feeling that they are part of society.

This involuntary side-lining has negative consequences for the economy and society. The economy grows when productivity increases, when we work more hours or add more value per hour of labour. If people who wish to work are prevented from doing so without good reason, we all lose out. This is why the WRR in its 2013 report *Towards a Learning Economy*[28] emphasized that *everyone* is needed to help build the economy – the more so because demographic changes will likely lead to structural labour shortages in the future.

---

[26] See, for example, the study of "dirty work" by Deery et al. (2019).

[27] The WRR report *Work in Perspective* made an important contribution towards this (WRR, 1990).

[28] WRR (2013a). A summary in English can be found at: https://english.wrr.nl/publications/reports/2013/11/04/towards-a-learning-economy

The slogan of Dutch labour market policies since the 1990s – "work, work, work" – needs updating, to focus on the *quality* of work. But what constitutes good work? Although perceptions here have changed as educational levels have risen and women have entered the paid workforce, we can distil from the sociological, economic and psychological literature and from international comparative studies[29] three basic conditions for good work: (1) control over income, an appropriate wage and income security; (2) control over work, sufficient autonomy and social support in the workplace[30]; and (3) control in life, good work-life balance. If work is accompanied by constant insecurity, we cannot describe it as good. The same applies when people have no control over their working lives, or if they have lost their work-life balance.

The automation, flexibilization and intensification of labour potentially have major consequences for the quality of work. Although technology can turn workers into mechanical appendages, there is no need for it to do so. Flexible working arrangements, when one can be called in to work at any time, can be hard to combine with caring for young children. But again, it does not have to. The question is how we can – now and in the future – create good work for as many people as possible. As David Coates writes, "Work is good for us, but work is only really good for us if it is 'good work'."[31]

1.3 Concerns About the Quality of Work

Dutch workers are generally satisfied with their jobs; three-quarters even say they "greatly enjoy" their work.[32] Asked the lottery player's question – "What would you do if you won a large sum of money?" – most answer that they would keep working.[33] The "bullshit jobs" made famous by American anthropologist David Graeber[34] is not yet an issue in the Netherlands, where only 5% of workers doubt the importance of their work.[35]

But dissatisfaction is rising.[36] Statistics Netherlands reports that strikes have reached their highest level in two decades,[37] with bus drivers, airline pilots, teachers, home care workers and university lecturers among those who have resorted to

---

[29] Such as OECD (2016a) and Eurofound (2017).

[30] For example, opportunities for participation and learning (Pot, 2017b). There is limited, although growing, interest in this area among European policymakers (Pot et al., 2017).

[31] Coates (2009).

[32] Wennekers et al. (2019).

[33] van Luijk (2011).

[34] Graeber (2018).

[35] Dekker (2018).

[36] de Beer and Conen (2019).

[37] There were 32 strikes in the Netherlands in 2017, more than in any year since 1989. 150,000 people took part, the highest number since records began in 1901. Logistics and manufacturing

industrial action. While some protests are classic wage disputes, others focus on workloads, especially the burden of overtime and administrative duties. In recent walkouts, primary-school teachers have been demanding "a fair salary, less work pressure". Theirs are not "bullshit jobs", they say. But they do have too many "bullshit tasks" within their jobs. What they want is the freedom to do their jobs well.

Disturbing exposés of contemporary working life are all-too-common. In *Hired*,[38] British investigative journalist James Bloodworth reveals what it is like to be an order picker at Amazon, where he worked undercover. The company monitors employee activities, including toilet visits, with digital wristbands. Breaks are limited and there are penalties for reporting sick. Zero-hour contracts are the norm and almost no one has a permanent job. Similar reports have been published in the Netherlands about what it is like to work for the taxi service Uber and online retailer Bol.com, in the meat-processing industry and in logistics.[39]

More work does not necessarily lead to less poverty. The proportion of the Dutch population classified as "working poor" has been rising since 1990.[40] In 2014, this applied to about 320,000 people (4.6% of all workers), of whom 175,000 were wage-earners and 145,000 were self-employed.

1.3.1 The Quality of Work as a Distribution Issue

Higher-skilled persons do not always have good jobs; lower-skilled persons do not always have bad jobs. There are, however, structural differences between these groups. Paul de Beer finds that lower-skilled people in the Netherlands, in both absolute and relative terms, were more likely to be employed "in 2016 than a person with similar characteristics (age, gender, domestic situation, origin) in 1990". But there was also a downside: "the chances of this person being in flexible employment and on low wages were higher in 2016".[41] The OECD notes in its report on the Netherlands that "non-standard work results in significant inequalities between workers. Workers on non-standard contracts earn less, suffer from higher insecurity and are less likely to participate in collective bargaining and training".[42]

There are further concerns about the declining quality of work. Workers today have less say over how they perform their duties; in other words, their autonomy at work is declining (Fig. 1.4). Although occupational health is generally good, the

---

were the sectors most frequently affected; the greatest loss of working days was in education (CBS, 2018e, 2019a).

[38] Bloodworth (2018). Or see, for example, Adler-Bell (2019, August 3).

[39] See Van Bergeijk, 2018. Investigative journalism platform Investico recently published *Uitgebuit: Het verhaal van de Nederlandse werkvloer* (Exploited: the story of the Dutch workplace; Woutersen, 2019).

[40] SCP (2018, October 3).

[41] de Beer (2018a).

[42] OECD (2019a).

proportion of employees reporting symptoms of burnout shot up from 11.3% in 2017 to 17.5% in 2018.[43] Although widespread across the working population, burnout is more common among the better educated. While work is a fine remedy for poverty, depression and poor health, it can also make you ill.

Public-sector professionals have been sounding the alarm about their working conditions – their wages being too low and their workloads being excessive – for some time. Especially teachers and healthcare staff want more autonomy to do their jobs well. The Professional Ethics Foundation has highlighted the mistrust police officers, teachers and nurses face from their superiors, which manifests in excessive control and enforced record-keeping.[44] What is at stake is "the recognition of one's own professionalism".[45]

Although job satisfaction in the Netherlands generally remains high, many people when asked the "lottery question" say they would continue working, but with the caveat "under different conditions". What workers want most is the space to do their jobs well. Compared to two decades ago, workers today have higher expectations. As well as good colleagues, they want jobs that are interesting, which allow them to make the most of their abilities and which give them a sense of achievement (Table 2.3).

Although not everyone needs to be ecstatic at work,[46] there are sound reasons to pay more attention to well-being in the workplace. Good work is about mutual engagement between employers and employees and about bringing out the best in people, with long-term benefits for workers, businesses,[47] the national economy and society. Better work improves occupational health, reduces absenteeism and encourages innovative workplace behaviour. Contented workers come up with creative ideas to improve products and services – all essential for a flourishing economy.

1.3.2   The Netherlands in Europe

Although the Netherlands is not performing badly on indicators that measure the quality of work, it could be doing much better. The country is a European leader in some areas, but by no means in all. Recent rankings by both the OECD[48] and the EU research agency Eurofound[49] place the Netherlands mid-table, with the OECD describing the country as an "average performer" alongside Mexico, South Korea,

---

[43] Houtman et al. (2020).

[44] www.beroepseer.nl

[45] Tjeenk Willink (2018).

[46] Davies (2015). In the words of *The Economist* (2019): "Work can be irritating but, as any unemployed person will tell you, it is better than the alternative. It gives purpose to people's days and, on occasion, can even be fun. But not every day."

[47] See, for example, Krekel et al. (2019).

[48] OECD (2016a).

[49] Eurofound (2017).

Japan, France, Belgium and Sweden; nations that score better include Denmark, Finland, Australia and Austria. According to Eurofound, some 40% of Dutch workers have "poor quality" jobs and are "under pressure" – more than in the UK or Belgium. What explains the Netherlands' middling position? Part I of this book seeks to provide some answers.

1.4 Better Work and Well-Being

Our focus on good work dovetails with national and international initiatives to look beyond gross domestic product and employment rates. While the United Nations Millennium Development Goals said nothing about work,[50] "decent work" is part of the Sustainable Development Goals (SDGs) agreed in 2015. SDG 8 reads: "Promote sustained, inclusive and sustainable economic growth, full and productive employment and decent work for all." While the long explanatory text mentions "decent work for all" several times,[51] what it means in concrete terms is up to individual nations to work out; implementation can and will differ across countries. The Dutch government has endorsed the Sustainable Development Goals, while ministries[52] and companies[53] have begun working to achieve them.[54]

1.4.1 Focus on Well-Being

While policymakers have long privileged economic growth and GDP, these indicators alone cannot gauge a nation's overall prosperity and the well-being of its inhabitants. GDP as a measure of economic performance was never meant to do this.[55] Since the French government's Commission on the Measurement of Economic Performance and Social Progress published its report[56] in 2008, international

---

[50] In 2005 a new goal 1B was added: "Achieve full and productive employment and decent work for all, including women and young people." See www.un.org/millenniumgoals/poverty.shtml

[51] Luebker (2017).

[52] At www.sdgnederland.nl we read: "Since January 2016, the [Dutch] central government has gone to great lengths to translate the SDGs into national policy. The report *Nederland Ontwikkelt Duurzaam* [The Netherlands developing sustainably], a 'plan of action for implementation of the SDGs', states that eight ministries have compiled an SDG inventory of government policy. Does this reflect the 17 goals and 169 subgoals?"

[53] See, for example, VNO-NCW (2018, November 30).

[54] The pursuit of better work is also in line with the European Pillar of Social Rights, signed in 2017. It includes the right to lifelong learning so that citizens can continue to participate in the labour market, guidance into work and good work-life balance.

[55] Coyle (2014), Hoekstra (2019), Hueck and Went (2015, January 25); Stiglitz (2018, December 3); Went (2015, January 30).

[56] Stiglitz et al. (2009).

organizations have been at the forefront in advocating for a broader view of prosperity and well-being. Numerous reports and books have addressed the limitations of GDP and proposed alternative ways to quantify happiness, well-being and prosperity.[57] To track more than just the evolution of GDP, national and international organizations have developed new indicators and composite indices.[58]

Interest in well-being has grown in the Netherlands as well. The debate in the House of Representatives following the WRR's report *Towards a Learning Economy*[59] led to a parliamentary committee on "Defining General Well-Being". The committee's report in 2016 led to further debate[60] and the House of Representatives voting to request Statistics Netherlands to develop a *Monitor of Well-Being*.[61] Since 2018, this report has been published annually on Accountability Day when the national government and its ministries present their annual reports to the House of Representatives.[62] The concept of well-being[63] has been gaining traction in local politics as well, with the City of Amsterdam's Research, Information and Statistics Department issuing its first *Monitor of Well-Being for the Amsterdam Metropolitan Region* in June 2018.[64]

1.4.2 Work Is Important for Our Well-Being

As Statistics Netherlands declared in its first *Monitor of Well-Being*, work is central to human welfare and a key factor in shaping well-being in its broadest sense.[65] The section on the distribution of well-being breaks down unemployment data by social groups; the chapter on policy themes and Sustainable Development Goals provides

---

[57] Clark et al. (2018a), Coyle (2014), Davies (2015), Pilling (2018).

[58] Stiglitz et al. (2018), Went (2019).

[59] WRR (2013a).

[60] Tweede Kamer (2016).

[61] CBS (2018c, d).

[62] "General well-being refers to the quality of life in the here and now, but also to the extent to which that is achieved at the expense of future generations or people elsewhere in the world" (CBS, 2018d).

[63] Many indicators and dashboards are being developed to measure well-being, happiness and broad prosperity, including the OECD's Better Life Index (www.oecdbetterlifeindex.org) and, in the Netherlands, Utrecht University and Rabobank's Comprehensive Indicator of Well-Being (Brede Welvaartsindicator, BWI). See also Went (2015, January 30).

[64] See www.amsterdam.nl/onderzoek-informatie-statistiek/projecten-data/brede-welvaart/

[65] The first edition of the *Monitor of Well-Being* states: "Both work and leisure time contribute significantly towards general personal well-being in the here and now. Work is important to people for generating income, for participation in society and for self-esteem. If people cannot or are no longer able to work even though they want to, this often has negative effects upon their general well-being at a later date. It is important for many people that they can find work, that they do not remain unemployed for too long, that they are in a suitable form of employment (permanent, flexible or self-employed) and that they can work free of excessive stress or insecurity"(CBS, 2018c).

indicators related to labour, workforce participation and leisure time. Having a job is a determining factor of well-being; so too is the kind of work one does. As the Taylor Review of modern working practices for the British government put it: "While having employment is itself vital to people's health and well-being, the quality of people's work is also a major factor in helping people to stay healthy and happy, something which benefits them and serves the wider public interest."[66] These findings all argue in favour of paying greater attention to the quality of work.[67]

1.5 In this Book

We argue that improving the quality of work for all people willing and able to work is a key societal and organizational challenge for governments, public institutions, businesses and organizations representing workers and employers. This dovetails with the OECD's new jobs strategy which "goes beyond job quantity and considers job quality and inclusiveness as central policy priorities"[68] – a strategy based on evidence that countries which focus on improving inclusion and the quality of work outperform countries that solely privilege labour market flexibility.[69] Focusing on good work for all is also in line with the International Labour Organization's "human-centred agenda for a decent future of work",[70] which advocates long-term investments in human development and well-being.

The OECD emphasizes that there are no standard policy recipes to achieve good and inclusive work. Each nation must pursue its own analysis of the opportunities and weaknesses in its labour market and formulate appropriate measures. In its submission to the Netherlands Independent Commission on the Regulation of Work, the OECD states that "the future of work will largely depend on the policy decisions countries make". The Netherlands, it adds, is "at an important juncture and urgent decisions need to be taken about the kind of labour market that is desired in the future".[71]

This book should be read in this context. It analyses key developments in the Dutch labour market, examines their potential consequences and formulates policy recommendations. Our analysis is based on international and interdisciplinary scientific research; on the working papers we commissioned from the Netherlands Organization for Applied Scientific Research, the Netherlands Institute for Social Research, Erasmus University Rotterdam, the University of Amsterdam and Tilburg

---

[66] Taylor et al. (2017).
[67] See also Pot and Smulders (2019).
[68] OECD (2018a).
[69] OECD (2018a).
[70] ILO (2019).
[71] OECD (2019a: 9).

University[72]; on policy reports, studies and evaluations from the Netherlands; and on conversations with policymakers and stakeholders, including discussions of our previous studies *Mastering the Robot*[73] and *For the Sake of Security*.[74]

We hope that the analysis of the Netherlands presented in this book will provide researchers and policymakers in other countries with actionable insights on the importance of good work and how new technologies, flexible labour markets and the intensification of work are affecting its quality – and what governments, employers, trade unions and others can do create better work. If the Netherlands, known for its knowledge-based economy and employee satisfaction, is wrestling with these issues, this will be the case in other countries as well. As the developments we analyse are occurring everywhere, we hope that the proposals and recommendations we present will provide some food for thought.

1.5.1   Covid-19 Pandemic

This book was written shortly before the outbreak of the Covid-19 pandemic. The crisis has not rendered our analysis out of date but has highlighted the urgency of our study. First, the Dutch labour market has become one of the most flexible in Western Europe; there is a chasm between people with and without permanent contracts and income security. Much of the economic shock is being absorbed by temporary and self-employed workers, disproportionately affecting young people, women, and ethnic minorities. The pandemic's economic impact, and the immediate financial support given by the Dutch government to the self-employed, reveals vulnerabilities in the labour market and the necessity of rethinking current social-security systems and reforming labour regulations to create stable work.

Second, the pandemic is revealing the need for renewed and expanded active labour-market policies as workers look for jobs in different sectors and governments face enormous challenges in helping job seekers find new employment. This requires adequate resources as well as administrative creativity when assistance must be provided digitally; in the absence of sufficient resources, those who are easily placeable are helped quickly while the most vulnerable are not.

---

[72] These working papers can be downloaded at www.wrr.nl.

[73] Went et al. (2015). Part of this work has been translated into English as *Mastering the Robot: The Future of Work in the Second Machine Age* and can be downloaded here: https://english.wrr.nl/publications/investigation/2015/12/08/mastering-the-robot.-the-future-of-work-in   -the-second-machine-age. See also Kremer and Went (2018).

[74] Kremer et al. (2017c). Part of this work has been translated into English as *For the Sake of Security. The Future of Flexible Workers and the Modern Organisation of Labour* and can be downloaded   here: https://english.wrr.nl/publications/investigation/2017/05/01/for-the-sake-of-security. The site contains a visual summarizing the book.

Third, while professionals in healthcare, social care and education are now deemed "heroes", they still suffer from highly demanding jobs, comparative low pay, high work pressure and relatively little control over their work. The current crisis once again underlines the importance of fair pay and sufficient autonomy for public professionals.

Fourth, the pandemic is revealing the importance of good work-life balance. Due to the measures taken to prevent the spread of the virus, many workers are now working from home, with many parents doubling as teachers. While working from home may become the new normal for many, it once again raises questions about healthy working conditions and investments in childcare.

Finally, from developing contact tracing apps to video-conferencing with co-workers, the Covid-19 crisis has been a catalyst for technological change. While the latest technological developments may ultimately have both positive and negative consequences for workers, it underlines our analysis of the importance of developing and implementing technologies in such a way that it leads to better work.

1.5.2 In the Following Chapters...

Drawing on the scientific literature, we first outline why work is important and what constitutes "good work" (Chap. 2). Then, in Part I, we examine how the quality of work in the Netherlands has been affected by the three trends at the heart of our study – the automation, flexibilization and intensification of labour (treated respectively in Chaps. 3, 4 and 5). In Part II, we discuss the consequences of these trends for the ability of different parts of the population to find and retain work (Chap. 6). In Part III, we discuss how globalization and new technologies inform the space available to national governments and labour organizations to invest in good work for everyone willing, able and needing to work (Chap. 7). Finally, Chap. 8 advances suggestions about how governments and other stakeholders can actively contribute towards "better work" for all.

Between the chapters are portraits of some common professions. By following the working day of truck drivers, home care workers and many others, these portraits reveal how the three trends at the heart of this book are experienced in daily life as well as just how important good work is.

A Day at Work: The Truck Driver

Max climbs into the cab of his truck between 5 and 6 am each morning. He works for a small family business, hauling loads ranging from sugar beet and lime to glass for recycling. Today's route takes him to several destinations in the Netherlands and then to Belgium. It is exactly 7 am when Max arrives at his first stop: a glass processing plant where he delivers coarse coloured glass and picks up a load of white rinsed fine glass.

Max joined the company two years ago as it allowed him to work more "normal" hours. But he still finds it difficult to lead a normal life. He spends between 50 and 60 h each week on the road, which makes it a tough job. "With breaks included, you're away from home for the best part of 65 hours. The planner back at the office designs the routes and schedules, so it's better to stay in his good books", Max says with a smile. The planner can follow drivers using their GPS trackers. "If he spots you cutting corners, he'll take it out on you." Tonight, Max wants to be home no later than 7 pm as it is his brother's birthday. To compensate, he has accepted a night shift for this Saturday, which pays a premium for unsocial hours. But this will force him to cancel his Sunday football match, ruining his weekend.

When Max arrives at the glass factory at around 11 am, he must first wait for another truck to unload. Pausing the meter above his head, he uses this time to work off half an hour of his break. Drivers must take a 45-min break for each 4.5 h they spend behind the wheel; they otherwise risk being fined. But for Max there is no chance to rest. He uses this time to clean the truck's tires, to loosen the tarpaulin to ready for unloading and to fill in forms. An hour after arriving, he can set off again, on his way to Belgium.

Max keeps his cabin spotlessly clean: "I spend whole days in here – this is my home." Behind the seats is a made-up bed; Max sleeps on the road an average of twice a week. Curtains hang from the windows and under the bed is a fridge containing his lunch. There will soon be a TV as well.

To his relief, Max arrives at the Belgian company just before the shift change, when the whole place shuts down. "It's always a hassle here. You wait for ages and then they complain that your freight compartment isn't clean." The piles of glass reach impressive heights. The glass itself is so fine that it looks like sand and the wind blows it around. It tickles and stings everywhere. "You should see my socks at home", says Max. "They're all shredded."

Once he has loaded and weighed the truck and filled in all the forms, Max is on his way again. He chats on his CB radio with other Dutch truckers who are approaching the same factory, annoyed as they will arrive during the shift change. Although Max is alone in his cab all day, "I never feel lonely with this thing." He spends the whole day chatting with colleagues driving nearby.

It is 2:30 pm and Max has been behind the wheel for 9 h now. He still has some time left, he says with a big smile. Suddenly, he must slam on the brakes. A car has just cut in front of him to exit from the motorway. Forty tonnes of fine glass protest, its weight pushing the huge vehicle forward as Max barely

(continued)

manages to keep control. Long days or not, Max must stay alert. A recent accident in which a fellow driver died has left a deep impression on him. He talked about it with his colleagues. "It makes you think. If it ever comes to it, I just hope I'm not trapped for ages. That would be horrible. I'd rather die instantly."

From a safety point of view, it might be preferable to completely automate freight transport with self-driving trucks. While Max often hears about this future scenario, he does not fear for his job in the short term. The individual loads and routes, combined with loading, unloading and other essential tasks, will make full automation difficult. "Even if it comes to that, you'll still need someone to check the machine."

At about 4:30 pm he delivers the fine glass and collects his final consignment of the day, a load of "coarse brown" which must go to Drenthe. But Max is finished for the day; this will be his first delivery tomorrow. He drives his truck back to the company depot, fills the tank – 540 litres, which takes a while – and completes more forms. Finally, at 6:15 pm, about 13 h after he began his working day, Max gets into his own car and drives home, just in time to celebrate his brother's birthday.

At the beginning of 2019, some 109,000 people worked as truck drivers in the Netherlands. Almost all were men, roughly half with only basic education and half with upper secondary schooling. The vast majority (nine out of ten) were employed, increasingly on flexible contracts which now account for almost a quarter of trucking jobs. While the number of jobs in the sector were falling for over a decade due to competition from Eastern Europe, economic growth and an ageing workforce have led to a shortage of drivers in the past two years. Truck drivers typically earn €1800–2400 gross per month, excluding overtime premiums. The average (modal) income in the Netherlands in 2020 will be just over €2800 euros per month, excluding holiday pay. Truck drivers work long and irregular hours. Although they experience little work-related pressure compared to other professions, it is increasing due in part to the wider use of digital tracking systems.

Chapter 2
The Importance of Better Work

For most people, work is a source of economic independence, social contact and identity. Who we are is largely determined by what we do. Work is often where we connect with others; some of us spend more time with colleagues than with friends or loved ones. Unemployment has major consequences for individuals, for their social environments and for society, while the importance of paid work is most tangible for those who do not have it.

This chapter draws on the extant scientific literature on the importance of having a job, in particular the importance of having *good* work. Above all, it seeks to pinpoint what good work entails. We first discuss the functions of paid work and the consequences of unemployment for individuals and societies – a subject about which a great deal is already known (Sect. 2.1). We then turn to what economists, sociologists and psychologists have written about good work (Sect. 2.2). From this literature we distil three core characteristics of good work, which also align with survey findings about what people in the Netherlands expect from their jobs (Sect. 2.3). We then discuss why good work is so important for individuals, companies, the economy and society (Sect. 2.4) before concluding the chapter (Sect. 2.5).

2.1 The Meaning of Paid Work

The importance of paid work is most obvious to those who do not have it: the unemployed. Social psychologist Marie Jahoda and sociologist Paul Lazersfeld visited Marienthal, Austria, in the 1930s in the wake of a local factory closure which had made the majority of the village workforce redundant (see Box 2.1). From their field research and an extensive literature study, Jahoda and Lazersfeld identified six

© The Author(s) 2021
M. Kremer et al., *Better Work*, Research for Policy,
https://doi.org/10.1007/978-3-030-78682-3_2

functions of work which are as applicable today as they were then.[1] First and foremost, work (1) furnishes an income. But apart from this, work also provides (2) daily structure, (3) personal development, (4) social contacts and experiences, (5) the opportunity to contribute to society and (6) status and identity. To a considerable extent, work determines a person's position in society.

Jahoda emphasized the social functions of work. Because people find their place in society through employment, it has taken over some of the functions of

---

Box 2.1 from Marienthal to Janesville: Studies of the Unemployed

During the depression of the 1930s, Marie Jahoda and Paul Lazarsfeld accompanied a team of researchers to Marienthal, an Austrian village where the only factory had been forced to close. The result was the first large-scale study of the consequences of unemployment. *Die Arbeitslosen von Marienthal: Ein soziographischer Versuch über die Wirkungen langandauernder Arbeitslosigkeit (The Unemployed of Marienthal: A Sociographic Experiment on the Effects of Long-term Unemployment)*[2] described both the practical aspects of joblessness such as managing household budgets and the slow tread with which the unemployed walked through the village and the shrinking of [their] life horizon. While the financial consequences of unemployment were great, what was even more striking was the suffering caused by loss of status, identity and self-esteem. The study found that people reacted differently to unemployment; some descended into a vicious cycle of inactivity and apathy, unable to take advantage of the limited opportunities available to them.

A half-century later, *Een tijd zonder werk (A Time Without Work)*[3] – based on ethnographic research in the cities of Rotterdam, Amsterdam and Enschede – studied long-term unemployment in the Netherlands in the 1980s. This study likewise found extended periods of joblessness leading to losses of status and identity, an altered sense of time and a contraction of the world. But it also identified an alternative culture of unemployment celebrating autonomy and individualism. Joblessness did not necessarily undermine status and identity; particularly young people made strategic use of welfare benefits as a de facto basic income to organize their lives in a way that suited them.[4]

The slipstream of the 2008 financial crisis has produced relatively few academic studies of the experience of unemployment. Among the notable studies are *Washington Post* staff writer Amy Goldstein's account[5] of the city of Janesville, Wisconsin, where a General Motors factory had closed its doors. *Janesville: An American Story* is as an account of the resilience of a local community. Retraining courses, Goldstein found, were no quick fix, as people who had undergone retraining found it harder to find new jobs.

---

[1] Jahoda (1982).

[2] Jahoda et al. (1975).

[3] Kroft et al. (1989).

[4] See also Engbersen et al. (1993).

[5] Goldstein (2017).

communal and religious ritual. Alongside the family, work offers a social context that allows people to experience, on a daily basis, that they are not islands unto themselves. Without work, people feel they have no purpose in life and that they are unable to contribute to the collective; they feel excluded from society.

Jahoda's six functions of work still apply although the meritocratization of society – the conferral of status by talent – since the 1930s has added a seventh function: work affords self-respect.[6] In *Respect in a World of Inequality*, Richard Sennett[7] writes that people without paid work find it hard to respect themselves – a feeling reinforced when people are judged above all by their earnings.[8] If people are out of work, the general consensus is that they only have themselves to blame; they should have stayed longer in school or performed better at the last job interview. A Dutch study by Judith Elshout[9] found many unemployed people sharing such views: their situation was "their own fault" while people without work were "losers".

American sociologist Michelle Lamont[10] reports that there are currently few sources of self-esteem outside of paid employment – the centrality of which has pushed aside other possible reasons to value oneself. Although many men and women in the Netherlands value leisure and family above paid work,[11] (Fig. 2.1) recent research shows that one's job remains the most important source of respect. The unemployed, people with disabilities, pensioners and homemakers (both male and female) all struggle more than working people with issues of self-esteem. Working people feel more useful and valuable, and are more proud of themselves (Fig. 2.1).[12]

Can volunteer work take over the functions of paid work? Although volunteering is generally good for one's health and well-being, this is less true for unemployed people, especially when they are young and have their lives ahead of them.[13] The Netherlands has a tradition of valuing voluntary work as a symbolic contribution to society; within the benefits system, experiments are currently underway to guide recipients towards the voluntary sector (see Box 2.2). But however valuable it may be and however much it may bolster self-esteem,[14] volunteering can never fully take over all the functions of a real job with a real payslip.[15]

---

[6] See also the "homo honoris" in Engbersen et al. (1993). Honneth (2001, 2007) emphasizes the importance of recognition, consisting of love, respect and appreciation. For the application of Honneth to practices at work, see Sebrechts (2018).

[7] Sennett (2003).

[8] Swierstra & Tonkens (2008).

[9] Elshout (2016).

[10] Lamont (2000).

[11] Conen (2018, 2020).

[12] Wielers et al. (2018).

[13] Jahoda (1982), van Willigen (2000), van der Aa et al. (2014), Casiday (2015), Detollenaere et al. (2017), Wielers et al. (2018).

[14] Wielers et al. (2018).

[15] Kampen (2014), Elshout(2016).

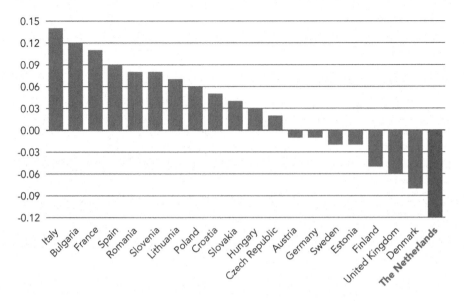

Fig. 2.1 The centrality of work across countries – total population aged 18-plus (indexed)
Source: Conen (2020)

Box 2.2 Experiments with Volunteer Work

Experiments with volunteering have long sought to give those without paid work a daily routine and meaning in life. The first experiment we know of took place in the UK in 1935 when the Quaker movement set up the Subsistence Production Society, a voluntary co-operative for 400 former miners. Rather than a wage, participants received a small cash allowance. While the project emulated many of the functions of work, it attained better results among older men; younger men often failed to show up. For the former, it brought structure to the day; for the latter, voluntary work undermined their social status. The younger men did not feel they were contributing to a greater goal.[16]

Since the 1980s, the Netherlands has seen numerous experiments with volunteer work for the unemployed, usually targeting long-term benefit claimants.[17] A study by the City of Rotterdam found that social assistance claimants were generally positive about the expectation to give back to the community, although a minority found it oppressive. Participants in an experimental programme generally felt more confident and valued, and expanded their social contacts; their employment prospects and health, however, did not improve.[18] In Amsterdam, the comparable programme *Meedoen werkt* ("Joining in works") made participants feel "more self-reliant" but only rarely led to them finding paid work.[19]

---

[16] Jahoda (1982).

[17] Kampen (2014).

[18] Bus et al. (2017).

[19] GGD Amsterdam & OIS (2017). See also the dossier www.socialevraagstukken.nl/meedoenindebijstand

2.1.1   When People Are Out of Work: Consequences for the Individual and Society

Because work has so many functions, it is unsurprising that unemployment has such far-reaching consequences. Numerous studies have shown that being out of work leads to poorer health, particularly mental health; controlling for socio-economic status, employment history and education, we see that joblessness clearly contributes to mental illnesses such as depression.[20] Conversely, unemployed people who find jobs experience huge health gains, comparable to the effect of participating in programmes designed to promote healthy behaviour.[21] Understandably, scientific attention over the past decades has shifted away from the pathogenic nature of work – its role in causing illness and disease – towards its remedial effects. Nowadays, a job is more often considered medicine.

The unemployed, as Jahoda already observed, are less embedded in "society" – which after all is largely created at work. The WRR pointed to this phenomenon in its 1990 report *Work in Perspective*,[22] by which time the erosion of traditional integrative links had made social bonding through work an urgent issue: "Labour-force participation – allowing always for new definitions of what constitutes employment – has become an increasingly important precondition and manifestation of social participation, cohesion and individual citizenship." People without jobs are less anchored in society, have smaller social networks and are more likely to be single. Sometimes they are excluded; sometimes they exclude themselves. Particularly for married men, losing their job increases the chances that they will lose their partner.[23]

Work in Perspective also found that low labour-force participation rates were threatening the solvency of the Dutch welfare state. A healthy ratio between working and non-working people is needed to maintain solidarity and to finance the social-security system. Unemployment and occupational incapacity entail costs that go well beyond the sums paid out in benefits, such as those associated with healthcare and social services. For example, people on benefits account for a considerable proportion of the spending on mental healthcare.[24]

The costs of health problems caused by unemployment are at least in part borne by society. It is therefore important to help as many people as possible into work, not only for their own good but for that of the general public. But it is crucial that this work be good work. We now turn to what this actually means.

---

[20] Harbers & Hoeymans (2013), OECD (2014, 2015a).

[21] Schuring et al. (2011), Kenniscentrum UWV (2011).

[22] WRR (1990): 43.

[23] Goñalons-Pons & Gangl (2018); see also de Hek et al. (2018).

[24] Einerhand & Ravesteijn (2017).

2.2   Good Work: Insights from the Social Sciences

Much has been written about what constitutes good work. Although there is no single, unambiguous definition, specific elements keep recurring in the academic literature and in large-scale international studies by the European Union and the OECD. This section describes criteria for good work as proposed by economists, sociologists and psychologists, and boils them down to three crucial characteristics.

2.2.1   Good Work as Seen by Economists

In economics, the quality of work is generally equated with pay levels.[25] High wages mean good work; low wages mean bad work. Paul de Beer[26] argues that economics has narrowed its view of work to income: "Although most economists do underline the importance of work for the individual, the dominant approach in economics, the neoclassical theory, provides little reason to do so. In most economic views of the labour market, work is primarily a way of making money." Nevertheless, meaningful jobs can be badly paid while well-paid work can also lead to burnout. As important as wages are for income and recognition, sociologists and psychologists have shown that there are more criteria to good work than pay alone.

Economics has indeed begun to pay more attention to well-being. In *The Origins of Happiness*,[27] Layard and colleagues explore how the quality of people's work affects their contentment and distil from contemporary studies three conditions for good work: (1) good organization, with sufficient variety in tasks, autonomy, support, appreciation and so on; (2) good work-life balance (flexible and "civilized" hours); and (3) good pay, with income security and opportunities for promotion. In sum, work is good if it makes people happy with their lives.

Arne Kalleberg[28], a sociologist inspired by economists, identifies five conditions for good work. First, the wage must be sufficient to cover basic needs, with the chance to earn more over time. It is not only the amount one earns, but the social mobility that the income allows. Second, good work provides social benefits such as health insurance and post-retirement pensions; Kalleberg emphasizes this as social benefits in the United States are generally linked to one's employment contract and not, as in the Netherlands and Europe more broadly, arranged collectively or through industry-wide agreements. Third, good work offers "opportunities for autonomy and control over work activities", including having a say over one's tasks. Fourth, "flexibility and control over rosters and working conditions" is increasingly

---

[25] Kalleberg (2011).

[26] de Beer (2001): 119.

[27] Clark et al. (2018b).

[28] Kalleberg (2011): 9.

important in light of on-call work in the 24/7 economy. Finally, workers must have some control over when their jobs end, as the flexible labour market thrives on short-term appointments.

All five conditions do not necessarily have to be met for work to be good; if one is missing, this does not automatically make it bad. Here Kalleberg aligns himself with neoclassical economic theory, which posits that employers can trade off positive and negative aspects of work, for example the price in security self-employed in the creative industry pay for their independence. Kalleberg nevertheless notes that the exchange is often not all that it should be; while employers offering precarious positions should be paying higher wages, this often does not happen. The conditions for good work are also increasingly divorced from one another. We can no longer confidently say that individuals earning high incomes will likely score well on the other indicators of good work. For example, there is now less job security across the board.

2.2.2 Good Work as Seen by Sociologists

According to Duncan Gallie,[29] sociologists assess the quality of work through two dominant lenses. Building on sociology's founding fathers (see Box 2.3), the first approach seeks to objectively determine the conditions under which workers' interests are advanced. Marx, for example, argued that without ownership over their work, workers will remain alienated from themselves and from their labour. The second approach is based more on what people themselves experience as good work. Good jobs are jobs in which people are happy; it is better to let people judge for themselves what constitutes good work as their preferences differ.

Gallie further argues that people are remarkably consistent in how they evaluate their work, with similar patterns visible in almost all European countries, among both men and women. Workers with modest educations, less discretionary space, fewer training opportunities, limited job security and greater difficulties combining work and care are less satisfied with their jobs. Objectively as well as subjectively, the quality of work can be reduced to three central elements: (1) discretionary space at work; (2) job security; and (3) work-life balance.[30]

2.2.3 Good Work as Seen by Psychologists

While sociologists study the quality of work through the lenses of social equality, opportunities and workplace performance, psychologists tend to focus on workers' health and well-being. Peter Warr's "vitamin model", for example, compares the

---

[29] See, for example, Gallie (2007a, 2013).
[30] Gallie (2007a).

Box 2.3 Alienation in the Iron Cage: The Quality of Work According to Classical Sociologists

Karl Marx, Émile Durkheim and Max Weber were engaged with the industrial relations of their day and the question of how to enforce good work.[31] Marx (1818–1883) was particularly affected by the kind of industrial labour he saw in English factories. The dangers of work lay primarily in various forms of alienation: alienation from the product being made, alienation from the work process, alienation from one's fellow workers and alienation from the individual creative process. It was vital that people be allowed to be social and creative. The answer to alienation lay not in liberation *from* work but in liberation *through* work. This was only possible if workers controlled the means of production so that they were no longer "wage slaves".

Émile Durkheim (1858–1917) is famous for his idea that specialization makes people more interdependent, creating an organic form of solidarity. But he also warned against the excessive division of labour, where workers become automatons and there is little contact between one function and the next. People should be able to choose their work freely as this will better match their individual abilities. Durkheim saw little point in seeking out conflict, preferring a higher level of moral consciousness through professional organizations modelled on the guilds of the Middle Ages.

Finally, Max Weber (1864–1920) described how bureaucracies – or other forms of far-reaching rationalization – restrict freedom of action, imprisoning people in an "iron cage" leading to "depersonalization" and loss of creativity. Weber sought a solution in charismatic leaders who could introduce new moral values.

Although the proposals advanced by these nineteenth-century sociologists to achieve better work ranged from moral appeals to the appropriation of capital, they were all concerned with scope for individuality and creativity, working according to one's abilities, and social relationships at work. It all sounds surprisingly modern and to the point.

psychological influence of working conditions to the effects of vitamins on physical health.[32] According to Warr, people have a natural need for nine "vitamins of work" without which good work is impossible. Some have health benefits but can be harmful when overdosed (see Table 2.1). For example, excessive performance requirements lead to stress, too much variety in one's tasks reduces concentration, and not everyone thrives with autonomy. The other vitamins – financial rewards, physical security, position and status – do not lead to overdose but have no further benefits beyond a certain dose.[33]

---

[31] See Hodson (2001), de Beer (2001).

[32] Warr (1987, 2007).

[33] de Jonge et al. (2013).

Table 2.1 Warr's vitamins of work

Aspects of work with constant effects on health and well-being	Aspects of work with sometimes adverse effects on health and well-being
Financial rewards Physical comfort and security Position and status	Opportunity to control work autonomously Clarity of goals and role Social support and contact Opportunity to use and develop skills Variety of tasks Performance requirements and feedback

Source: De Jonge et al. (2013)

Another strand of psychological research on workplace well-being builds on motivation theory. Abraham Maslow's pyramid of needs, advanced in *A Theory of Human Motivation* (1943), is often used to outline a hierarchy of needs, the fulfilment of which leads to good work. With physiological needs at its base, the pyramid progresses through the needs for safety, belonging, love and esteem before reaching its apex: self-actualization. Self-determination theory as advanced by Edward Deci and Richard Ryan has also found considerable resonance in workplace research.[34] According to this hypothesis, people are driven by three basic psychological needs: (1) autonomy, meaning the freedom to design an activity as one sees fit with a degree of independence; (2) competence, meaning confidence in one's own ability and the experience of control; and (3) belonging, meaning social interaction and trust in others.[35] Safeguarding all three in the workplace should result in better performance (quality of work and productivity) and in better health and well-being.[36]

2.2.4 Good Work as Seen by International Organizations

International organizations such as the OECD and Eurofound have built on the scientific findings outlined above to define and operationalize good work in their research on the quality of work. In recent reports such as *Divided We Stand*[37] and *In It Together*,[38] the OECD has increasingly focused on pay and income inequality as well as the insecurity of workers in flexible labour markets. In its understanding of the quality of work, the OECD privileges the socio-economic aspects of employment (see Table 2.2). Eurofound in studying the quality of work has identified seven key indicators, each with several sub-characteristics (see Table 2.2). Compared to the OECD, Eurofound places greater emphasis on physical working conditions, how work is organized and social innovation in the workplace.

---

[34] Deci & Ryan (1985, 2008), Deci et al. (2017).

[35] These characteristics apply to everyone – including for example people with disabilities (Frielink 2017).

[36] Deci et al. (2017). See also www.selfdetermination.org

[37] OECD (2011).

[38] OECD (2015d).

Table 2.2 International job quality indices

Eurofound	
1. Physical environment	*2. Social environment*
Posture-related (ergonomic) Ambient (noise, temperature, vibration) Biological and chemical	Adverse social behaviour Social support Management quality
3. Work intensity	*4. Skills and discretion*
Quantitative demands Pace determinants and interdependency Emotional demands	Cognitive dimension Decision latitude Organizational participation Training
5. Working time quality	*6. Prospects*
Duration Atypical working hours Working time arrangements Flexibility	Employment status Career prospects Job security Downsizing
7. Earnings	
OECD	
1. Earnings quality	
Average earnings Earnings inequality	
2. Labour market security	
Risk of unemployment, linked to level of unemployment insurance Risk of extreme low pay	
3. Quality of working environment	
Job strain: Demands (time pressure and physical risk factors) in relation to available resources (work autonomy and learning opportunities)	

Source: Eurofound (2017): 37. and OECD (Cazes et al. 2015)

2.3   Conditions for Good Work

Three core conditions for good work recur in the scientific literature. While their importance may fluctuate for individuals over the life course, research shows that there are minimum levels for work to be considered good. All three conditions do not need to be maximized. Good work can also be good-enough work.

2.3.1 Income Security

The first condition for good work is material. People need to be paid enough to live on: work that results in poverty cannot be called good. Wages should also be proportionate to the effort involved: is there a balance between what people do and how much they are paid? Warr calls this fairness.[39] To some extent, fairness is relational; people tend to compare what they earn with others. Comparative earnings are therefore a key indicator. If a person's wages are much lower than those of close colleagues or people with the same level of education, it is hard to claim their work is good.

Security is part and parcel of the material dimension of the quality of work. Although people with steady jobs can experience insecurity – "in a reorganization you can be out of the door just like that" – temporary contracts are seen as indicators of bad work as they bring little financial stability and slim career prospects.

Security is enhanced when workers have opportunities to find other or better-paid work through retraining and on-the-job learning and when job loss is accompanied by financial compensation, for instance through an adequate redundancy package. Redress for loss of income due to termination of contract or incapacity to work, as well as guidance into other work where appropriate, are conditions for good work.

2.3.2 In the Workplace: Freedom and Belonging

The second condition for good work concerns the workplace itself. A job can be secure and well paid but can hardly be called good if one has no space to decide when and how tasks are performed, if the workplace atmosphere is toxic, if job requirements are so basic that boredom sets in, or if one lacks opportunities for development. Although workers don't need to be in a constant state of bliss, they generally want to feel that they are making a contribution.[40] Whether one is well or poorly educated, highly gifted or cognitively impaired, being able to make the most of one's abilities is a basic human need.[41] People like to use and develop their skills. Being under-challenged is not only a waste of human talent; it is often demeaning. Conversely, people can also be over-challenged: if there are not enough people for the task, if the task is too complex, or if it demands the constant managing of one's own and other people's emotions, the work can no longer be considered good.

While both Kalleberg and Eurofound emphasize the importance of social mobility through work, we prefer Warr's vitamin model which recognizes there can be too much emphasis on advancement. Mobility in itself is not an end; people can be

---

[39] Warr (2007).
[40] Jahoda (1982).
[41] Deci & Ryan (1985).

satisfied with the work they have. Good work strikes the right balance between stress and boredom.[42] It concerns appropriate job requirements, not just avoiding burnout but also preventing "bore-out".

To keep alienation – occupational estrangement from oneself and/or others – from setting in, workers need a degree of control or ownership over their work. As Marx wrote, being able to use our creativity makes us human.[43] Good work means that people can perform their tasks without constant control from managers or technology – a common problem today, especially for workers in the gig economy who must ultimately answer to an algorithm.[44] While an appropriate amount of personal latitude can shield people from excessive workloads and stress, not all workers need the same amount of autonomy, or all of the time; the need for autonomy is stronger in some people than in others, and can evolve over the course of a career. Too much autonomy can also make workers exhausted and insecure[45] – especially when their authority does not match their responsibilities. But with the right amount of autonomy, psychology's classic demand-control model[46] (see also Sect. 2.4) predicts that workers will be more productive. Their input in shopfloor meetings and participation in decision-making is crucial as it allows workers to shape how tasks are organized in a way that makes the most of their abilities.[47]

People want to feel connected to those they work with; this is a basic human need.[48] Respect and appreciation, courtesy and social support are essential to good work.[49] People value workplace social relationships, which must be free of discrimination, aggression and bullying. If workers' have bad relations with their bosses or colleagues, it is not good work.

2.3.3 Work-Life Balance

The third condition for good work is work-life balance. Good work entails working hours appropriate for one's stage in life. Some people want to reduce their working hours when raising young children or if elderly parents require their care. Others want to work more, which can be facilitated by good public care provision for children and the elderly. Yet others wish to continue working after the normal retirement age. Not everyone can or wants to follow the standard life-course of "study, work, rest". Good work means fluidity and flexibility so that family life and personal

---

[42] Warr & Clapperton (2010).

[43] Hodson (2001).

[44] Bloodworth (2018), O'Connor (2016, September 8).

[45] Kubicek et al. (2017).

[46] Karasek (1979).

[47] Felstead et al. (2016), Gallie & Zhou (2013), ETUI (2019). Workplace participation or democracy is emphasized by the ILO: the right to "decent" work is one thing, but it is even better if workers can help shape this right.

[48] Deci & Ryan (1985).

[49] Warr (1987, 2007).

Table 2.3 Three conditions for good work

Condition	Indicators
1. Control over income	Reasonable pay
	Job security
	Security of work
Material dimension of work	Social security
2. Control over work	Autonomy
	Use and develop skills
	Social support
Immaterial dimension of work	Absence of aggression and discrimination
3. Control in life	Part-time work
	Paid leave
	Influence over working hours
Work-life balance	Good childcare and elderly care

development can be combined with a career.[50] This includes flexibility in the place and timing of work.

The line between work and private life has been blurred in the flexible labour market, where working hours and locations are often no longer fixed. While flexibility is often demanded unilaterally by the employer, good work is about flexibility *for* the employee, not about having to be available for work at all hours.[51] It is also important that personal problems do not constantly interfere with work, that workers are not repeatedly called away to care for a confused parent or to pick up a sick child from school. Employees must be allowed enough rest and time to work well.

Table 2.3 summarizes the three key conditions for good work and links them to 12 indicators. We will return to them in our analysis of the Netherlands in subsequent chapters.

2.3.4 The Three Conditions for Good Work

Do the above conditions for good work, as distilled from the scientific literature and summarized in Table 2.3, align with the wishes of Dutch society? Surveys find that people in the Netherlands, more than in any other European country, do not place paid work first on their list of priorities[52] (see Fig. 2.1). On average, they attach greater importance to family, friendships and free time – a privilege of prosperous countries where joblessness does not risk basic livelihood.[53] Both Dutch men and women wish to be able to combine paid work with free time and care responsibilities.[54]

---

[50] Epstein & Kalleberg (2004), Schmid (2017).

[51] A recruiter for flexible jobs in the UK has set up an innovation unit to create greater flexibility in the design of shifts, rosters and jobs for people currently lacking this opportunity: "Shift workers in retail and manufacturing, for example, and frontline staff such as nurses are often left out of the debate" (*Financial Times,* 11 October 2018).

[52] Conen (2020): figure 1.

[53] Wielers & Koster (2011).

[54] Portegijs & van den Brakel (2016).

Table 2.4 Work orientations in the Netherlands, employed labour force (in %), 1990–2018

	1990	1999	2008	2018
Extrinsic work values				
Good pay/high income	75	76	77	78
Good working hours	45	35▼	57▲	68▲
Job security	38	24▼	42	
Good holiday arrangements/extensive leave	36	26▼	47▲	45▲
Intrinsic work values				
A job in which you can use your abilities	74	75	85▲	
An interesting job/position	67	63	77▲	
A working environment in which you know you can achieve something	44	41	67▲	63▲
Social values				
Pleasant workmates	94	92	96	
A job useful to society	44	37	56▲	

Note: ▼/▲p < 0.01; compared with 1990
Source: European Values Study, authors' own calculations, weighted data, Conen (2020)

Table 2.4 shows that Dutch people want work that pays well. But it is even more important that their work is interesting and that it makes the most of their talents. A good salary is of great importance to more than three-quarters of the population, but people also want interesting work "in which you can use your abilities". All things considered, Dutch workers attach more importance to the intrinsic aspects of work than do many other Europeans.[55] In other words, the value of work lies mainly in the work itself. Workers in the Netherlands, more than in the rest of Europe, want their work to be "social"; they want pleasant colleagues. A sense of belonging at work is an important condition for good work.[56]

Although the expectations of employees today do not differ markedly from those of their 1970s predecessors, women's growing participation in the labour force has generated new expectations regarding work-life balance.[57] People attach greater value than ever before to reasonable working hours and generous holiday arrangements so they can combine their personal and working lives (see Table 2.4). It is also striking how much having an interesting job and the ability to "achieve something" at work have grown in importance over the past three decades.

It is sometimes claimed that younger people see work very differently, that they attach less importance to job security. This is a "millennial myth" – this generation, too, wants good work that provides a secure livelihood.[58] Everyone, regardless of

---

[55] Conen (2020).

[56] There are differences between social groups. Men on average attach greater importance to extrinsic values than women, who more often privilege intrinsic and social values. Highly educated people also score higher on intrinsic values than those with less schooling, for whom extrinsic values are more important. See Conen (2020).

[57] Freese (2008), Freese et al. (2008).

[58] Conen (2020), see also van der Klein (2017).

age, appreciates a steady job, a good employer and a reasonable salary.[59] Everyone, regardless of age, appreciates the value of security. In sum, the quality of work, according to Dutch workers, concerns pay and security; autonomy and belonging in the workplace; and being able to combine work with private life.

2.4 Consequences of Good Work for the Individual, the Economy and Society

Good work is not only good for workers; employers and society gain as well. Figure 2.2 shows how.

2.4.1 Health and Well-Being

Good work is good for workers' health and well-being, which means less absenteeism, higher productivity and lower costs for the welfare state. Numerous epidemiological studies show a causal relationship between the quality of work and the health

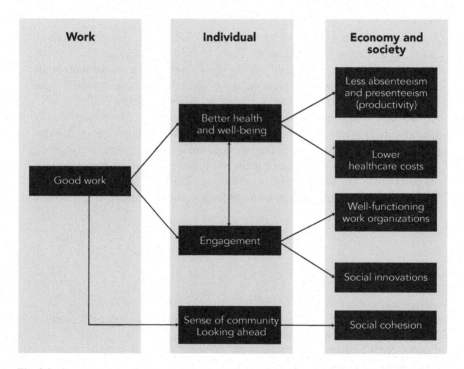

Fig. 2.2 Consequences of better work for the individual, the economy and society

---

[59] Freese (2008), Freese et al. (2008).

and well-being of workers.[60] Although this applies to physical health as well, it is especially – and increasingly – the case for mental health.[61]

Occupational health is associated primarily with conditions in the workplace and the extent to which workers have control over their working lives. There is a direct link between high – and above all continuous – work-related stress and medical complaints.[62] Mental-health issues can arise when employees are insufficiently challenged, when they do not feel that their tasks match their abilities, or when they lack opportunities for advancement.[63] Poor relationships with colleagues and bosses increase the risk of illness and can have major implications for a person's mental health and subjective well-being.[64]

Box 2.4 Burnout: A Product of Changes in Work and Society
The best-known negative effect attributed to bad work is burnout: mental and emotional exhaustion often accompanied by physical fatigue, cynicism towards work, insufficient sleep and flagging self-confidence. Burnout has many causes. Broader social developments play a role; in the performance society, work is an indicator of success and having a busy job is a status symbol.[65] Meanwhile, we devote our leisure time to even more activity, from sports to maintaining a social media presence, leaving us scant time to recover from work.[66]

Other underlying causes of burnout can be traced to the changing nature of work, in particular its acceleration. The shift from an industrial to a service economy means that people are working less with their hands and more with their heads and hearts. Work nowadays is more likely to be mentally than physically taxing,[67] altering the pattern of occupational illness.

Workers today have fewer opportunities to tune out. More likely to be working with others, they are expected to keep their interactions civil, even under trying circumstances.[68] Many workers are increasingly engaged in emotional labour, tasks that require them to suppress their own feelings or to express emotions they are not experiencing. This can lead to all kinds of exhaustion from burnout to compassion fatigue, the diminished ability to feel empathy.

[60] Eurofound (2017): 36.
[61] van Echtelt (2020).
[62] Bierings (2017), Gallie & Zhou (2013), Smulders & van den Bossche (2006), Béjean & Sultan-Taïeb (2005), Shvartsman & Beckmann (2015).
[63] Hupkens (2005), Smulders et al. (2013).
[64] Schaufeli et al. (2009).
[65] Pfauth et al. (2016, April 12).
[66] van Echtelt (2014).
[67] Houtman et al. (2008).
[68] van Bergen (2016).

A great deal of research has been done on occupational factors that affect health. Of the frameworks seeking to predict which employees are at increased risk of illness, the demand-control model,[69] the effort-reward imbalance model[70] and the job demands-resources model are probably the best known.[71] All recognize that certain negative factors (job requirements) increase the incidence of medical complaints and that certain positive factors (resources) reduce it.[72]

Excessive workload is undeniably a negative factor: employees under great pressure are more likely to suffer symptoms of burnout.[73] While such pressure is usually manageable for short periods, prolonged exposure to stress puts the body in a constant state of maximum preparedness, which renders relaxation difficult.[74] Working to tight deadlines is fine so long as workers are allowed enough rest between them. Interruptions such as phone alerts are also not a problem unless they occur continuously and undermine concentration, which increases the chances of burnout.[75]

To deal with the causes of workplace stress, employees need resources and control options at their disposal. With support from managers and colleagues, they are less likely to suffer from health issues.[76] Being able to talk freely about difficulties helps, which can also make it easier to hand work over to colleagues.[77] But colleagues can also be part of the problem when relationships are strained or when there is bullying in the workplace.[78] Autonomy at work can provide protection against illness and burnout. Heavy workloads can be better managed when workers are able to decide when and how they perform their tasks; workers entrusted with responsibility also feel more appreciated.[79] This is probably why people who are their own boss are less likely to burn out.[80]

---

[69] Karasek (1979).

[70] Siegrist (1996).

[71] Demerouti et al. (2001), Schaufeli & Taris (2013).

[72] van Echtelt (2014).

[73] Bierings & Mol (2012), Schaufeli & Bakker (2013b), Smulders et al. (2013).

[74] van den Broeck et al. (2010).

[75] Newport (2016), TNO (2017), van Bergen (2016).

[76] Bierings & Mol (2012), Crawford et al. (2010), Demerouti et al. (2001).

[77] Halbesleben (2006).

[78] Houtman et al. (2008).

[79] Muller et al. (2015), Bierings & Mol (2012), Smulders & van den Bossche (2017).

[80] TNO (2016).

Box 2.5 Emotional Labour in the Service Economy

"Emotional labour" is increasingly widespread in the service economy, where more and more workers are expected to manage their feelings to present a particular image to clients and customers. In *The Managed Heart*, sociologist Arlie Hochschild[81] shows how flight attendants are trained and controlled to be pleasant (smile!) at all times. Emotional labour, she warns, can lead to alienation, especially if one's feelings do not match how one is expected to behave. This effect increases when a worker is being watched by a boss or colleagues. Since Hochschild coined the term, emotional labour has been studied in workplaces ranging from call centres to schools and hospitals. As the service economy expands, aspects of emotional labour are encroaching onto less obvious professions, for example movers and plumbers who must deal with customers of all kinds.

Although emotional labour can make work meaningful – it may add an extra or deeper dimension to the job – it can also lead to stress and burnout. This is especially the case when there is "emotional dissonance" – when workers, like actors, must feign emotions they are not actually feeling. People who work closely with others are more likely to take sick leave and suffer burnout. This is why emotional capital – the ability to feel and manage emotions – has become an increasingly important asset in the workplace.[82]

The material aspects of work influence psychological well-being. Low earnings can lead to poverty while the poor are more likely to suffer poor health.[83] Job insecurity, especially flexible contracts, can negatively affect mental health.[84] International research consistently finds a link between long-term temporary working and the greater risk of health problems. Studies in the Netherlands are less clearcut on this point, perhaps because people with chronic medical conditions are less likely to be working due to the country's robust social-security system. Temporary agency work appears to have negative health effects while self-employed professionals report better health.[85]

Work-life imbalance has psychological consequences. People who work long days are more likely to burn out,[86] while disrupting an existing equilibrium between care-giving and work often undermines health, well-being and workplace functioning.[87] Having to be continuously available for work can generate considerable stress for "task combiners". While combining work with care-giving does not necessarily

---

[81] Hochschild (1983).

[82] For more on this, see Heuven (2013), Cottingham (2016).

[83] de Hek et al. (2018), Broeders et al. (2018).

[84] Gallie (2013), Kalleberg (2018), see also Kremer et al. (2017a).

[85] Chkalova & van Gaalen (2019).

[86] Eurofound (2018).

[87] Henkens & van Sollinge (2017).

lead to stress or mental health problems, those who feel their work and care responsibilities are out of balance are more likely to experience symptoms of burnout.[88]

Much also depends on the worker's network of social support. Do they have
people they can turn to at home for help with work-related stress, and people at
work who can assist when they have domestic troubles? Tellingly, burnout is less
common among task combiners, perhaps because their families offer more support.[89] But if there are problems at home – for example with the children or finances –
the risk of burnout increases.[90] The incidence of sick leave is also higher among
working care-givers; the longer they combine care duties and work, the longer they
are off sick.[91] Conversely, good work can have a protective effect, for example by
keeping working care-givers from being overburdened by their care responsibilities.
In short, the right combination of personal and work activities can energize employees and improve their productivity, motivation and engagement.

What are the consequences for society if work is not good? The resulting health
problems increase absenteeism. Alongside workplace conflict, health problems –
especially psychological ones – are the main reason people take time off from
work.[92] A significant proportion of absenteeism is due to problems with the work
itself[93]: overwork and stress are increasingly cited as reasons for reporting sick.[94]
The Dutch National Institute for Public Health and the Environment estimates that
unfavourable working conditions cause 4.6% of the total burden of disease in the
country, the same order of magnitude as environmental factors (5.7%), physical
inactivity (3.5%) and obesity (5.2%).[95]

Absenteeism is detrimental not only for workers but for employers and society.
The Netherlands Organization for Applied Scientific Research calculates that an
employee idle for a year due to burnout costs at least €60,000[96] and that all work-
related absenteeism costs an estimated €5 billion annually. Of this, €2.7 billion can
be attributed to "psychosocial workload". In addition, healthcare costs for people
with occupational disorders amount to €1.6 billion, and for occupational disabilities, €2.1 billion. In total, work-related health conditions cost the Netherlands €8.7
billion in 2018.[97]

Good work can contribute to keeping people at work and keeping them in work
longer, as well as enabling those with health problems to return to the workforce.[98]

---

[88] Pot & Smulders (2019); see Chap. 3.

[89] Bierings & Mol(2012).

[90] Chandola (2010), Meijman & Zijlstra (2006).

[91] de Klerk et al. (2015).

[92] Gallie (2007a), Eurofound (2017).

[93] Johnson et al. (2018); see also Chap. 6.

[94] Pressure or stress at work was cited as the cause of absenteeism in 42.5% of cases in 2017; in
2015 it was 37% (TNO 2019).

[95] RIVM (2019).

[96] See Wester (2017, June 19).

[97] TNO (2019).

[98] OECD (2018a).

In addition to absenteeism, work-related psychological complaints can lead to "presenteeism" – the employee turning up to work but doing little once there, for example due to chronic fatigue. Improving the quality of work, the OECD concludes, reduces absenteeism and losses in productivity[99] as workers become more physically and mentally present. In short, investing in good work benefits employees, employers and society alike. Good work is good for everyone.

2.4.2   Engagement

One consequence of good work is engagement,[100] deftly described in workplaces past and present by the sociologist Richard Sennett[101] in *The Craftsman*. Employee engagement affects how organizations function.[102] Engaged employees work harder and deliver better results.[103] Effectory – a firm that has surveyed employees across Dutch companies and institutions, including the entire central government – no longer only asks about job satisfaction, which it deems a too-passive concept. Nowadays, Effectory asks about enthusiasm at work and commitment to the organization.[104] Alongside the formal contract, every employment relationship contains a reciprocal "psychological contract", "a perception of promises made between employer and employee, expressed or implied, about their exchange relationship."[105]

Employers able to engage their employees, typically through non-hierarchical relationships, consultation and worker participation, promote "organizational citizenship behaviour". Staff are then more inclined to take on work left by absent colleagues, to not cause problems for others and to commit themselves to the company.[106] When people feel safe, secure, supported and appreciated at work, they often do more for the organization than is required by their formal contract.[107] Such engagement is good not only for the functioning of the company, but benefits its clients.[108]

---

[99] See also EU-OSHA (2014).

[100] Bakker & Schaufeli (2015); see also www.arnoldbakker.com

[101] Sennett (2008).

[102] Bakker & Schaufeli (2015).

[103] Kalleberg (2018).

[104] www.effectory.nl.

[105] Rousseau (1990).

[106] See also Felstead et al. (2016).

[107] Dekker & Freese (2018); see also research by economists such as Stiglitz on the "efficiency wage", https://en.wikipedia.org/wiki/Efficiency_wage

[108] See also Schaufeli & Bakker (2013a) and www.arnoldbakker.com

Good work contributes to innovation and economic growth by encouraging workers to think about how products, services and work processes can be improved.[109] Eurofound finds that "job quality contributes to developing organisational commitment and motivation among workers, as well as shaping a climate that is supportive of creativity and innovation".[110] Social innovation – structuring work organizations in ways that bring out the best in people (see Box 2.6) – is crucial for our knowledge and service economy, which primarily depends on human capital.[111] Innovations often happen when employees have ideas about how work processes can be improved. But this only happens when workers enjoy real autonomy. Offices are cleaned better and faster when cleaners can suggest improvements.[112] Starbucks' Frappuccino was the brainchild of an employee given room to experiment after returning from a holiday in Greece.

Insecurity at work inhibits innovative behaviour. Companies that depend on flexible workers tend to focus on bureaucracy and controlling their staff.[113] Temporary contracts also undermine innovative behaviour.[114] Staff who do not know whether they will be employed in a few months have few incentives to brainstorm improvements or to provide feedback on how things could be done better. Lack of autonomy interacts with job insecurity to adversely affect innovation and economic growth.

Box 2.6 Social Innovation in the Netherlands: Past, Present and Future[115]

At the beginning of this century, Dutch employers' organizations and trade unions agreed to promote "social innovation".[116] They joined the Smarter Work Platform, and later, the Netherlands Centre for Social Innovation, in which academic institutions also participated. In a 2005 report, the Social Innovation Task Force described social innovation as "renewing the work organization and maximizing its use of skills with the aim of improving business performance and talent development."[117] The Netherlands Centre for Social Innovation received government support; one of the national employers' association (AWVN) played a major role in the initiative, focusing on co-creation.

(continued)

---

[109] Pot et al. (2009).

[110] Eurofound (2017): 36.

[111] van Hoorn (2015), WRR (2013a).

[112] Gallie & Zhou (in press).

[113] Kleinknecht (2014).

[114] de Spiegelaere (2017).

[115] With thanks to Frank Pot.

[116] "Exercising control over labour and technology occurs under a variety of headings: different organization, smarter organization, working differently, smarter working, social innovation, innovative work organization, empowering people, high-involvement organization, and so on" (Pot 2019b).

[117] Taskforce Sociale Innovatie (2005).

Box 2.6 (continued)

As a concept, social innovation is meant to offset the general bias towards technological innovation. It is about "the participative and interrelated renewal of work, organizations and personnel policy in order to improve human functioning and so take organizational performance, the quality of work and labour relations to a higher level. Obviously, this will almost always be done in conjunction with technological innovation."[118] "Organizational performance" here primarily refers to labour productivity and innovative ability; "quality of work" to enriching tasks, developing skills and mitigating stress-related risks. An evaluation of 10 years of social innovation in the Netherlands found that organizations committed to the concept had gone some way to achieve these goals.[119]

The number of socially innovative companies nevertheless remains limited. In 2019, the Minister of Social Affairs and Employment announced that he would turn to the Social and Economic Council of the Netherlands – an advisory body of employers, employees and independent experts – for advice on the "broader and better application of social innovation", meaning smarter working, flexible organization, co-creation and dynamic management.[120]

2.4.3   Sense of Community

Finally, good work is good for the individual's sense of belonging to the community and for social cohesion. Insufficient income and insecure work limit opportunities in the housing market and, especially for men, in the life-partner market. People with permanent positions are more likely to have children.[121] For young flexible workers, putting off starting a family is almost the norm; as a German Minister of Family Affairs once said, temporary contracts are "the best contraceptive".[122] The same applies to possibilities for combining work and care; countries with paid parental leave have higher birth rates.[123] Workers with both uncertain and irregular hours can never be sure if and when they will be called into work and so experience particular difficulties combining work and care.[124] The consequences of good work thus extend to social and family life.

---

[118] Pot (2012).

[119] Xavier & Pot (2012).

[120] See www.ser.nl/-/media/ser/downloads/werkprogramma/ser-adviesaanvragen-2019.pdf?la=nl& hash=6B5619DD5614B3E30413DAE37B8E746B

[121] Verweij & Stulp (2019, August 29); SER (2016b).

[122] van der Klein (2017).

[123] Rovny (2011), Olivetti & Petrongolo (2017).

[124] Kremer (2017), Ballafkih et al. (2017).

Lack of good work can fuel social discontent. More and more workers in jobs with low wages, little security, scant autonomy and few or no control options are turning their backs on society and growing pessimistic about the future.[125] Why is this happening? First of all, bad work is widely experienced as demeaning. People in such jobs feel little respect and appreciation, and often sense that they are interchangeable: "If you go, there are ten more waiting to take your place".[126] Negative workplace experiences – tasks one is overqualified for, discrimination or "flexism" (the unequal treatment of people with temporary positions) – are easily projected onto society as a whole. Second, social unease grows when people do not experience control over their own lives, their futures and that of their children.[127] This leaves them unable to look ahead, consigned to be "prisoners of the present".[128] As work is central to everyone's existence, job insecurity easily engenders insecurity in all aspects of life.[129] Finally, bad work can induce feelings of marginalization, especially when others are perceived to have better work. If their work seems peripheral, people have no incentive to engage. Better work can draw people towards the heart of society.

Sharp distinctions between good and bad jobs can put social cohesion under particular pressure. Indeed, qualitative job polarization may trigger all kinds of new social problems from the increased mistrust of institutions and incidence of mental ill-health[130] to the creation or deepening of social divisions along education, gender and ethnic lines. Good work for *all* is crucial for society.

2.5 Conclusion: Good Work Means Control

People in the Netherlands do not want work to dominate their lives, crowding out family and leisure time. But paid work continues to have important social functions. Work provides status and gives people the feeling that they are contributing to something larger than themselves. Work is a major source of self-esteem, satisfaction and a sense of belonging – but only if it fulfils certain requirements.

The scientific literature reveals three key conditions for good work, all of which align with the expressed wishes of Dutch workers and the needs of the country's economy.

1. *Control over income.* Good work provides financial security, also in the long term, and a fair wage.

---

[125] See Engbersen et al. (2017).

[126] Hodson (2001).

[127] See also Vrooman (2016).

[128] Silva (2013).

[129] van Dijk et al. (2018).

[130] Wilkinson & Pickett (2009), Pickett & Wilkinson (2018), Therborn (2013), see also Kremer et al. (2014).

2. *Control over work.* Good work allows for appropriate workplace autonomy and supportive social relationships.
3. *Control in life.* Good work allows sufficient time and space to combine work with care responsibilities and a private life.

For work to qualify as good, all three conditions must be met; they cannot be traded off against one another. While one condition might (temporarily) trump another in individual cases, proportionality is crucial. While autonomy is a hallmark of good work, workers can also suffer from too much latitude. Although good work allows workers to have private lives away from the workplace, it also allows reasonable demands to be placed upon workers.

People without (good) work suffer psychological and social consequences. Good work increases workers' well-being and makes them feel visible, recognized and part of society. Work that is not good is problematic not only for the individual worker but for society. The economy benefits from productive workers, not from those who are made ill or exhausted (which ultimately undermines the finances of the welfare state). Engaged workers benefit the economy by contributing to well-functioning companies and workplace innovation. Good work benefits social cohesion by enabling workers to build social relationships, feel recognized and look ahead rather than living on society's margins. To maximize social cohesion, *everyone* must have good work.

The following three chapters focus on the quality of work in the Netherlands. Where does the country have the most to improve? How are new technologies, flexible contracts and new workplace pressures affecting Dutch workers? We focus in turn on control over income (Chap. 3), control over work (Chap. 4) and control in life (Chap. 5).

A Day at Work: The Primary-School Teacher
Marijke, a self-proclaimed teacher in heart and soul, has been in the class-room for more than 25 years. She is at school by 7.30 am each day, where she teaches a third-grade class. Today she has the help of a trainee teaching assistant who comes in once a week. Marijke prepares the lessons while the teaching assistant sets up the classroom. The 29 miniature desks are arranged in six groups, crammed into the available space.

The children start trickling in at 8.20 with their parents. Within minutes the place is bustling. Some parents read or play with their children; others need to see "Miss" about something or ask her "a quick question". Then Marijke claps her hands and shouts, "Let's start!"

The first lesson today is reading. The assistant takes a handful of pupils who are behind in their reading out of the classroom to teach them separately. Those left behind read independently in groups. Marijke calls those children whom she suspects have dyslexia up to her desk, one by one. Half an hour later the class is reunited. The reading books are put away and language text-books come out. After some commotion and instruction, the children again work on their own. This gives Marijke and the assistant space to help those who get stuck one-to-one. Hands are going up all the time. The maths lesson after the break is similar: a short introduction followed by independent work. Marijke walks around the classroom, at times giving pupils individual attention, but "always less than you would like". The children are allowed to ask each other for help "but kids just tend to give the right answer rather than explaining how it works".

Children differ not only in achievement, but in learning skills, working pace and behaviour. Identifying and responding effectively to such differences is the big challenge facing teachers, says Marijke. The magic words are differentiation and customization. With 29 faces looking at her, that is a task and a half. "On the days without an assistant, I can't give the kids all the guidance they need."

The children are tested regularly to monitor their development. While their scores reveal deviations from average performance, Marijke says they do not take into account the child's individual circumstances. While she takes the results with a pinch of salt, Marijke realizes her attitude is a luxury she can afford due to her experience; things are harder for her younger colleagues. The tests take up a lot of teaching time – three to four times a year for 29 children in Dutch language, reading and maths – and generate a lot of administrative work. Each pupil's results and how they affect the way he or she is taught must be recorded in a digital tracking system. Marijke does some of this work at home.

"Appropriate education" – recently added to Marijke's job description – aims to keep children with learning difficulties, from Down's syndrome to autism, in mainstream education as much as possible. It requires additional expertise. The teaching profession is changing, says Marijke. Co-ordination is essential for pupils across the spectrum of abilities to flourish throughout their

(continued)

school careers. Teaching is increasingly becoming a team effort, at the expense of the individual teacher's autonomy.

The relationship with parents is also more intensive than when Marijke entered the profession, with both under-involved and over-involved parents creating further stress. But Marijke is no shrinking violet and knows how to manage both. "Parents demand attention – and rightly so, as long as it's about their child, not themselves – but they also need to realize that there are 20 to 30 other children who also deserve attention."

This afternoon, one parent arrives too late to pick up his child. Marijke must thus play babysitter. She then has a meeting with another parent about examining her child for suspected autism. While Marijke knows how to keep the meeting to the agreed 20 minutes, not all of her colleagues are so adept at time management. She then sits down with the trainee teaching assistant to discuss her progress. They then tidy the classroom together and prepare for the next day. As they are doing so, another teacher enters, in need of a shoulder to cry on. After she has left, Marijke expresses her own concerns: "Teachers want the best for the kids, so it can be hard to draw boundaries. Especially for the younger ones. They experience real emotional distress."

At 5.15 pm Marijke shuts down her computer and checks her to-do list for the day. Only half of the items can be crossed off. Later tonight, at home, she will go through her e-mails, including some from parents. It is 5.30 pm when she finally leaves the school, 10 h after arriving.

The Netherlands has 155,000 primary-school teachers, more than 80 per cent of them women. Most have vocational degrees; two-thirds work part-time. Teaching leads all professions in work-related stress. The rate of sick leave is 50 per cent higher than the average for all occupations. A full-time primary teacher earns between €2600 and €4200 gross per month. The average (modal) income in the Netherlands in 2020 will be just over €2800 euros per month, excluding holiday pay. Since 2017, primary-school teachers have been campaigning to reduce their workload and for pay rises to bring their salaries in line with those of secondary-school teachers, who also typically have vocational degrees.

Part I
Good Work: Development and Current Status

Chapter 3
Control Over Income

The Netherlands does not top international tables when it comes to the quality of work.[1] Compared to many other countries, the Netherlands has low unemployment, which remained the case in the wake of the 2008 financial crisis and the recent Covid-19 crisis. Security of employment – a person's general employability or chance of having a job – is relatively high. Statistics Netherlands reports that many jobs have been created in recent decades, and that the Dutch have never worked so much as now.[2] The quantity of work does not seem to be a problem.

The Netherlands' middling position with regard to the quality of work is mainly due to the flexibility of its labour market. While jobs exist, they are increasingly insecure. This chapter delves into the workings of the Dutch flexible labour market, including security of employment, opportunities for training and professional development, social security and wages. What has changed in recent decades? How have new technologies and flexible contracts affected income security? Have identifiable groups of workers been affected differently?

3.1 Insecure Work

Just under two-thirds (64%) of all Dutch workers have permanent contracts; just over a third (36%) have some form of flexible work. The pre-pandemic economy was generating both permanent and temporary jobs, most notably on-call and casual work. The number of self-employed persons (those without employees of their own) was also rising, albeit at a slower pace than a few years ago. In 2018 there were 1.1

---

[1] OECD (2016a), Eurofound (2017).
[2] CBS (2019a).

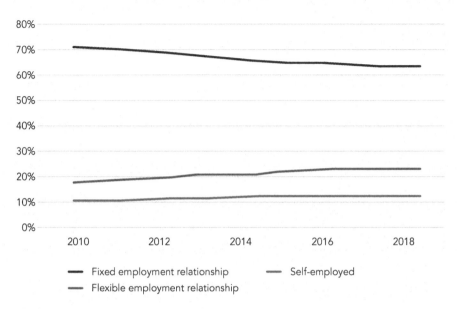

Fig. 3.1 Working people by type of contract, 2010–2018
Source: cbs StatLine

million self-employed persons in the Netherlands.[3] About half of them also had
income from a pension, benefits or a job with an employer (Fig. 3.1).[4]

While more and more people across the board find themselves in the flexible
labour market, temporary contracts – especially agency and on-call work – tend to
be concentrated in specific groups: the young, the less skilled, women and people
with migration backgrounds.[5] Insecure work is thus distributed unevenly; the higher
one's level of education, the more likely one will have a permanent contract
(Fig. 3.2). The gaps are also widening: while a quarter of high school graduates had
flexible contracts 10 years ago, by 2018 it was more than one-third (35%). For those
with higher education, the corresponding figures were 11% and 15%. The recent
rise in permanent employment has mainly benefited the highly educated.[6]

A higher proportion of high-school graduates are employed in the Netherlands
than in Germany or France.[7] Nevertheless, this group remains on the margins of the
economy and are the first to lose their jobs in a downturn. Temporary workers,

---

[3] These are people whose primary occupation is classified as "self-employment without staff".
When those who undertake freelance or similar work for extra income are included, the number is
1.5 million.

[4] cbs StatLine; Kremer et al. (2017c).

[5] Kremer et al. (2017c), van Echtelt et al. (2016), Euwals et al. (2016), Wennekers et al. (2019).
Men, people with migrant backgrounds and the lower skilled are also more likely to remain on
temporary contracts for extended periods (Bolhaar et al. 2016).

[6] cbs (2019c, May 29).

[7] https://data.oecd.org/unemp/unemployment-rates-by-education-level.htm

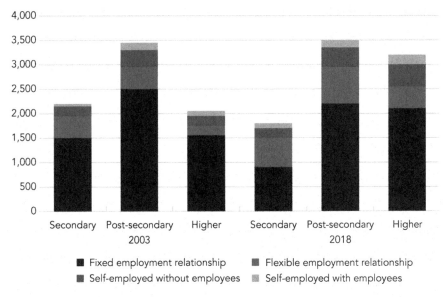

Fig. 3.2 Form of employment by level of education, 2018 versus 2003 (x 1000)
Source: Commissie regulering van werk 2019

especially those employed through agencies, are less happy with their work and lives than the workforce as a whole; the vast majority would prefer a permanent contract.[8]

In contrast, the self-employed tend to be content with their work. Although it was not always their choice to start out on their own, over time most are happy to be their own boss.[9] They particularly value the freedom and autonomy that accompanies self-employment, working in a way and at a place and time of their own choosing (see sect. 3.2). Self-employment is also democratizing, with people from all walks of life setting up on their own. Nevertheless, the typical self-employed person remains highly educated, male and aged over 45.[10] There are considerable differences within this group. The IT consultant who goes freelance at the age of 55 with a substantial pension pot and home equity, a working partner and his previous employer as customer cannot be compared to a self-employed builder or an up-and-coming freelance talent in music or journalism. The differences in income and asset base between self-employed individuals are huge – far larger than those between employees.[11] While no category of worker is as diverse, the self-employed,

---

[8] van Echtelt et al. (2016), CBS (2017b, October 24).

[9] According to the TNO Self-Employment Survey (Van der Torre et al. 2019), one in ten of these people would prefer conventional employment.

[10] CBS (2018g).

[11] Rijksoverheid (2015), Kremer et al. (2017c), CBS (n.d.). According to Statistics Netherlands, the incomes of the self-employed in 2019 were "clearly more skewed" in their distribution than those of working people (https://longreads.cbs.nl/welvaartinnederland-2019/welvaart-van-werkenden/)

compared to their employed counterparts, all share one thing: less income security. The market in which they specialize may collapse, think about the effects of the Covid-19 pandemic, or they may be struck down by illness or their partner might leave them.

3.1.1 Insecurity

Insecurity is the price many flexible workers pay. Research by one of the authors of this book (Kremer) amongst self-employed individuals and employees on temporary contracts shows that this phenomenon means different things to different flexible workers. It sometimes has a positive ring to it.[12] High-earning professionals who turn freelance towards the end of their careers and recent university graduates who have landed their first temporary contract may well experience insecurity as *expectant tension*. Not knowing what is coming is preferable to stone-cold certainty

---

Box 3.1 Insecure Work with Online Platforms

Online platforms such as the taxi-hailing app Uber and Werkspot, an app for jobs about the house, claim that workers are free to use them or not. While the idea is that people can work on their own terms, when and where they want, in practice this is not always the case. People are often judged by their availability, the ability to refuse work can be limited, and reviews by sometimes fickle customers can result in jobs no longer being offered. The fear of losing work is stress-inducing and leads to exceedingly long working days. There is never a guarantee of work, never mind how much – less of a problem for people who do platform work on the side than for those trying to live on it.[13]

For people struggling to start out, platforms can be a relatively easy way to access work. But there is considerable controversy over the quality of much of this work. Legal proceedings about the rights of platform workers are underway in many countries, with local and national governments occasionally stepping in to regulate services. Some platform workers have begun organizing themselves[14] to fight for more rights and greater security. These groups also give platform workers a venue to share their experiences and to support each other. When your boss is an algorithm, there are no opportunities to meet colleagues around the coffee machine or water cooler.

---

[12] Kremer (2017).

[13] Gray & Suri (2019).

[14] See, for example, Arets & Frenken (2019).

about what they will be doing a year from now – "my worst nightmare" according to one young woman. Uncertainty for these people means "change", which gives them the feeling of personal growth.

But insecurity certainly has its downsides, too. Insecurity for many people means *financial stress*. Will there be food on the table tomorrow or in 6 months' time? Such uncertainty can affect sleep and mental health, but can have broader economic impact by for instance postponing consumer spending.[15] If one is unsure about one's income 6 months from now, buying a new TV or booking a holiday is no easy decision.

Work-related insecurity also leads to *life-course insecurity*. People want to look ahead and make plans for the future, but this can be difficult for freelances and temporary workers. People in the Netherlands typically think about starting a family from about age 25, but this is usually beyond the means of young self-employed or temporary workers.[16] A German government minister once described flexible work as the best form of contraception, and this also applies to the Netherlands. Particularly women in temporary employment tend to postpone having children.[17]

Finally, uncertainty often means *lack of recognition and appreciation*. Colleagues and especially employers often treat flexible workers differently than permanent employees, a phenomenon known as flexism. Examples include being denied training or access to important workplace meetings. In the Dutch political debate, employability has long been seen as more important than job security.[18] But for many workers, a permanent contract has not only practical value – it allows one to rent or buy a home – but symbolic significance. When it means moving from one temporary job to the next, flexible contracts give people the feeling that they are expendable: "If you go, there are ten people waiting to take your place." In the words of a temporary healthcare worker: "I'm a puppet and if I'm sick or can't come into work, someone else will. That has opened my eyes."[19]

Most people value security – a crucial feature of good work. But there is a significant gap between most people's wishes and reality.[20] While the flexible labour market may help more people find work, especially temporary and on-call work clearly have adverse social and economic consequences (see Chap. 2). These range from discouraging innovation in the workplace because people have scant incentive to take initiative, to putting off starting a family and general societal dissatisfaction.

---

[15] Dekker and Vergeer (2007) show that greater job insecurity leads to lower or postponed consumer spending as well as slower economic recovery after a recession.

[16] van der Klein (2017).

[17] Chkalova & van Gaalen (2017).

[18] WRR (2017).

[19] Kremer (2017: 107).

[20] Conen (2020).

3.2 Social Security and Insecurity

The safety net provided by the Dutch social-security system has been steadily withdrawing its protections against personal financial insecurity. Although the self-employed can claim basic subsistence benefits, these are much lower than the work-related benefits employees contribute to. They can only be accessed after 3 months without work, and only when the applicant has neither assets nor an earning partner. Self-employed individuals are also entitled to a basic state pension, but not to disability benefits or a state earnings-indexed pension.[21] While many European countries wholly or partly exclude the self-employed from such schemes, the Netherlands is among the countries with the fewest statutory provisions for this group. In Belgium the self-employed must join a social insurance fund of their choice; in Germany they can join sector-specific disability insurance schemes.[22]

Self-employed persons in the Netherlands have generous tax allowances, designed to stimulate entrepreneurship and to allow them to individually cover themselves against occupational risks.[23] In practice, few take out private disability insurance. This is not because the self-employed are foolhardy[24] – many are deeply worried about incapacity to work – but because they are deterred by high premiums (due to negative selection), strict acceptance criteria and the small print in available policies: "Will I actually be paid if I become unable to work?"[25] There are few alternatives to the commercial insurance market. A tiny proportion contribute to "mutual aid funds" (see Box 3.2); others are saving towards a private pension. Few make use of opportunities to join existing pension initiatives.[26]

Self-employed individuals without their own insurance cover and savings thus rely on the public purse when they are no longer able to work. Once they reach retirement age, they can draw a basic state pension although this on its own is barely enough to keep them out of poverty. In the event of unemployment or disability, they can only apply for a basic subsistence benefit if they have no earning partner to support them.[27]

---

[21] Goudswaard & Caminada (2017).

[22] See also European Commission (2017).

[23] Rijksoverheid (2015).

[24] Conen & Debets (2019); see also Kremer (2017).

[25] According to the TNO Self-Employment Survey (Van der Torre et al. 2019), four in ten have no unemployment or disability risk cover of any kind: they are not insured, do not deposit money in a mutual aid fund and have no investments or savings. The great majority cite high costs. Sufficient assets or the ability to fall back on a partner's income are rarely mentioned (Rijksoverheid 2015).

[26] Berkhout & Euwals (2016), Goudswaard & Caminada (2017).

[27] Self-employed persons with assets can claim basic welfare benefits more easily than employees; there are special arrangements for this group (Self-Employed Workers Benefit Decree).

Box 3.2 Mutual Aid Funds: Insurance for the Self-Employed
Local mutual aid funds have recently emerged to provide independent entrepreneurs with an alternative to expensive private insurance against disability. Membership is limited to a maximum of 50 people, each contributing a small sum each month (between €34 and €112). The idea is that this keeps the arrangement transparent because everyone knows each other. In case of a member falling ill, the fund usually pays a modest amount (between €750 and €2500) per month for a maximum of 2 years. The first mutual aid fund was set up in 2006; there are now about 500 across the Netherlands, with a total of more than 22,000 members.[28]

The Dutch interdepartmental policy study *Self-Employed Persons without Staff* concluded in 2015 that this group's distinctive tax arrangements and exemption from social insurance premiums sets them apart from regular employees. This applies at all income levels. A self-employed person with gross earnings equivalent to the national minimum wage will retain 87% of this income after statutory deductions, an employee just 72%. At twice the national average (modal) income, the self-employed retain 55% and employees, 46%. This does not take into account amounts reserved for private pension contributions and sickness or disability insurance, which are voluntary for the self-employed. But even when these are included, a self-employed person with a modal income retains approximately €11,000 a year more than an employee. On the other hand, the self-employed must offset potential loss of income during periods when they have no assignments. For their clients, using freelances can have significant cost benefits; calculations by the OECD[29] show that doing so can reduce labour costs by up to 37% – although the actual amount depends on the individual entrepreneur's bargaining position and can thus vary considerably. For those at the bottom of the market, it is the employer who most likely benefits. At the top of the market, the advantage lies with the supplier.[30]

According to the interdepartmental policy study, the rapid growth of Dutch self-employment may well have been fuelled by these tax and social insurance differentials. Depending on who is best able to take advantage of the arrangement, issuing and taking on assignments on a self-employed basis can be financially attractive for clients, workers, or both. The study concludes: "On balance, the effect upon the government finances of the growth in the number of self-employed persons without

---

[28] ten Houte de Lange (2018, July 3); van der Meer (2017); www.broodfonds.nl

[29] OECD (2019a).

[30] The OECD calculates in its report for the Netherlands Independent Commission on the Regulation of Work: "Considering an unmarried individual without children and earning the gross average wage for employees, the firm could pay a total employment cost of EUR 40,911 (with a payment wedge of 22%) for an unincorporated self-employed contractor instead of EUR 64,960 for a standard employee (with a payment wedge of 51%). This represents a total labour cost saving for the firm of 37%" (OECD 2019a: 21).

staff is very likely to be negative."[31] Although this group currently makes scant use
of the benefits system, this could change in the future. As this would undermine
public support for the system, there is no justification for retaining differential treatment. As the same study points out, "From the protection point of view, in many
cases there is little reason to treat self-employed workers and employees differently.
The self-employed, like employees, run health risks at work and experience similar
problems in assessing their sickness, disability and longevity risks."[32] The exclusion
of the self-employed from the Dutch social-security system – that is, up until the
Covid-19 pandemic – not only affects them as individuals; it may prove detrimental
to the system's long-term solidarity and financial sustainability.

3.2.1 Workers on Temporary Contracts

Are workers on temporary contracts better covered by the Dutch social-security
system? While they have proportional access to its provisions, the rules around benefits and incapacity insurance are insufficiently geared to today's fluid and hybrid
labour market.[33] If on-call workers have monthly fluctuations in their earnings –
sometimes placing them above subsistence level and sometimes well below it – they
face bureaucratic hurdles when applying for benefits to supplement their income.
Similarly, those who go from one temporary job to the next and claim benefits
between contracts must face labyrinthine rules that generate a great deal of uncertainty. The social-security system seems incapable of providing the level of flexibility needed to cope with the fickleness of temporary work.

   While temporary workers have a full package of rights on paper, things are not
always so clear-cut in practice. Take expectant parents: they have a legal right to
parental leave but their temporary contracts are not automatically extended for the
period of leave.[34] Employees on extended sick leave are entitled to assistance rein-
tegrating into the workplace, but only for the duration of their contracts. What is the
chance that their employer will keep them on once the contract has expired? In
practice, formal legal equivalence is often not what it seems.

   The social-security rules are often cited as a reason for the burgeoning flexible
labour market in the Netherlands.[35] The prevalence of temporary work, for example,

---

[31] "The emergence of individual self-employment has, to a limited extent, been accompanied by
positive external effects. On the other side of the coin, however, are lower tax and national insurance yields and higher expenditure on tax allowances. On balance, the effect on the public finances
of the growth in the number of self-employed individuals is very likely to be negative"
(Rijksoverheid 2015: xiii).

[32] Rijksoverheid (2015): xiii.

[33] See, for example, Bannink (2018).

[34] Plantenga (2017).

[35] The prospect of entitlement to a state pension or benefits can make individual self-employment
an attractive option. See Kremer (2017), Conen & Debets (2019).

is often attributed to the country's stringent rules surrounding sickness and incapacity.[36] When workers with permanent contracts fall ill, employers must continue paying their salaries for 2 years and help them to reintegrate into work. While this
arrangement has cut the incidence of long-term sick leave, it also makes especially
small and medium-sized enterprises hesitant about hiring people on a permanent
basis. While research commissioned by the Ministry of Social Affairs shows that
75% of employers are insured against long-term sick leave, 45% still see it as an
obstacle to recruitment[37] – the financial obligations less than the labyrinthine paper-
work and the reintegration requirement. This then begs the question why it is mainly
larger companies that make use of flexible contracts.[38] Having studied all the possible explanations for the Netherlands' leading position in flexible work, Paul de
Beer concludes that it is mainly because companies copy each other.[39]

For all workers in the Netherlands, the social-security system itself has become
a source of insecurity.[40] Compared to other countries, the Netherlands has sound
arrangements for unemployment – albeit primarily for the first years of joblessness;
the longer-term unemployed are better off in Belgium, Germany and Sweden.[41] But
in recent decades, every change to the Dutch social-security system has reined in its
provisions.[42] The changes have also been continuous: the rules around occupational
disability benefits alone underwent 16 major revisions between 1995 and 2010.[43]
However justified some of these amendments may be, for ordinary citizens they
reduce the continuity and predictability of their social rights. Each incoming government has announced the further retrenchment of social-security along with
stricter rules.

3.3   Repair or Revise

The flexibilization of work, in particular the rise of individual self-employment, has
brought renewed urgency to the long-standing debate over the need for a social-
security system better suited to the modern labour market. There are essentially two
options: repair the current system or completely revise it. Which is preferable
largely depends on how one sees the growth in the number of the self-employed.
Are these 1.1 million largely uninsured independent workers an unintended consequence of recent laws and regulations, so that it should be possible through legal

---

[36] OECD (2018a).

[37] Brummelkamp et al.(2014).

[38] See Koster (2020).

[39] de Beer (2018b); see also Dekker (2017) and Chap. 7.

[40] van Lieshout (2016).

[41] OECD (2015c).

[42] See also ter Haar (2017, February 2).

[43] Vrooman (2010).

restrictions, stricter enforcement and the elimination of tax advantages to reduce their numbers? If so, the favoured option might be to repair the system, for instance by requiring the self-employed to insure themselves against incapacity. Here the Netherlands could follow the Belgian example. There was such a requirement for a brief period around the turn of the millennium,[44] abolished as the costs were perceived to be too high. It could perhaps be reinstated in some form.

If such a system is introduced, all self-employed individuals would have to pay into it and fulfil its other obligations. Social insurance of this kind only works with a viable level of participation and a fair spread of good versus bad risks; even those with a relatively low chance of becoming incapacitated would have to contribute, precluding any kind of voluntary opt-out arrangement – which would also be unwise for psychological reasons. In *Why Knowing What to Do is Not Enough*,[45] the WRR outlined human limitations such as foresight, assessing risks and converting knowledge into action – limitations that also apply to the self-employed. Solidarity among the self-employed would also be undermined if participation in a national disability insurance scheme were voluntary.

This combination of financial, psychological and social factors lend support to the second option: revising the social-security system to make it universal, covering all workers and citizens regardless of employment status so that the self-employed participate as a matter of course.[46] This is the alternative most likely to be favoured by those who consider the 1.1 million self-employed as a more or less inevitable (and irreversible) product of the contemporary labour market. As more and more people alternate between or concurrently juggle temporary contracts, self-employment, part-time work and care responsibilities, a social-security system geared solely to contracted employment is even less appropriate; the system needs to be realigned to accommodate all working and life situations (see Chap. 5). Changes to the location, organization and meaning of work all call for a form of social security no longer determined by one's source of income or contractual arrangements. The diversity of work in today's world requires a universal base of certainties.

"Contract-neutral" social security could be achieved through a system in which everyone participates in the most basic forms of social provision. It would involve a minimum level of government-organized insurance and investment applying to all citizens – not just the active workforce – to protect them financially against illness, disability and unemployment, to provide them with a pension, to enable them to

---

[44] The 1997 Self-Employed Persons' Disability Insurance Act applied to everyone in this category, whether or not they employed staff of their own. The statute was repealed in 2004.

[45] Keizer et al. (2019).

[46] This is the option preferred by the membership of ZZP Nederland, an association representing the individual self-employed. More than 82% of its membership is against compulsory occupational disability insurance; 90% would rather see basic provision for all workers so that the self-employed can take out optional supplementary insurance if they wish. See www.zzp-nederland.nl/nieuws/achterban-zzp-nederland-geen-aov-plicht-maar-positief-over-basisvoorziening-   arbeidsongeschiktheid-voor-werkenden.

organize their care responsibilities and to allow them to pursue training to strengthen their position in the labour market. On top of these standard statutory arrangements, people could take out supplementary insurance according to their own wishes and possibilities. Self-employed workers who cherish their autonomy would retain the freedom to make their own choices, as would all other workers. As it consists of a basic product with additional options and toppings, this variant of social security is also known as the "cappuccino model".[47]

Any future reset of the social-security system would require further elaboration of its financing and of the roles played by employers' organizations and trade unions, which could focus more on personal development, learning on the job and better reintegration following long-term sick leave. A further advantage of a reset is that it could address other urgent issues in the labour market, such as intergenerational solidarity, migration and the burden of social premiums.

3.4 Security of Employment and Professional Development

Learning on the job is necessary to improve both security of income and employment. In workplace training and professional development, the Netherlands compares reasonably well to other European countries; only the Scandinavian countries tend to score better.[48] Workers undergo training and attend courses fairly frequently, often paid for by the employer: four in ten have done so recently.[49] Informal learning is often more important than formal instruction; professional development is not just about returning to school or following compulsory courses, but about developing one's abilities in the workplace: learning by doing, through peer advice and feedback from managers and colleagues.[50] Such informal learning, however, seems to have declined slightly between 2004 and 2017.[51] According to the OECD, it is doubtful whether Dutch workers' professional development is sufficient for an advanced knowledge economy.[52]

While lifelong learning has been on the Dutch agenda for five decades, participation in courses and training has levelled off since the beginning of the century. At present, there are some 140 training and development funds in more than 100

---

[47] The "cappuccino model" and its variants have been debated for some time. For their advantages and disadvantages, see Geleijnse et al. (1993), CPB (2005). For a discussion of its underlying principles, see Van der Veen (2016). The Netherlands Bureau for Economic Policy Analysis has described several variants from a flexible labour-market perspective (Euwals et al. 2016). The IBO report (Rijksoverheid 2015) also describes several variants, including a system that begins with the worker's degree of self-reliance.

[48] Eurofound (2017).

[49] van Echtelt et al. (2016).

[50] de Grip (2015, June).

[51] de Grip et al. (2018).

[52] OECD (2017).

sectors, contributing financially to the professional training of workers and some-times also offering courses and training projects themselves. Take-up on the good schemes is about 45%; on the bad ones, it is virtually zero, with very few people even being aware of their existence.[53] In the context of lifelong learning, it is crucial that training can facilitate movement between sectors. In 2019, the Dutch govern-ment allocated more than €200 million to provide everyone in the country with a personal development budget.

One problem is that those who are most in need of training are the least likely to receive it. Highly educated workers continue to have more opportunities for both formal and informal learning; people with the least schooling, on temporary con-tracts, ethnic minorities and those suffering health problems have fewer chances to develop professionally.[54] Particularly agency temps and on-call workers have virtu-ally no chance to learn on the job. Flexible contracts have affected employers' will-ingness to invest in staff, especially for formal learning.[55] Employers may also be hiring workers on a temporary basis so they don't have to invest in them.[56]

Future-oriented learning is not about teaching everyone hard technological skills, but the human competencies needed to thrive in the service economy: how to solve problems, negotiate, persuade, deal with others, and to cope with one's own and other people's emotions. Although not everyone needs to learn to code, people need to know something about robots and artificial intelligence: what they can do, what they cannot do, and how people can work with technology. As tasks and duties will inevitably evolve, everyone needs to be able to learn on the job. Above all, people must learn how to learn (see Chap. 6).

It is a myth that the formally less educated are less able to develop in the work-place. Learning often occurs naturally as tasks and duties evolve. High-school grad-uates are often consigned to jobs with scant learning potential. But when managers believe they can do more and better, and support them in this, their performance improves and they are often just as satisfied with their work as their more highly educated peers.[57] Research has consistently shown that people, regardless of previ-ous educational attainment, learn and develop more when the workplace is orga-nized to support professional development.[58]

Learning on the job and professional development require good colleagues and supportive bosses as well as a sense that there is something to learn. Professional development should be seen as a means to gain and retain control over one's work-ing life and as a way to bring out the best in people within the organizational setting rather than an obligation to bolster one's employability (see Chap. 4).

---

[53] According to the Grip, "good" funds also "draw attention to the availability of that money and the possibilities". See Bouter (2019).

[54] van Echtelt et al. (2016).

[55] Boermans et al. (2017).

[56] See also Dekker (2017).

[57] Boermans et al. (2017).

[58] Gallie & Zhou (2013), Felstead et al. (2016).

3.5 Wage Development

Wages in the Netherlands up until the Covid-19 pandemic were rising after years of stagnation. Wage development depends on many factors, among them the relative strength of workers, employers and their representative organizations. International comparison reveals that strong trade unions bring higher wages and greater pay equality.[59] In many countries, however, organized labour has long been in decline and unions are struggling to attract young workers in particular. Union membership in the Netherlands has plummeted, from 37% of the workforce in the late 1970s to the current 18%.[60] According to Paul de Beer: "To attract more members, they have to show that they can do more for their members. But to be able to do that, they need more members. It is difficult for unions to work their way out of this situation... Recruitment is usually indirect: people join a union because they are asked by colleagues who are already members. As unions shrink, their presence in the workplace declines and that reduces their ability to recruit."[61]

The weakening of the trade-union movement is a concern for employers' organizations which see staff involvement and support as indispensable. The Dutch employers' association AWVN is thus seeking to help unions recruit new members. In 2018, a think-tank organized by the AWVN, consisting of about 60 people from academia, politics, the trade-union movement and business, advanced ten proposals including "when signing their contract, new employees are offered trial membership of a union of their choice for a period of one year. Employers would encourage this by providing extensive information when hiring people."[62]

Until the Covid-19 crisis, wages in the Netherlands were rising moderately, although not equally for all. According to Statistics Netherlands, the average disposable income of households with a high-school graduate primary breadwinner was recovering more slowly than in other households: "In 2016 they had average income 4.6% higher than in 2013. For households whose main breadwinner had post-secondary or higher education, those figures were 5.3% and 5.7%, respectively. More and more people have found or returned to work since the crisis. For those with post-secondary or higher education, that usually means a greater rise in income than for the less well-educated"[63].

Wage inequality is not a matter of education alone. Wage differentials between professions are widening,[64] as was highlighted by primary-school teachers

---

[59] Kalleberg (2018).

[60] de Beer & Berntsen (2019).

[61] van Agteren (2017, October 26).

[62] AWVN (2018).

[63] CBS (2018b, June 7).

[64] Bol (2017).

demanding salaries more in line with their secondary-school colleagues in their recent wave of industrial action. Wages particularly lag behind in jobs involving a lot of repetitive or closely supervised work.

3.5.1 A Living Income

According to a survey by the professional association v&vn,[65] more than two-thirds of nurses and social care workers in the Netherlands believe they earn too little. Many can only make ends meet with the premium they receive for working evening, night and weekend shifts.[66] Their work requires commitment and dedication, is essential for society, and is difficult or impossible to automate.[67] Feeling insufficiently valued and rewarded, some look for other jobs; important services and facilities are thus unable to find enough staff.

The Dutch statutory minimum wage has been falling further behind average (modal) income for decades.[68] But compared to many other European countries, few workers in the Netherlands live in poverty: about 5.3% of the working population, or 320,000 in all.[69] Although this proportion has been growing steadily since 1990, it remains lower than in Germany (9.4%) or the United Kingdom (12.4%). But it is higher than in Denmark (3.5%) or Belgium (4.3%).[70] The working poor in the Netherlands are often poorly skilled and/or have migration backgrounds, and work mostly in catering, retail and transport, and sometimes in the public sector.[71] While their growing numbers can in part be attributed to their wages not rising as fast as the wages of other groups, the flexible labour market and the gig economy has created new groups of the working poor. More than one in nine self-employed persons are at risk of poverty.[72]

---

[65] v&vn (2017).

[66] More and more people must work at night, which can be detrimental to their health and social life. The Netherlands Health Council observed in an advisory report (Gezondheidsraad 2017) that "Nearly 1.3 million people sometimes or regularly work at night. Night work disrupts the body's circadian rhythm, which can lead to adverse health effects."

[67] Graeber (2018) refers to the "caring classes".

[68] oecd (2015b) and data from Eurostat (https://ec.europa.eu/eurostat/statistics-explained/index.php?title=Minimum_wage_statistics/nl#Algemeen_overzicht)

[69] Poverty is defined using the "modest but adequate" criterion formulated by the Netherlands Institute for Social Research. This is based on a "basic needs" budget to cover expenditures on essentials such as food, clothing, housing and insurance, plus a minimal amount for leisure and social participation. In 2014 the norm for a single person was €1,063 per month. The "working poor" are people in paid work living in a household classified as "in poverty", excluding school-children and students with a part-time job. See scp (3 October 2018): www.scp.nl/Nieuws/Aandeel_werkende_armen_in_Nederland_gegroeid_en_overtreft_dat_van_Denemarken_en_Belgi

[70] Vrooman et al. (2018).

[71] Snel (2017).

[72] cbs (2019e, March 5).

3.5.2 How New Technologies and Flexible Contracts Affect Income

Technological developments affect distinct groups in the labour market in different ways. Wages for jobs largely involving routine tasks are falling behind those that require problem-solving skills.[73] Wiljan van den Berge and Bas ter Weel[74] of the Netherlands Bureau for Economic Policy Analysis predict that some tasks now performed by the better-educated will also be replaced by new technology.

Job polarization can be exacerbated by the greater use of robots and artificial intelligence.[75] As some workers with post-secondary education face shrinking opportunities in the labour market, this puts pressure on workers with lesser qualifications – and their incomes. At the same time, new services and products are also increasing demand for less educated personnel.[76] Much also depends on the choices made by companies, institutions and governments about how technology is used: to complement or substitute human labour (see Chaps. 6 and 7).[77]

The flexibilization of labour puts pressure on wages. While economists often assume that employers pay higher wages for insecure work, this is rarely the case.[78] Not all self-employed individuals have the bargaining power to enforce fair fees for their labour, especially in times of high unemployment. This group also lacks collective means to enforce better pay. This is also true for temporary workers, for whom a succession of temporary contracts does not automatically lead to incrementally higher pay, as is generally the case in collective agreements covering permanent staff. The Dutch central bank, among many others, has concluded that the flexibilization of labour exerts downwards pressure on wages.[79]

---

[73] Fouarge (2017).

[74] van den Berge & ter Weel (2015a).

[75] van den Berge & ter Weel (2015b).

[76] van den Berge & ter Weel (2015a: 107).

[77] "Unlike replacing technologies, which take over the tasks previously done by labor, augmenting technologies increase the units of a worker's output without any displacement occurring, unless demand for a given product or service becomes saturated" (Frey 2019: 13).

[78] Kalleberg (2011).

[79] DNB (2018) writes on its website: "An analysis of data from eight Dutch industrial sectors over the period 1996–2015 shows that the fall in the wage share is linked to increased labour-market flexibility. One possible explanation for this is the weaker bargaining position of workers in the flexible shell, compared with employees on permanent contracts."

3.6 Conclusion: Control over Income Requires More Security and Less Inequality

Control over income	The Netherlands in Europe	The Netherlands over time
Reasonable pay		
Employment security		
Job security		
Social security		

░ Neutral   ■ Positive   ■ Negative

Income security is a crucial condition for good work. While work in the Netherlands is generally rewarded fairly, there are big differences in the financial value placed on various tasks and professions. These differences may be exacerbated by the automation and flexibilization of work; wage inequality may thus grow in the future. Although learning on the job and professional development are necessary for all workers to maintain their employability, they are still not the norm, most glaringly for workers who are already vulnerable. Despite the Netherlands' relatively low unemployment rate – which stood at 3% until the Covid-19 crisis – there remain concerns about income security, mostly centring on the rise of precarious work. Although employability in the Netherlands remains high compared to many other countries, job security is low – a product of the growing number of self-employed individuals and the expansion of temporary work and the gig economy.

The uncertainties associated with the flexible labour market are unevenly distributed: there are sharp divisions by education, age and sex. While almost everyone wants job security, the availability of secure positions has plummeted, especially for the less educated. Nor is the current social-security system equipped to deal with the uncertainties. The Netherlands needs a modern system incorporating risk-sharing and protection for all categories of workers; this means revisiting the responsibilities of employers, workers and the state (see the recommendations in Chap. 8).

A Day at Work: The Order Picker

Consumers no longer need to leave the comfort of their homes to make purchases. Supermarkets and department stores have their empty shelves restocked automatically. Distribution centres – the large square sheds that have sprouted across the countryside – are the hubs in the enormous logistics operations that make this happen. Behind their anonymous façades, distribution centres are a hive of activity, with truck drivers delivering goods, unloaders taking them inside, stackers shelving the products and order pickers collecting items to be sent to customers.

Anke and Jos are order pickers at a distribution centre for a department store chain. Some 350 people are employed here, spread across two huge warehouses: one for large items, with electric pallet trucks whizzing around, and the other for smaller products.

Much has changed over the 20 years Anke and Jos have been picking orders here. At first they walked around with pen and paper; then came handheld scanners. Now almost everything is automated. Each picker works in his or her allocated section of the aisle between the shelving racks. An automated system sends them crates. On their computer screen they see which articles to place in each crate, and in what quantity. Flashing red and green lights indicate where these products are located in the racks. At the touch of a button, the packed crate moves on and the next one appears.

"We don't have to walk as much and this system is less prone to errors", says Jos. "But it's not as enjoyable. Having a quick chat or a joke with your workmates is almost impossible now." This is tough for Jos because what he likes about work is the social contact. Now it is limited to three breaks per shift and further hindered by language barriers. As the centre increasingly employs people of different nationalities, speaking Dutch is no longer a requirement to work here. The products are all numbered and the headsets can be tuned to three languages: Dutch, English and Polish.

With all the changes, the workload has increased. There is a personal productivity target – 650 crates a day – and the computer can track everyone minute by minute. "Whenever there's a mistake", Anke says, "they can look back and see who made it." The central display in the warehouse is showing that one employee has done nothing for 8 min. "Maybe he's gone to the toilet", comments Anke.

Prompters come around several times a day to tell workers how they are performing. While Jos can feel them watching, he claims it does not make him work faster. "Although of course I'd rather hear that I'm doing well than that I haven't done enough." Some companies pay a performance bonus, but not this one. The pickers earn the minimum wage, or not much more. Jos would not recommend this job to others. "You work yourself to death for a pittance. It's hard to support a family on these wages."

Anke and Jos both have permanent contracts, but these are now few and far between. All new staff are agency temps and are out if they do not meet their targets. If they perform well for some time, they can apply for permanent positions.

(continued)

The order pickers work morning and evening shifts, currently only on normal working days although there are plans to introduce night and Saturday shifts. There are no specific educational requirements. It is not a difficult job, says Anke, "but you do need a feel for it". The work, however, is physically demanding. The pickers must still walk many kilometres a day and lift a lot – "it makes a difference whether you have to pick up tights or plates" – and the pace set by the red and green lights requires their full focus through each shift. At the end of the day they return home completely worn out. Many of their colleagues are seeing physiotherapists because of back, shoulder or wrist complaints.

Anke and Jos wonder whether they will make it to retirement age in this job. But even after all these years, Anke retains her enthusiasm. But she adds, "If I found something else less physically demanding tomorrow, I'd take it." This is not a job you get better at the longer you do it, she explains. You learn it in your training period and it remains pretty much the same thereafter until at some point, as you get older, you start "sagging". The system registers that you have slowed down. If you have been there for a long time and have a good reason to take it a little easier, the firm takes this into account. You can be put "on cardboard" (clearing away empty boxes) or the pallet trucks. But if your productivity decreases long-term, you must leave.

In the summer, temperatures in the warehouses can reach tropical levels. People sometimes pass out. With all her experience, Anke keeps an eye on the new workers. "They forget to drink because they're so focused on hitting their target."

Order pickers are typically paid €1600-€2000 gross per month. The average (modal) income in the Netherlands in 2020 will be just over €2800 per month, excluding holiday pay. Most order pickers only have secondary education. There is a shortage of workers in this sector, attributable primarily to the physical demands and monotony of the work. The introduction of electronic monitoring systems has increased the workload. While automation is a long-term trend in the industry, the number of jobs is not declining proportionally. A large Dutch supermarket chain reopened one of its distribution centres at the end of 2018 as an almost fully-automated operation. Where once it had employed 450 people, there are now just a handful. But shortly afterwards, the same firm announced plans to build an entirely new distribution centre where, from 2020, 1000 order pickers will be needed to meet the growing demand for home deliveries.

Chapter 4
Control Over Work

"Busy, busy, busy." Ask people about their working lives and they will often respond with this staccato summary. With titles such as *Busy: How to Thrive in a World of Too Much, One Second Ahead, Mindfulness at Work* and *Crazy Busy*, self-help books promise to make our lives less stressful. More and more workplaces are offering courses in yoga and mindfulness or stress tests to help people stay on top of the pressure.

Compared to their counterparts in most European countries, Dutch workers are doing quite well. Their workloads are average, many enjoy a relatively high degree of autonomy, their tasks are varied, and most receive support from colleagues and managers. Only in the Scandinavian countries, especially in Finland, do people enjoy more control over their work.[1] Yet burnout is on the rise. Moreover, if almost half of all workers report that they lack sufficient autonomy, is their work really good enough? Are more people losing control over their work, or does this problem only affect specific groups concealed below the surface of the overall averages? This chapter explores these questions and examines how the automation, flexibilization and intensification of labour may affect people's control over work.

4.1 Busier than Ever? The Intensification of Work

The Netherlands Organization for Applied Scientific Research[2] finds the "burden of work" among Dutch workers to be high and continuous (Fig. 4.1). Almost four in ten claim they frequently have to work hard and rapidly, for example to meet successive deadlines. This is the narrow, quantitative definition of the intensification of work. If we include a qualitative definition of intensification, almost eight out of ten

---

[1] Houtman et al. (2017); see also Eurofound (2017).

[2] Houtman et al. (2020).

© The Author(s) 2021
M. Kremer et al., *Better Work*, Research for Policy,
https://doi.org/10.1007/978-3-030-78682-3_4

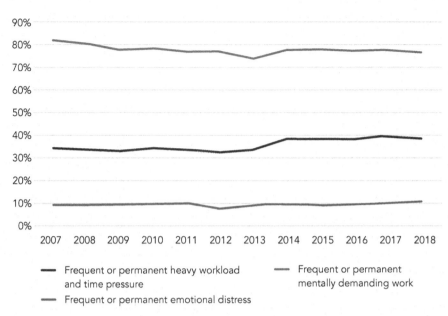

Fig. 4.1 The intensification of work, 2007–2018
Source: Houtman et al., 2020

workers find their work intellectually taxing, while one in ten consider their work emotionally challenging, placing them in tough situations that demand a high level of engagement.

Working people have not suddenly become busier. Their working lives were already demanding but have become more so over the past decade. In 2008, 34.5% of working people reported that they had to work fast; by 2018, this figure was 38.6%. The prevalence of mentally taxing work declined slightly in the same period, from 81.8% to 76.6%. The opposite applies to emotionally demanding work; its prevalence rose from 9.4% to 10.7%, particularly affecting workers in service and caring professions.

People who have emotionally demanding jobs also often consider their work rewarding and valuable. At the same time, they are far more likely to experience symptoms of burnout.[3] Fig. 4.2 shows aspects of the quality of work associated with burnout. Although the term "hard work" is still largely used to refer to physically demanding activity, the hard work in today's service economy is found primarily in intellectually and emotionally strenuous jobs.

These statistical time series apply to the entire workforce and are based on what people report. But work often changes of its own accord, unnoticed. These figures may thus also reflect human adaptability, of becoming accustomed to our tasks. Drawing on specialist expertise,[4] Van den Groenendaal et al. has mapped out the changes over recent decades in six common occupations: homecare worker,

---

[3] Pot and Smulders (2019).

[4] Conversations with labour experts and information from the Claim Assessment and Assurance System (cBBS) operated by t e Employee Insurance Agency (uwv).

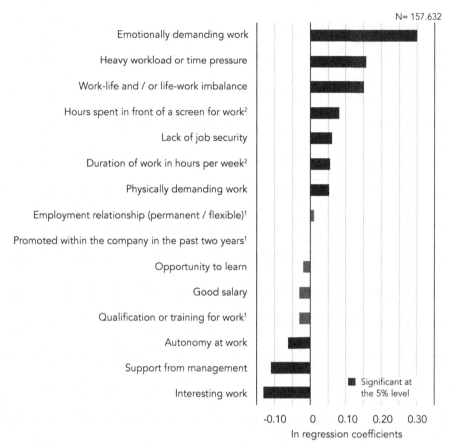

Fig. 4.2 Relationship between quality of work and burnout complaints
Note: All variables are measured on a three or four-point scale, unless otherwise indicated with "binary scale" or "ratio scale"
Source: Pot & Smulders, 2019

primary-school teacher, IT systems administrator, mobile security patrol officer, domestic truck driver and order picker.[5] In all six occupations, workers now face stricter quality requirements, greater time pressure and more emotionally demanding tasks; they all need better communication skills, greater stress-resistance and keener judgement of human nature. The only burden to have decreased is the physical workload. Although observed across the board, these trends differentially affect the surveyed occupations (see Box 4.1 and the professional portraits between the chapters in this book).

---

[5] These professions were chosen as they vary in educational and gender profile.

Box 4.1 Changing Requirements in Four Professions

The mobile security patrol officer must monitor a greater area and more premises than ever before. They now do this alone, carrying hand-held computers to remain in direct communication with the control room. They also need to be able to de-escalate confrontations with members of the public, who have become increasingly aggressive towards them.

The homecare worker must deal more frequently with illness and death due to their ageing client base. This makes the job emotionally tougher. At the same time, their schedules have become tighter – to the extent that these often part-time employees are inclined to help clients on their own time.

The primary-school teacher spends as many hours in the classroom as in the past, but now with much more diverse pupils: children from different countries and with a wide range of special needs. They have been required to take on a lot of additional work including extracurricular activities and updating the electronic student monitoring system.

The IT systems administrator has become busier because technology is increasingly central to organizations. Under greater pressure from bosses, clients and colleagues, they must deal promptly with incidents and consult more widely with a variety of people.[6]

4.2 Autonomy as Achilles' Heel

Whether people can cope with the quantitative and qualitative intensification of their work depends, among other things, on whether they feel they receive enough in return. The "burden of work" is not simply a synonym for workload but refers to the strain caused by the mismatch between task requirements (a lot of work and difficult work) and opportunities for control (the extent to which the worker has a say over how they do their work).[7] While workers may be as busy as ever, this need not be a problem so long as they feel in charge, that they have a certain degree of freedom in their activities. As Ulbo de Sitter wrote in his 1981 book *Op weg naar nieuwe fabrieken en kantoren* (*Towards New Factories and Offices*): "Simply put, it is not the problems which cause the stress but the obstacles to solving them."[8] We thus refer to an appropriate degree of freedom; not everyone thrives by being part of a self-managing team, while too much autonomy can itself cause stress.[9]

Compared to other European countries, Dutch workplaces offer a high degree of autonomy; only Finland scores higher.[10] Nevertheless, almost half of all workers in the

---

[6] van den Groenendaal et al. (2020).

[7] Wiezer et al. (2012).

[8] Quoted in Pot (2019a).

[9] Kubicek et al. (2017).

[10] Houtman et al. (2017); Eurofound (2017).

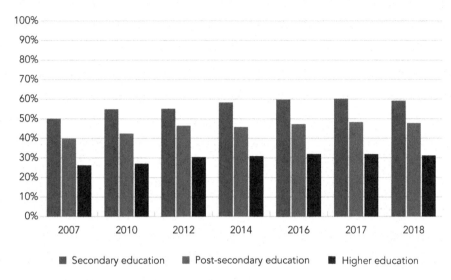

Fig. 4.3 Lack of autonomy by level of education, 2007–2018
Source: Houtman et al., 2020

Netherlands still say that they lack sufficient autonomy. This figure has grown in recent years, from 38.3% in 2007 to 44.3% in 2018.[11] Declining autonomy is most pronounced among high-school graduates, who were already more likely (59.2%) to report being too strictly regulated and having too little space and freedom in their work (Fig. 4.3). The same applies to 47.7% of Dutch workers with post-secondary vocational education. A striking 31.1% of university graduates also say they lack autonomy at work – a percentage that has also been rising. Women on average have less autonomy in their work than men (Fig. 4.4), largely due to the professions and sectors in which they work. Along with hospitality and transport, work in female-dominated areas of the public sector – healthcare and education – provide the least occupational freedom.[12] These fields also have a relatively high percentage of personnel – almost a quarter – whose work combines limited autonomy with demanding requirements: a toxic combination that leads to high levels of stress and absenteeism.[13]

Declining autonomy can hinder workers as they try to manage the intensification of their working lives. Seth van den Bossche and colleagues warn of its economic consequences: "Since autonomous personnel are often more innovative and productive, it is important to ensure that employees retain sufficient autonomy, especially in times of crisis."[14] Work only brings out the best in people when they have control over how they do this work (see Chap. 2).

---

[11] Houtman et al. (2020).

[12] TNO (2018).

[13] TNO (2016).

[14] van den Bossche et al. (2015: 350).

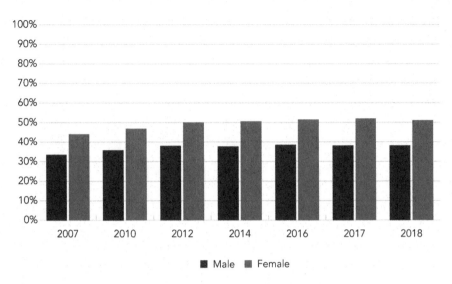

Fig. 4.4 Lack of autonomy by gender, 2007–2018
Source: Houtman et al., 2020

4.2.1 Declining Autonomy at Work: Explanations

How can it be that worker autonomy in the Netherlands is falling across the board? One possible explanation is the flexibilization of the labour market, in particular the growth of temporary and agency jobs.[15] Temporary staff generally have less control over how they do their work; when people are insecure in their positions, employers can exert greater pressure.[16] In this light, growing self-employment can be seen as a strategy by workers to maintain their freedom. Across Europe, "wanting autonomy" is the leading reason why people go freelance.[17] Self-employed individuals often find work organizations too restrictive, bureaucratic or hierarchical, and prefer the freedom that comes with "being their own boss".[18] The greater job satisfaction they experience, and the fact that they less frequently suffer health problems and burn-out, is mainly due to the control they exercise over their work.

The self-employed are the canaries in the coal mine of work organizations - to bring up another "bird metaphor" (see Chap. 1). When former employees strike out on their own, it may signal insufficient workplace autonomy. Research suggests that if companies and institutions allowed their employees as much autonomy as

---

[15] van den Bossche et al. (2015).

[16] Gallie (2017).

[17] Josten and Vlasblom (2017); Benz and Frey (2008).

[18] Kremer et al. (2017c).

freelances, they would be just as satisfied with their work.[19] Not only would employees feel less incentive to leave; the organization would benefit from giving staff greater initiative. Werner Liebregts and Erik Stam refer to "intrapreneurs" – enterprising employees within organizations who "can impel the growth of (new or established) companies" – who "may go on to become independent entrepreneurs later in their career. Whatever their position, working people must remain creative to generate new value. They are increasingly responsible for the investments made in their own careers. In addition to investing in expertise for specific tasks, this also means investing in entrepreneurship as well as collaborating in new contexts so as to create new tasks."[20]

Another explanation for declining workplace autonomy lies in New Public Management – the infiltration of management techniques and models from the private sector into the public and semi-public sectors.[21] Although meant to improve services, control costs and provide greater transparency for taxpayers, the introduction of accountability systems, protocols and performance measurements adversely affect the quality of work.[22] The "organized mistrust" they reflect results in ballooning administrative workloads for public-sector professionals, combined with shrinkage of their discretionary space. The control the government seeks to exert over them comes at the cost of the control they want over their own work.

The Professional Ethics Foundation (*Stichting Beroepseer*) believes that the practices of New Public Management have led to "professional distress", with experts in areas such as mental healthcare, education, youth services and science witnessing the "de-souling" of their professions.[23] This has repercussions not only for professionals personally, but for the public at large. As the Council for Health and Society reiterates, the erosion of the quality of professionals' work will ultimately have adverse consequences for the quality of public healthcare and other services.[24]

The autonomy of many workers in the private sector has declined as well, most notably affecting workers in logistics, business services and retail. Global competition encourages revenue models and work processes that privilege short-term thinking and accountability to "impatient capital".[25] This means that employers embrace

---

[19] Parent-Thirion et al. (2020)·

[20] Liebregts and Stam (2017).

[21] Osborne (2010); Pollitt and Bouckaert (2004).

[22] WRR (2004); Tummers et al. (2009); Noordegraaf and Steijn (2013); Bredewold et al. (2018); Tjeenk Willink (2018).

[23] The foundation's first publication, *Beroepszeer: Waarom Nederland niet goed werkt* (*Professional Distress: Why The Netherlands Is Not Working Well*; Van den Brink et al. 2005), marked the beginning of a long series of important studies. For more titles, see www.beroepseer.nl.

[24] RVS (2019).

[25] Kalleberg (2011).

temporary work and assume greater, more structured control over work processes. Especially in the wake of the 2008 financial crisis, many firms sought to "tighten the reins"[26] – visible in the above-mentioned changing protocols governing the work of security guards and truck drivers.[27]

Finally, the use of new technologies can result in declining autonomy, particularly at the bottom end of the labour market. Firms today often use technology to monitor their employees, reducing their control and freedom at work.[28] Truck drivers are required by law to have a tachograph in the vehicle – a device that allows the employer to keep track of their driving behaviour, location and efficiency. Order pickers at distribution centres are monitored so the firm can see how many items they pick per hour; those who fail to meet productivity targets rarely have their contracts extended.[29] These are examples of the Taylorization of work, in which people increasingly function as "robots made of flesh". Technology can increase the pace of work and constrain workers' room for manoeuvre while making it easier for management to penalize them if they perform below set standards.[30]

But technology can also help increase workers' autonomy and scope for control. In the chemical industry, Eurofound[31] research across five countries found that digitization gives employees greater latitude in the conduct, documentation and monitoring of processes. The use of cobots – collaborative robots that work with people – can make human tasks less routine and physically demanding as well as more challenging and interesting, pushing workers to draw on their teamworking, analytical, creative and problem-solving skills. Technology can thus take work in either direction: more or less interesting, augmenting or undermining workers' autonomy (Box 4.2).[32]

---

[26] van den Bossche et al. (2015).

[27] van den Groenendaal et al. (2020).

[28] van den Bossche et al. (2015)

[29] van den Groenendaal et al. (2020)

[30] Gallie (2017).

[31] Eurofound (2018).

[32] Went et al. (2015); see Chap. 7.

Box 4.2 Bringing out the Best in People? Not for Everyone

Good work means enabling people to use their abilities to the fullest extent possible. One indicator is the degree of autonomy people are allowed in their work. Another is the extent to which people are working below their abilities, with a third of Dutch workers claiming they do not use all their professional talents and skills at work.[33] Some also work at a level below that implied by their educational attainment, although this percentage is comparatively low.[34]

Women's capacities are under-utilized at work. From the age of 35, women in the Netherlands are more likely than men to work at a level lower than is appropriate for their education.[35] This is sometimes their own choice as they wish to devote more time to their children and so "choose" a less demanding job. But all too often, women encounter the glass ceiling which prevents them from rising to the top of an organization, or a "sticky floor" which keeps them bogged down in its lower regions.[36]

People with migration backgrounds often have jobs requiring a standard of education inferior to their actual qualifications. Statistics Netherlands concludes that the Dutch labour market has an inherent "ethnic sanction": after adjusting for their course of study and the grades they obtained, a person with a migration background needs a higher level of educational attainment than someone of Dutch origin to secure the same job.[37]

Finally, people with occupational disabilities are less likely than their able-bodied peers to be working at a level below that implied by their educational attainment. In many cases, this is probably because their health problems or disability prevented them from obtaining qualifications matching their intellectual ability. This group reports more frequently than their able-bodied peers that insufficient use is being made of their skills and know-how. This is in part due to the lack of workplace adjustments and adaptations, and in part due to prejudice and discrimination.[38]

4.3 Camaraderie at Work

Compared to workers in other countries, Dutch workers experience a high degree of social support at work, both vertically from managers and horizontally from colleagues. The figures are higher in Ireland and Norway, but lower in Germany.[39]

---

[33] Poulissen et al. (2017).

[34] OECD (2017).

[35] CBS (2016, January 19).

[36] Portegijs et al. (2016).

[37] Falcke et al. (2017).

[38] Poulissen et al. (2017).

[39] Eurofound (2017). In 2018, some 96.6% of Dutch workers enjoyed substantial social support from colleagues; 85.6% enjoyed support from managers Houtman et al., 2020.

Social support is not only a buffer against the intensification of work; it can reduce symptoms of burnout (see Fig. 4.2), improve occupational well-being, and is necessary for co-operation within the work organization. People who work well with others are the building blocks of social innovation, and the Netherlands values good workplace relationships like no other nation.[40] Although this desire for camaraderie is frequently fulfilled, the country also has one of the highest scores in Europe for aggressive workplace behaviour.[41] We explore this apparent contradiction in more detail below.

4.3.1 Aggression at Work

Workers in the Netherlands are more likely to encounter aggressive workplace behaviour, mostly in verbal form, than their peers in Germany, Belgium and France. It is difficult to explain. One probable factor is the size of the Dutch service sector, which is particularly prone to aggressive conduct. Across different service subsectors, the rate of violence is higher in the Netherlands than in other countries. The Dutch "direct culture" may also play a role.[42]

To some extent, it is colleagues and managers who make work a battleground. 16% of Dutch employees experience inappropriate behaviour at work from colleagues and managers, including harassment, bullying, unwanted sexual advances and physical violence.[43] People with migration backgrounds, especially the first generation, who are affected most (one-fifth), also report more discrimination by people they work with or report to.[44]

Clients, in the broadest sense of the term, are the principal source of workplace aggression: a quarter of employees experience harassment, bullying or unwanted sexual advances from clients.[45] The problem is the most severe in the health and social care sector. In the past 3 years, *Algemeen Dagblad*, one of the largest newspapers in the Netherlands by circulation, has reported cases of aggressive behaviour against disability care workers, prison guards, psychiatric care workers, paramedics, pharmacists and medical receptionists. While working with people is intrinsic to the service economy, it demands resilience and strength of character.

In the public sector, the aggression is largely due to increasingly vocal clients. Parents for example expect a great deal of say in their children's schooling; public policy encourages this empowerment. Combined with cuts to services that leave public-sector workers less time and space to do their jobs well, this can lead to

---

[40] Conen (2018); see also Conen (2020).

[41] Houtman et al. (2020).

[42] Eurofound (2017); see also Houtman et al. (2017).

[43] Houtman et al. (2017); see also Houtman et al. (2020).

[44] Hooftman and Houtman (2017).

[45] Houtman et al. (2017).

problems escalating more quickly and more often.[46] The flexibilization of the labour market also fuels aggressive behaviour as clients find themselves dealing with a different employee each time they interact with the organization. The resulting frustration is one reason why nine out of ten employees in disability care face aggression – not just from clients, but also from their relatives and friends.[47] Research by the Dutch teaching union AOB states that "parents are a factor in the workload that should not be underestimated" and that conflicts with assertive parents are one of the major causes of teacher burnout.[48]

Private-sector workers are also experiencing increased pressure and aggression from customers. Again, this is because many occupations have taken on a service dimension.[49] Security guards may be confronted by violent criminals, but more often by irritated drivers delayed at checkpoints. Truck drivers can experience road rage and then angry customers when they arrive late at their destination. Broader social changes are penetrating the workplace. When citizens become assertive consumers, in some cases encouraged by government policy, this can suppress human empathy for the person standing in front of them. We are treated everywhere as buyers of products and services, as consumers with a right to be demanding – "the customer is king (or queen)". But this is only possible because there are people working to provide these goods and services. In our current consumer society, we sometimes forget that we are not only consumers but working people.

The pressure empowered citizens and consumers place on workers in healthcare and the service economy can be further increased by digitization and social media. People working via online platforms in the gig economy are subject to the "reputation mechanism": the systemic use of customer reviews to encourage them to perform well. But other organizations, including governments, have begun using such mechanisms for direct review as well. Consumers and patients are often more motivated to write negative reviews than positive ones. The digital culture of constant evaluation can thus reinforce feelings among workers that they are always walking on eggshells and that their colleagues have become competitors. It was largely for this reason that staff at the Dutch department store De Bijenkorf, led by their trade union, resisted the introduction of a rating system for sales personnel.[50]

4.3.2 Camaraderie in the Age of Flexible Work

Platform-based work can undermine workplace camaraderie. When one's boss is an algorithm and one's colleague a competitor, it is difficult to build or experience any sense of fellowship. New technologies can also lead to more solo work, for example

---

[46] See also Tummers et al. (2016).
[47] See CNV ZORG AND WELZIJN (2018).
[48] Algemene Onderwijsbond (2017).
[49] van den Groenendaal et al. (2020).
[50] RTL Nieuws (2018, May 23).

security guards who now patrol with handheld computers rather than partners, and order pickers who receive their instructions from portable devices which direct them along the most efficient walking route, leaving them few opportunities to chat with colleagues.[51]

Temporary work can also hinder bonding in the workplace. The sociologist Richard Sennett in *The Corrosion of Character*[52] paints a portrait of a "short-term society" in which contacts are always temporary and fleeting. But although it is true that temporary workers, especially agency and on-call personnel,[53] receive less support from colleagues and managers than permanent staff, collegial atmospheres can be maintained when everyone is in the same boat, as is often the case in hospitality or cleaning.[54] Contact with managers, however, remains problematic; in much precarious work, the actual employer is nowhere to be seen.[55] In flexible work, the problem lies primarily in vertical relationships at the workplace (see Chap. 6).

Labour market flexibility has ushered in counter-movements. As noted in the WRR publication *For the Sake of Security*, many self-employed individuals participate in various forms of "work community-light".[56] Wanting to be one's own boss is not the same thing as wanting to be alone in the world of work. Freelances meet in coffee bars and shared offices, join mutual aid funds and form groups to help members with work and facilities.[57] Sometimes these contacts evolve into a kind of "work organization 3.0" that allows members both independence and basic ties to collectively cover risks.

4.4   Differences in Control over Work: Education and Occupation

When people have little control over their work, this constitutes bad work. Are bad jobs growing in the Netherlands, as Arne Kalleberg observed for the United States?[58] We observed earlier that work has been intensifying, especially in terms of time pressure and emotional labour, while workplace autonomy is declining. While *everyone* seems to have a little less control over work, there are important differences between workers, particularly according to their educational attainment and occupation.

---

[51] See the professional portraits in van den Groenendaal et al. (2020).

[52] Sennett (1986).

[53] Houtman et al. (2020).

[54] Camaraderie can also emerge in response to unfair treatment by the employer (Kremer, 2017).

[55] van der Gaag (2018).

[56] van der Meer (2017).

[57] One example is Zorg&Co. See van der Meer (2017).

[58] Kalleberg (2011).

At the bottom end of the labour market, work is generally unchallenging and workplace autonomy is in short supply. Especially young people, people with non-western migration backgrounds and people with less formal education are more likely now than in the past to have routine, boring jobs with little autonomy.[59] Figs. 4.1 and 4.3 show the decline in intellectually challenging work. Autonomy at work is lowest among high school graduates and has also declined the most for this group, although it has declined for workers with post-secondary education as well. While jobs have been created at the lower end of the market, these are mainly bad jobs offering little in the way of challenge.

There are also specific occupations in which control over work has eroded. Figure 4.5 shows the "burden of work" (both the quantitative and qualitative

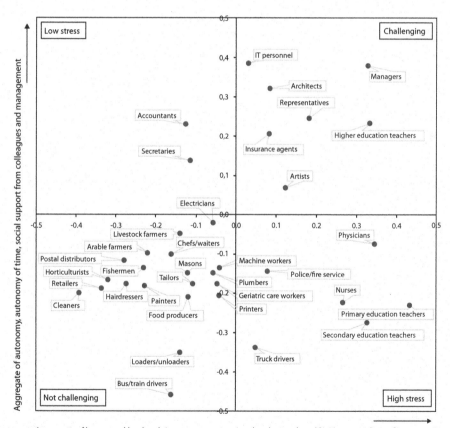

Aggregate of heavy workload and time pressure, emotional and mental workload, overwork, conflicts

Fig. 4.5 Burden of work and resources in various occupations, 2014–2018 (ages 15–74)
Source: Houtman et al., 2020

[59] Smulders and van den Bossche (2017).

intensification of work) on the x-axis and the resources available to deal with this burden (social support, autonomy) on the y-axis. The professions under greatest pressure are in the bottom-right corner: primary and secondary-school teachers, nurses and truck drivers. While care workers for the elderly, printers, loaders/ unloaders, and bus and train drivers are not far behind, they enjoy somewhat more social support and/or autonomy. These are precisely the occupations that have been demanding better conditions in recent years, sometimes through industrial action. In the top-right corner are professionals such as architects and managers who also work intensively, facing tight deadlines and complex situations. But they generally have more resources at their disposal, which allow them to better cope with the increasing demands.

Strikingly, the occupations in which workers have the least control are mainly in the public and semi-public sectors. The 2018 annual review of working conditions by the Netherlands Organization for Applied Scientific Research found healthcare and education (alongside hospitality) to be the sectors where workers most often face heightened demands alongside limited autonomy. Conditions have also been deteriorating over the previous decade.[60]

4.5   Who Is Responsible for Control over Work?

However helpful training courses, stress tests and self-help books may be – and however much we may ultimately be racing against ourselves – control over work is not an individual problem but one that suffuses the modern work organization. We should be focusing not only on how workers handle stress, but on how to minimize risks in the first place. First and foremost, it is up to companies and institutions to create healthier work organizations. But to date, improvements have been lacklustre. Who or what is holding back progress?

The Netherlands, like other corporatist European countries, has a highly developed system of social dialogue that makes extensive use of legally binding collective labour agreements that cover about 80% of all employees. Many actors participate in this system, including the government; employers' organizations and trade unions (the government's "social partners"); and working people alongside their professional associations. We discuss each in turn below.

4.5.1   Government

The government's first pillar, the Working Conditions Act, has since 1989 covered the quality of work (Section 3, Well-Being at Work). Initially focused on extending learning opportunities and reducing stress-related risks, measures were added in

---

[60] TNO (2019).

1999 to prevent workplace bullying and discrimination. These are just a few of the provisions in the Act's 44 sections, most of which cover the physical aspects of work (hazardous substances, heavy lifting and so on).[61] The Working Conditions Act holds employers responsible for the quality of work and obliges them to conduct risk assessments. The question is whether legislation is paying adequate attention to the non-physical aspects of work that also undermine workplace well-being.[62]

While the Social Affairs and Employment Inspectorate is responsible for ensuring compliance with working conditions legislation, it lacks the human and financial resources needed for comprehensive enforcement. Its inspections reveal that many firms do not even undertake the mandatory risk assessments. Overall, the inspectorate concludes, the business community is falling short of its legal obligations.[63] Although the inspectorate's remit includes workloads, workplace aggression and discrimination, it rarely checks – certainly not in actual workplaces. Inspections still tend to focus on the physical aspects of work.[64] While work today is more likely to entail psychosocial risks, the law and what enforcement there is focus on their *detection* rather than on how the work organization can be improved to bring out the best in people.[65]

The government's second pillar consists of legislation governing sick leave and reintegration in the workplace. Employers are obliged under the threat of fines to take care of staff on sick leave. This system, unique to the Netherlands, has successfully reduced absenteeism. The guidance provided by occupational physicians, however, is directed mainly at individuals, not the work organization, and it remains questionable whether the medicalizing of individual employees is the right approach. Improving the design of companies and institutions cannot be left to doctors alone; it sometimes requires more structural changes for which labour or organizational experts are needed.

The government's third pillar is the law on staff councils. These bodies are highly developed in the Netherlands and allow employees to influence the quality of their work through legally binding rights of advice and consent. Not all work

---

[61] Regarding "psychosocial" and other forms of mental or emotional pressure, Section 3.2 of the 1999 Working Conditions Act states: "The employer shall operate a policy aimed at preventing employment-related psychosocial pressure, or limiting it if prevention is not possible, as part of the general working conditions policy."

[62] Frank Pot argues that more effort should be made to publicize Section 3 of the Working Conditions Act, where it "calls for work to be adapted to the employees' individual characteristics and for monotonous work and activities that need to be carried out at a particular speed to be avoided or limited" (Pot, 2019b).

[63] Inspectie szw (2019).

[64] As an exception, 81 organizations were inspected between 1 November 2015 and 1 March 2016 to see whether employers had developed policies to manage work pressure; 80% were found not to have done this systematically enough (Inspectorate szw, 2016).

[65] The OECD cites the Working Environment Act in Denmark as an example of good practice (OECD, 2018a: 182).

organizations are required by law to implement this form of employee participation; many small firms are exempt, while workers in the platform economy, self-employed individuals and flexible temporary staff generally fall outside of its remit.[66] Workers with insecure flexible jobs rarely take part in decision-making, are less familiar with this form of participation and are not strong enough to enforce changes.[67] The larger the proportion of temporary personnel on a company's books, the less likely it is to have a staff council.[68]

4.5.2   Social Partners and Professional Associations

Employees can exert influence to improve their control over work.[69] After all, who is better placed to do so? The question is whether employees are sufficiently powerful and whether existing forms of staff representation focus enough on the quality of work. Compared to especially the Scandinavian countries and France, the Netherlands has low trade-union membership; unions generally lack meaningful presence in individual workplaces. At the national level, trade-unions advise the Social and Economic Council of the Netherlands (SER) and campaign to shape Dutch and European regulations. The SER[70] is an advisory body comprising representatives of trade unions and employers' organizations as well as independent experts, one of the main platforms for social dialogue in the Dutch system of broad consultation known as the "polder model". In its 2016 report *People and Technology*, the SER advocated combining technological and social innovation.[71]

  Collective labour agreements provide further opportunities for improving the quality of work. Although discussion about implementation has yet to begin, two agreements recently concluded in the metals sector contain provisions to promote workplace "social innovation". Many industries publish working conditions catalogues specifying occupational health, safety and well-being requirements tailored to their particular contexts, along with recommendations and examples of best practice.[72] Renewing their traditional interest in their members' professional

---

[66] Heidsma and Zaal (2019).

[67] van der Gaag (2018).

[68] Tros et al. (2019).

[69] "Workers' participation is all the more necessary as the advent of artificial intelligence is expected to bring new challenges to workplaces" (Ponce Del Castillo, 2017).

[70] https://www.ser.nl/en/SER/About-the-SER/-/media/544A7D818CA04A2FA1DFCCE9E0F09057.ashx

[71] SER (2016b).

[72] Working conditions catalogues are available in the meat, poultry, fish processing, agricultural, parks and gardens, cleaning, window-cleaning, construction and infrastructure sectors, among others. They advocate alternating or rotating tasks and ergonomic improvements. The catalogues do not question the nature of the work itself, although they do occasionally refer to the Working Conditions Act – specifically Section 3.1d, which calls for the avoidance of monotonous work (Pot, 2018a).

development would allow unions to more effectively participate in the debate on how technology can improve the quality of work and workplace well-being.[73]

While professional associations – for example V&VN, representing nurses and social care workers in the Netherlands – often emphasize professional development and workplace autonomy, they are not always large enough or sufficiently resourced to press their demands home within individual companies and institutions.[74]

4.5.3   Workers

Effective staff representation improves the quality of work and protects workers from occupational stress.[75] There are three levels at which workers can strengthen their positions within organizations: on the shopfloor, in the staff council and in the boardroom. Particularly the system of staff councils could be better exploited to improve the quality of work. Companies with staff councils generally have working climates where employees can take initiative.[76] Staff councils can facilitate consultation and teamwork on the shopfloor; the more influence employees have over the organization of their own work, the more effectively their representative bodies operate.[77] But it remains unclear to what extent staff councils are able to influence decision-making. While they already have a broad statutory remit, they may – judging by their past track record[78] – be hard pressed to tackle broader issues such as emotional stress or how technology is used in the workplace.

Employees do not always feel represented by existing structures. Organizations have thus begun experimenting with more pro-active forms of participation alongside, instead of, or within staff councils.[79] Examples include the banking group ABN AMRO's participant pool and Haarlem City Council's theme groups that draw many more employees than only staff council members into work-related discussions.

How far can workers influence corporate governance? From his research on how employee participation has affected the market value of 700 European companies in the period 2006–2008, Robert Kleinknecht[80] concludes that employee participation

---

[73] Crouch (2018).

[74] V&VN, the Dutch professional association for nurses and social care workers, is very active and has more than 100,000 members. It addresses workload, education, autonomy and professional pride.

[75] ETUI (2019); Eurofound (2013).

[76] Smulders and Pot (2016).

[77] Tros et al. (2019); Smulders and Pot (2016).

[78] Pot (2019b).

[79] Tros et al. (2019).

[80] Kleinknecht (2018).

heightens managers' awareness of long-term goals. In the Netherlands, the debate thus far has focused mainly on gender balance in governance (see the SER advisory report *Diversity in the Boardroom: Time to Accelerate*).[81] Elsewhere, French President Emanuel Macron, former UK Prime Minister Theresa May and former US presidential candidate Elisabeth Warren have advanced proposals to reserve more places on company boards for staff or trade union representatives.[82] In the Netherlands, one suggestion is for a nurse to sit on the board of every healthcare institution[83] – an idea that has long been on the agenda in the US.[84]

Finally, it is possible to create work organizations in which the personnel take charge from the outset. Although workers' co-operatives are not as common in the Netherlands as they are in Italy or Spain, interest is growing: groups of the self-employed have begun pooling their resources while new initiatives are emerging in the platform economy (see Box 4.3). Some companies have introduced initiatives combining profit-sharing and representation.[85] More recently, social enterprises with a different approach to doing business than traditional firms are emerging,[86] although they may encounter legal and regulatory obstacles from the requirement to establish staff councils[87] to the ban on employees who are also claiming benefits from sharing in the profits. To strengthen control over work, initiatives to democratize work must be supported.

The three structural developments at the heart of this report – the automation, flexibilization and intensification of labour – can all undermine control over work. To ensure that this does not happen, different actors need to play their part.

---

[81] SER (2019a).

[82] Kowalsky (2019).

[83] In 2018, MPs Corinne Ellemeet and Sophie Hermans tabled a parliamentary motion calling for all healthcare institutions to appoint a "chief nursing officer" to the board. They believe that nurses, with their wealth of knowledge and experience, should be listened to.

[84] Graystone (2019).

[85] See, for example, Kremer, M. (Kremer, 2015, February 2).

[86] See also the WRR exploratory study of philanthropy (de Goede et al., 2019) which proposes studying the desirability of a new statute for social enterprises.

[87] The SER can grant exemptions from this requirement, but rarely does (Tros et al., 2019).

Box 4.3 Workers' Co-Operatives
Co-operatives enable self-employed individuals and platform workers to enter into collective agreements about rates and other matters. A platform co-operative is owned and managed by the platform's users. Examples include Stocksy, a website operated by a group of photographers, and Green Taxi, formed by 800 taxi drivers in Denver, Colorado. Smart, originally founded in Belgium, claims to represent 85,000 freelances, many of them artists and performers. Co-operatives have effectively functioned as trade unions when new platforms appear on the market, forcing for instance food-delivery services Deliveroo and Take Eat Easy to accept collective agreements covering their members.[88]

There are businesses where the staff are in charge in other industries as well. *Schoongewoon*, founded in 2012, is a group of ten local workers' co-operatives in the cleaning sector. Everyone participates in the firm's decision-making and shares in its profits; all say they prefer this work to their previous job – not because their wages are higher (they are not) but because they feel that they are their own boss, that there is mutual trust and everyone helps each other.[89] In the home care sector, the *Helpgewoon* co-operative is organized along similar lines.

4.6   Conclusion: Control Over Work Requires More Autonomy and Camaraderie

Control over work	The Netherlands in Europe	The Netherlands over time
Autonomy		
Use and develop skills		
Social support		
No aggression/discrimination		

▨ Neutral   ■ Positive   ■ Negative

Dutch workers are constantly trying to adapt to the changing and growing demands of their jobs, which are leaving them with more to do and less time to do it. Although the Netherlands, on aggregate, scores well in "control over work", it does not do so

---

[88] Arets (2019, February 25).
[89] Stavenuiter and Oostrik (2017).

consistently. Aggression in workplaces is increasing while almost half of all workers experience limited and declining autonomy. While new technologies and flexible contracts are part of the story, the government itself is part of the problem when public-sector professionals are suffering the brunt of New Public Management and the organized mistrust it entails. With little autonomy at work, people are less able to cope with its intensification. All in all, it is a recipe for burnout and absenteeism.

Lack of control over work is not an individual problem that can be solved through stress tests and self-help books. It concerns work organizations and, more broadly, society. How can we ensure that companies and institutions take responsibility for the quality of work they provide as they make strategic decisions about the automation, flexibilization and intensification of labour? After all, the prime responsibility for the quality of jobs and workers' ability to exercise meaningful control over their work rests with management. Much remains to be done, not least by employers' organizations and trade unions; workers also need greater influence over their organizations (see recommendations in Chap. 8).

It is crucial that people have control over their work – for their own health and well-being as well as for the functioning of the work organization. For the same reasons, workers need to be able to put boundaries around their work so that they may exercise control over the rest of their lives. That is the subject of the next chapter.

A Day at Work: The IT Worker

"Data is the new gold", says IT worker Gerco, "and I help mine that gold." Gerco was hired on a freelance basis by the German energy company Innogy, the parent company of Essent – a leading supplier of gas and electricity to the Dutch market. Innogy wants to make the most of its data on its 2.5 million customers in the Netherlands, such as their energy consumption and their responses to special offers. Gerco is part of a "Big Data Team" of 20 specialists organizing and analysing this material, converting it into behavioural predictions.

Aged 48, Gerco is self-employed and currently engaged by several clients, mostly on long-term projects. He works for Innogy about three days a week, partly at home and partly at its offices in Den Bosch. Today there is a short sub-team meeting at 9:30 am to identify problems and define new tasks. Because of its international composition, the team works in English. After the meeting, Gerco takes a seat at one of the workstations in the "flexible space" where the Big Data Team has gathered. He is working on a program for an improved data library. "Programming is not so creative", he explains. "It's mainly making use of solutions other people have already come up with. Programmers are constantly googling." He types in a question, goes through the search results and finds a possible answer. Then he cuts and pastes, polishes, does a test and finds that it works. A big laugh: "We are very pleased with Google."

(continued)

The self-managing team works in "three-week sprints", each with new goals. From these are derived specific tasks, which are delineated and allocated through mutual agreement. At 11 am there is a stand-up meeting in a cramped, glass-walled conference room to mark the end of the current sprint. Against the back wall is a 3×2-metre board with the project timetable, covered with stickers and Post-It notes. The team members report briefly on their progress and discuss successes, problems, solutions and new estimates. Post-Its are moved and new ones added. The conclusion: they are still on schedule. Everyone returns to their own computer.

Shortly after noon, someone calls out something about lunchtime. Gerco drags himself away from his screen. It is rare for anybody to work through lunch with just a sandwich at their computer. In the canteen, six members of his team sit together at a table. 45 min later, everyone is back in the office. Gerco continues to work on his program. Now that he has found the right route, he can set about perfecting it.

Information technology is developing rapidly. Gerco keeps up to date by reading and talking with colleagues, but above all by doing. He had to learn the trade largely on the job – his degree is in Mechanical Engineering, not IT. His criticism of many training courses and companies is that they tie employees down to a specialist domain, say Java, when broad knowledge is essential to keep up. "As a freelance, I'm in on a wide range of projects. You learn from that."

Becoming self-employed was a deliberate choice for Gerco. He has joined 4Synergy, a group of 45 freelance IT specialists who work together to acquire and share knowledge. He is saving for a rainy day and is insured against illness through a mutual aid fund. His rate varies between €700 and €1200 gross per day, depending on the type of assignment.

At about 2 pm, Gerco has an appointment with a colleague from Innogy. The Big Data Team needs permission to link its cloud platform to the firm's data files. This is a major information security issue. The two men sit together in a small interview room, each behind his own laptop. The jargon flies: "gateway", "AWS management console", "user landing". The perfect solution cannot be achieved at the moment, but Gerco says that the alternative they have found is more than adequate: it sounds an alarm if anyone tries to break in. But his colleague doubts this will satisfy his superiors. Gerco is not happy. Co-ordination with the company often leads to delays, he sighs.

He returns to his computer. Stress is not a problem for Gerco. Nor does he have the idea that companies are racking up their demands or expecting orders to be completed faster. It is rare for him to work in the evening or on weekends.

Gerco notes that technology is taking over more and more work, including that of people in IT. "The hardware specialists, especially in non-graduate positions, are losing their jobs. For example, because servers are being replaced by the cloud." Which does not mean that he, as a cloud specialist, is

(continued)

sitting pretty. "In ten years' time that could be replaced by artificial intelligence." So? "So I have to make sure I stay up to date and in demand. How? By continuing to work. Beyond that, you can't plan things."

It is 5 pm. Gerco finishes his program and then goes home.

The number of IT workers in the Netherlands continues to grow; at the beginning of 2019 there were 395,000 of them, 85% of them men. They are relatively highly educated: 62% have a university degree, 22% a post-secondary vocational qualification. The number with permanent contracts is declining. In 2017, they accounted for 73% of the profession, while 15% were on flexible contracts and 16% were self-employed. According to a 2014 survey of IT professionals by the technology website Tweakers, almost 60% have a gross income of between €2000 and €4000 per month. The average (modal) income in the Netherlands in 2020 will be just over €2800 per month, excluding holiday pay. Freelance IT workers are more likely than employees to earn less than €2000, but also more likely to earn more than €4000.

Chapter 5
Control in Life

The Dutch value clear boundaries around their work. However much they may be committed to their professions and occupations, they want to live a life and to be able to look after young children and elderly parents. It is thus hardly surprising that control over one's working hours has become a key policy issue in recent decades.[1] This has largely been driven by women moving en masse into the paid labour market, although working men certainly want more control over their lives as well. One in ten workers in the Netherlands now say that their working and private lives are out of balance.[2] As deadlines pile up at work, so too does the washing up at home; as a result, people sometimes feel inadequate on both fronts.[3] Some people – especially the highly educated, women and parents – feel perpetually rushed.[4]

Eurofound[5] observes that it is relatively easy for people in the Netherlands to set limits on their work and to combine work with private life. This is largely due to the country's part-time work culture. Dutch women entered the workforce en masse only in the late 1990s, at about the same time as women in Spain and Ireland. The inroads women have made since then are largely due to the part-time economy, with shorter hours widely accepted even in the middle and upper segments of the labour market.[6] But it is not only women who find it easier to enter paid work; the part-time culture also benefits other groups such as people with occupational disabilities (Box 5.2).

---

[1] The clearest changes concern the importance of good working hours (45% in 1990, 60% in 2018) and good holiday arrangements (36% in 1990, 45% in 2018) (Conen, 2020).

[2] Houtman et al. (2020).

[3] Houtman et al. (2017).

[4] Overall, 36% of workers sometimes feel rushed, 54% that they are sometimes too busy, and 39% that they are failing to some extent. Highly educated persons, women and parents more often express such sentiments (Roeters, 2018).

[5] Eurofound (2017).

[6] Visser (2002).

© The Author(s) 2021
M. Kremer et al., *Better Work*, Research for Policy,
https://doi.org/10.1007/978-3-030-78682-3_5

The question remains whether this has not created what economist Janneke Plantenga calls the "part-time trap".[7] Public provisions in the Netherlands, from school hours to pre-school childcare, tend to be geared to part-time work which has become the norm, in policy as well as in practice. As a result, many workers do not truly choose the hours they work. The part-time culture has also impeded progress in areas such as comprehensive childcare and paid leave.

This chapter focuses on part-time work as well as the other ingredients necessary to improve control in life including paid leave, good childcare, care for the elderly and workers' ability to determine their own working hours. How are new technologies, flexible contracts and the intensification of work affecting people's control in life?

5.1   Part-Time Work, or Looking After Number One

The work-life balance enjoyed by most people in the Netherlands can be attributed to the part-time economy, more specifically to the part-time economy for women. Three-quarters of working women are employed part-time (Fig. 5.1); their average working week has now risen to 28 h, which is no longer low by European standards. Twenty-two percent of working men also work part-time, a level unique in Europe. Overall, men work an average of 39 h a week (Fig. 5.2).[8]

The Care and Work Act, introduced in 2006, allows people to adjust their own working hours, providing what is effectively a right to work part-time. The possibilities were further expanded by the Flexible Working Act in 2016. This means that the Netherlands, together with the UK, now has the most comprehensive legislation for part-time work.[9] By law, workers enjoy substantial autonomy to determine for themselves where and what hours they work. Combined with the Dutch part-time economy, the law ensures that people have more time for their families, voluntary work and other activities.

Does the lack of affordable childcare force especially women to work part-time? The answer, largely, is "no": part-time work is what most women prefer. It is their wish, primarily because it allows them to spend more time with their children. Despite this, the Netherlands Institute for Social Research has calculated that the average female working week would be 2.3 h longer if all women were able to work the amount they preferred.[10] Moreover, 13% of women – and 7% of men – explicitly state that they want to work more hours.[11] Whereas public policy in recent decades

---

[7] Dohmen (2017, October 20).

[8] Portegijs and van den Brakel (2018).

[9] OECD (2019b).

[10] Portegijs et al. (2016).

[11] Portegijs and van den Brakel (2018). According to Statistics Netherlands, 662,000 people want to work fewer hours, notable among them the self-employed. In the first quarter of 2019, 766,000 people wanted to work more hours, although not all were immediately available (www.opendata. cbs.nl).

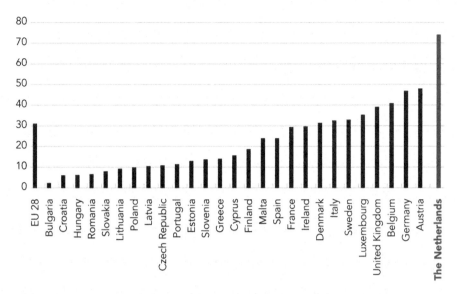

Fig. 5.1 Proportion of women in part-time work in the Netherlands and the rest of the European Union, 2017
Source: SCP

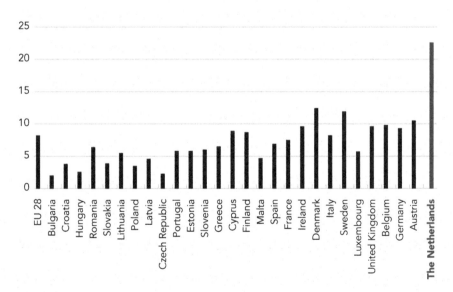

Fig. 5.2 Proportion of men in part-time work in the Netherlands and the rest of the European Union, 2017
Source: SCP

has focused on opportunities to work less, perhaps more attention is now warranted for possibilities to work more. While part-time work as a choice is a hallmark of good work, this choice is inevitably shaped by prevailing social, economic and institutional conditions. We examine the most important of these below.

5.1.1 Childcare

Would people in the Netherlands work longer hours if childcare was less expensive and of better quality? The provision of public care for young children – professional childminding, crèches, kindergartens, nursery schools – is seen primarily as a surrogate for parental care (the term kinder*opvang* implies a "relief" or "stand-by" service). The main aim of childcare in the Netherlands has always been to support women's participation in the workforce – unlike in Scandinavia, where the child's social, emotional and cognitive development is paramount.[12] The quality of Dutch childcare has long worried pedagogues.[13] Most workers in the sector only have modest qualifications,[14] and it is only quite recently that Dutch public childcare has been assessed as "satisfactory" to "good".[15] Pedagogues claim that compared to other countries, the quality of Dutch childcare is only "average".[16]

Dutch parents often find the costs of childcare prohibitive, and they are right: only in the UK do parents spend more of their income on childcare. A couple with one full-time and one part-time earner can easily find themselves spending a fifth of their earnings on childcare, even if it is only for a few days a week.[17] While parents generally consider the quality of the care good, they are critical of the high staff turnover – a product, in part, of labour market flexibilization.[18] Dutch parents have low expectations.[19] Because of the part-time economy, children only attend nursery a few days a week; "safe" and "fun" are thus good enough. If childcare focused more on the child's educational development, parents might make more use of it, allowing them more time to work.

---

[12] See also WRR (2013a).

[13] Vermeer and Groeneveld (2017).

[14] The *National Childcare Quality Monitor* concludes: "The provision of professionalization activities is middling on average, with little frequent substantive educational consultation with colleagues or fellow childcare workers and managers" (Slot et al., 2017: 12).

[15] Slot et al. (2017).

[16] Fukkink (ed.). (2017).

[17] OECD (2016b); see also OECD (2019b). Dutch government spending is also relatively low; see also McKinsey Global Institute (2018).

[18] Roeters and Bucx (2018).

[19] Dohmen (2017, October 20).

Box 5.1 Childcare in Northern Europe
Pre-school in Scandinavia has historically focused on children's social and cognitive development, and Finland, Sweden, Iceland and Denmark consistently top international tables for the quality of childcare. The idea is that – certainly from the age of two – children are better off attending nursery than staying at home. In Denmark, all children older than 6 months are entitled to at least 20 h of public childcare a week, even if their parents do not go out to work.[20] In line with this thinking, higher professional demands are placed on staff in the sector, who usually have vocational degrees. In contrast, their Dutch counterparts are more likely to have post-secondary qualifications at best, while many are on temporary contracts.

5.1.2   Care for the Elderly

Would people in the Netherlands work longer hours if care for the elderly were better organized? In previous generations, women were stay-at-home mothers and available to look after elderly relatives if need be. Now that most members of both sexes are working outside the home, more and more people are combining paid work and informal care-giving – one in three women and one in five men, 2 million people in all. This number will only continue to rise with the aging of the population and people staying in work for longer.[21] So long as their care-giving only consists of basic tasks and errands that are not too time-consuming, most working informal care-givers manage to cope. But the heavier the burden becomes – 8 h or more a week – the more likely some will stop working altogether and many more will work fewer hours or take sick leave.[22] Workers with heavy informal care responsibilities experience a great deal of time pressure and are less satisfied with their lives.[23]

Compared to most other European countries, the Netherlands spends large sums on long-term care for the elderly. A significant percentage of those aged 75 and over live in residential nursing facilities or receive professional care in their own homes.[24] While the policy aim is for people to continue living independently for as long as possible, the Dutch social care system is not organized to support informal care-givers; it focuses on the elderly themselves, not on their working sons or daughters. What assistance informal care-givers receive comes from local government in the form of information, emotional support and at times short-term respite care – none of which does much to keep the informal care-giver in work.

---

[20] Kremer (2007); Rostgaard (2014).

[21] de Boer et al. (2019).

[22] Among those combining work with intensive informal care-giving, 17% started working less and 7% gave up work altogether (Josten & de Boer, 2015).

[23] de Boer et al. (2019).

[24] Spasova et al. (2018).

Structural facilities to help working informal care-givers such as day-care centres and hospital-based services have been phased out. Referring to what they call
the "participation society", recent Dutch governments have called on people to take
greater responsibility for care and to make less use of facilities provided by the
welfare state. For the foreseeable future, the care demands placed on families are
more likely to increase than decrease.[25]

5.1.3 Fair Sharing

Do people work more if their partner does more at home? The policy ideal in the
Netherlands has long been the "fair sharing" of both paid and unpaid work. But
although the Dutch have been European leaders in talking about men's responsibilities[26] and shared caring is the stated ideal of much of the population,[27] things differ in
practice. Women usually reduce their working hours once children are born while
men work more. In only 18% of households with children do both partners work
equal hours. While Dutch men have begun caring more for their children than men in
most other European countries except in Scandinavia, Dutch women more frequently
remain responsible for household tasks and especially family organization. The differences are most apparent in informal care-giving, where 17% of working women
and 10% of working men look after sick or needy elderly relatives, partners or
children.[28]

5.1.4 Good Work

If one chooses for it, working part-time can protect workers from the intensification
of work.[29] But would part-time employees work longer hours if they had better
jobs? Women tend to have less autonomy at work and are more likely to be working
on a temporary or on-call basis and in sectors with high workloads such as primary
education and healthcare. Some jobs are so emotionally stressful that people eschew
full-time positions. In primary education, a leading reason to prefer part-time
appointments is that teaching is "too demanding for a full-time job".[30]

Sometimes only part-time work is available, for instance in home care, after-
school childcare and cleaning. Entry-level jobs for young women leaving school or
college are often part-time,[31] while cleaning often also employs men and ethnic

---

[25] Bredewold et al. (2018).

[26] See, for example, Commissie Toekomstscenario's Herverdeling Onbetaalde Arbeid (1995).

[27] Portegijs et al. (2016).

[28] Portegijs et al. (2016).

[29] Piasna (2018).

[30] Arbeidsmarktplatform PO (2019).

[31] Merens and Bucx (2018).

minorities who must hold several part-time jobs to make ends meet. Part-time work has become the norm in some occupations and sectors, not because it helps workers gain control in life but because it is cheaper for employers.

While the Flexible Working Act sets the standard and encourages the practice of part-time employment,[32] it is less well-known that this statute provides opportunities for both reducing and increasing working hours, for example by working from home. Legal proceedings to enforce this right are less common than cases seeking fewer hours and are also less likely to succeed as employers can give many reasons for opposing such requests.[33] Employees are often unaware that they can demand more official hours as an alternative to structural overtime. From the perspective of good work, being able to work more, if one wishes, is as important as the right to work less.

The quality of work can be a significant factor encouraging people to work fewer hours. It is striking that 70% of the lower skilled labour force in the Netherlands, male and female, have part-time jobs – a rate unsurpassed anywhere else in Europe.[34] Women in this group are less likely than other women to be working at all. When they do, they have on average the shortest working weeks: 22 h, compared with 25 h for women with post-secondary qualifications and 28 h for university graduates.[35] One reason, it seems, is that many women with lower educational attainment have "traditional" views of family life, preferring to spend a lot of time with their children; their husbands are less active in the household than other men. But there is also the fact that the work they do, or could do, is not very attractive. With better jobs, they might want to work longer hours.

In short, part-time work can help people gain control in life – but only if it is a genuine choice, not something forced on people because childcare is too expensive or poor in quality, because their jobs are too draining to do all day, every day, or because there are no full-time positions on offer.[36]

Although part-time employment allows people to more easily draw boundaries around their working lives, it comes at a price. Ultimately there is a price for society as well. The Dutch part-time economy is among the main reasons why women are less likely to be in good jobs and senior positions, and more likely to be paid less, to have lower pensions, to receive less compensation when they become incapacitated

---

[32] Kamerstukken ii, 2010/2011, 32 889, No. 3.

[33] Burri (2020).

[34] OECD (2019b).

[35] Portegijs et al. (2016).

[36] The *Emancipation Monitor* (Portegijs & van den Brakel, 2018) maintained by the Netherlands Institute for Social Research reports that nearly eight out of ten women working part-time would, subject to certain conditions, like to work more hours. One in three cite inadequate household income as their motivation. Similar numbers would work more hours if they could better combine it with their personal lives, for example through more suitable hours, working from home and/or shorter commutes. Affordable quality childcare would make a difference for one in six mothers; one in five informal care-givers say they will work more once their help is no longer needed.

Box 5.2 Part-Time Employment as an Opportunity to Work
Part-time employment provides opportunities for people with difficulties
adapting to the demands and rhythms of paid work, or who need a stepping
stone to full-time employment. They include people who wish to start working again after serious illness, the long-term unemployed and people with
occupational disabilities. According to the OECD, it is because of the part-time
economy that people with serious mental health issues in the Netherlands are
more likely to be working than in other countries.[37] But in most cases, these
people would like to be working longer hours to be able to make a decent
living.[38]

or unemployed, and to be, overall, less financially independent.[39] Only 60% of
women (compared to 79% of men) have incomes that are at least 70% of the net
full-time minimum wage.[40] This means that they have less financial bargaining
power and run greater risks if their home situation changes due to separation or
divorce. The Dutch solution to provide work-life balance thus has a price for both
individuals and society.

5.2   Paid Leave

Workers in the Netherlands do not receive financial compensation for providing
informal care. If parents choose to work part-time to look after the children, they
bear the costs in lost income. Things are different in Scandinavia and Germany,
where the dilemma of combining care with work has been solved through *paid* care
leave, which can sometimes be taken on a part-time basis. The right to paid leave
applies to both parents; sometimes it is subject to a "use it or lose it" clause to
ensure that fathers take advantage of the provision to strengthen their bonds with
their children and so that women do not fall further behind in the labour market.[41] In
contrast, the Netherlands only has parental leave for new mothers and, as of 1 July
2020, 5 days of paid partner leave, plus the option of taking up to 26 weeks of parental leave unpaid.

---

[37] OECD (2015a).

[38] Schaafsma et al. (2015).

[39] Burri (2020).

[40] Portegijs and van den Brakel (2018). Persons in the Netherlands are considered economically
independent if their individual net income from employment and/or self-employment equals or
exceeds the threshold for individual minimum income. The threshold is currently set at 70% of the
statutory net minimum wage, an amount equal to the net subsistence benefit payable to a single person.

[41] OECD (2019b).

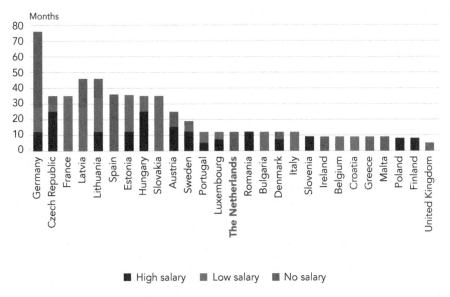

Fig. 5.3 Overall parental leave entitlement in months, EU countries, 2017
Source: Blum et al., 2018

Figure 5.3 shows that the Netherlands lags behind much of Europe in its parental leave arrangements. Germany, for instance, provides a total of 14 months of parental leave on a state-funded benefit,[42] which parents can divide between themselves. In Sweden the combined paid leave period for both parents is 16 months; the government pays a basic allowance, supplemented by employers. To comply with EU policy, the Netherlands is now revisiting its policies on parental leave. From 2022, all parents will continue to receive half their wages for the first nine weeks they take off (out of a total leave entitlement of 26 weeks) during the child's first year of life – a still limited arrangement compared to many other European countries.[43]

The idea behind paid parental leave is that by giving both parents time and money to look after their new child, they divide care duties equally and both remain active in the labour market. The structure of the arrangement is crucial; it needs to include clauses ensuring that both partners actually take time off and that they are adequately compensated when they do so. As for its duration, the leave should be neither too short nor too long, so parents do not lose touch with the world of work. Eight to twelve months per person is probably a sensible period.[44]

Leave arrangements for informal care-giving are even less developed than for new parents. Here the Netherlands is more in line with the rest of Europe. The Dutch system includes rights to emergency leave, short-term care leave (on 70% of

---

[42] This is about €1800 per month.

[43] See also OECD (2019b).

[44] Akgunduz and Plantenga (2013).

salary) and long-term unpaid leave (approximately 6 weeks a year). But only one in ten informal care-givers make use of the paid leave they are entitled to, while many more use their vacation days or report sick in order to fulfil their care responsibilities.[45] Apparently, the almost unpaid arrangements available to them do not meet their needs. Few collective labour agreements include provisions for informal care, although there has been slightly more recognition in recent years of the "combined pressure" of work and care.[46]

The growing group of flexible workers rarely claim paid leave. A self-employed person has no employer and is not covered by a collective labour agreement. A temporary employee has only limited rights, while having intensive care duties at home would seem unlikely to help them secure a permanent contract.[47] Plantenga concludes: "A self-employed worker with a sick partner or a single parent with a temporary contract and an unwell child see the hard face of the current social-care infrastructure."[48] In the flexible, part-time Dutch economy, parents and informal care-givers bear the costs of lost income.

It is not inconceivable that looking after young children, elderly parents and sick partners will eventually become the privilege of the happy few. But for single parents with limited skills or low-earning or sick partners, choosing to work fewer hours is not always a viable option. The National Institute for Family Finance Information calculates that a person with an average income who works one day less a week to care for a sick father living elsewhere in the country will easily be €245 out of pocket each month. Particularly if workers must reduce their hours to care for a sick partner who depends on benefits, there is a genuine risk that they will descend into poverty.[49] While people with good jobs may have enough of a financial cushion to move into part-time work, especially if it is only temporary, what about the shop assistant with a sick father or partner? Such people often lack control or even influence over their working hours.[50] More than a third of working informal care-givers have no say at all over their working hours; more than one in five are rarely or never able to take time off.[51] Having the time and money needed to provide care could well become a new issue of distributive justice.

Unpaid care is already apportioned unevenly. More and more women are fulfilling informal care responsibilities in their "spare" time. Much of this labour – as well as voluntary care work in home care and hospitals – falls on people already working in the social and healthcare sector, one in four of whom provide some form of

[45] de Boer et al. (2019).

[46] Heeger and Koopmans (2018).

[47] The self-employed in the Netherlands are entitled to 16 weeks of maternity leave, during which they receive the Maternity Benefit for the Self-Employed.

[48] Plantenga (2017): 271.

[49] Heeger and Koopmans (2018). The National Institute for Family Finance Information has calculated that informal care-givers can lose €1100 per month (Nibud, 2014).

[50] See also de Klerk et al. (2017).

[51] de Boer et al. (2019).

unpaid care on top of their paid work.[52] The burden of care, both paid and unpaid, thus disproportionately falls on a specific group of workers.

Box 5.3 Do the Dutch Really Work So Little?
It is often claimed that the Dutch work less than anyone else in Europe. While this is true, the differences are not as great as many people think. The average Dutch person now works 29 h a week, the same as the average Belgian and only an hour less than the average Dane.[53] While the average Dutch worker in the 1960s logged about 1800 h per year, by 1990 this had declined to around 1400 h per year, a number which has since remained relatively stable. But collectively, the Dutch are working more than ever before (Fig. 5.4). This is because participation in the labour market, especially by women, has risen since the 1990s to a level comparable to that in the Scandinavian countries[54]. Many working people thus also run households, take care of children and help out when loved ones are ill.

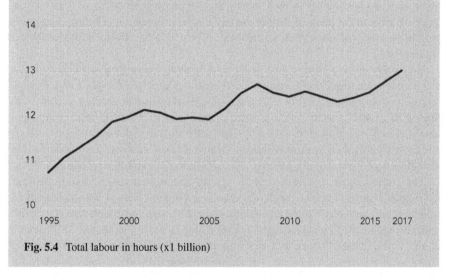

Fig. 5.4 Total labour in hours (x1 billion)

---

[52] de Klerk et al. (2017).

[53] https://ec.europa.eu/eurostat/documents/4187653/9699107/weekly+paid+hours+2016.   The European average is 33. In Denmark it is 30. The gap between the Netherlands and other European countries is narrowing.

[54] In 2017, some 72.9% of women aged 15-64 who were not studying were working. The figure for men was 84.8% (Portegijs & van den Brakel, 2018).

Paid work need not double the load for people with care responsibilities at home. Workplace flexibility and support from colleagues and managers may shield them from the strain. Those who have a good day at work can return home ready to take on the challenges of looking after a sick partner or a disabled child. Good jobs that give workers space for care-giving make unpaid care work possible.

5.3   Control Over Working Hours

While part-time work, paid leave, childcare and home care services all have the potential to give working people greater control in life, people also need some control over where and when they work.[55] Above all, this means flexibility *for* the worker, not *by* the worker. About half of all working people in the Netherlands say they can largely determine their own hours; only workers in Denmark, Sweden and Norway fare better.[56] The other half, however, have no control over their hours. For them, requesting time off to look after a sick child or an evening shift to take an elderly parent to the hospital during the day can be problematic. Control over one's working hours is also unevenly distributed, primarily along the axis of educational attainment.[57]

Especially insecure temporary workers lack control over their working hours, a real problem for the 550,000 casual and on-call workers (see Chaps. 1 and 3) over-represented in the hospitality, cleaning, supermarket and healthcare sectors.[58] In theory, these workers can refuse shifts; in practice, they fear that they are replaceable and will no longer be called.[59] Especially in the above-mentioned sectors, employers roster their staff to eliminate "inactive" time at work. The work itself is also often intensive, leaving workers too exhausted to maintain a private life.[60]

The combination of insecure contracts with uncertain hours – "double flexibility" – makes things even worse. In the words of a flexible home-care worker with a school-aged daughter: "You don't know what your week will look like. You can't make arrangements for your daughter. Everything is subject to change."[61] Research in the United States underlines the importance of regular, predictable working hours, with workers, on average, willing to surrender 20% of their pay in return for greater control over their hours.[62]

---

[55] Some 45% of respondents in 1990 considered good working hours important; in 2018 it was 68% (Conen, 2020).

[56] Eurofound (2017).

[57] Houtman et al. (2020).

[58] On-call workers also include many school, college and university students; 70% are under the age of 25. We are not talking about them here, but about adults working to build independent lives.

[59] Kremer (2017); van der Gaag (2018).

[60] Piasna (2018).

[61] Kremer et al. (2017c): 104.

[62] Mas and Pallais (2017). See also Datta (2019), who concluded from research in the US and the UK that although atypical workers may like flexibility, they still prefer permanent jobs and that many would settle for less pay if it means greater job security.

Another form of labour flexibilization, self-employment, can be considered more accommodating *for* the working person. People who became their own boss often report they did so to combine work and care; better able to balance their personal and professional lives, they tend to be more satisfied with their situations, especially if they chose it themselves.[63] Among informal care-givers, the self-employed outnumber those with salaried positions.[64] It suggests that employers still do not take work-life balance seriously enough, although research shows that companies and institutions that allow personnel to tailor their work to their home situations have lower staff turnover, more enthusiastic employees and less absenteeism.[65]

5.4   Blurring Boundaries

The self-employed sometimes have difficulties demarcating their working and private lives. This became apparent in the interviews conducted for our previous publication, *For the Sake of Security.*[66] In their free time, freelancers often feel they should be generating turnover: "The work goes on all the time". This feeling of working all the time is the flip side of working from home.

Almost one-third of employees in the Netherlands regularly work overtime – most notably managers, teachers and university graduates aged 25–35.[67] Many must bring work home to finish their allotted tasks.[68] But it is not always clear anymore what people see as overtime. In one study, highly educated professionals did not consider reading and replying to e-mails as work.[69] They did this in front of the television in the evening and on Sundays, to be ready for work the next day – a clear case of blurring boundaries. While many professionals feel perpetually on call,[70] they need time to recover and would benefit from clear dividing lines between their work and personal lives.

The internet and portable devices are further blurring the boundaries of work. Digital technology is a double-edged sword; in a joint report, Eurofound and the ILO[71] found smartphones, tablets, laptops and the like affecting the quality of work in both positive and negative ways. On the one hand, these technologies can improve

---

[63] Annink (2017).

[64] Josten and Vlasblom (2017).

[65] Kamerstukken ii, 2010/2011, 32 889, No. 3.

[66] Kremer (2017): 116.

[67] CBS (2018h, July 24).

[68] van Echtelt et al. (2016).

[69] Gregg (2011).

[70] Duxbury and Smart (2011).

[71] Eurofound & International Labour Organization (2017).

work-life balance, reduce commuting time and stimulate productivity.[72] Tele-working makes it easier for parents of young children to remain working full-time.[73] On the other hand, these technologies can lengthen working days, increase work-loads and fuel work-life conflicts.[74] Many countries have thus begun imposing lim-its on how far workers can be contacted outside of their official hours. Since 1 January 2017, employees in France have the legal right to switch off their phones outside of working hours; several companies in Germany including BMW and Volkswagen entitle their employees to be "unreachable". In the Netherlands, a 2019 parliamentary bill introduced the "right to inaccessibility" – a prerogative already included in some collective labour agreements.

5.5   Conclusion: Control in Life Requires More than Just Part-Time Work

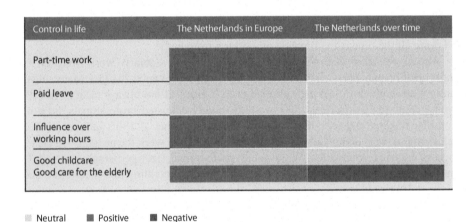

It is easier to balance work and private life in the Netherlands than in many other countries. This is largely due to how public policy supports working part-time – meaning people are not forced to devote themselves entirely to work during life's busy periods. The question nevertheless remains whether certain groups – espe-cially moderately and less educated women – would not work longer hours if there

---

[72] Cal Newport (2016) argues that the omnipresence of the internet and portable devices means we are no longer in the phase of "deep work". Work has become fragmented; our brains must con-stantly process information, which takes time and energy.

[73] Chung and van der Horst (2017).

[74] Houtman et al. (2017).

was better public care for the young and the elderly. This would not only enable these groups to work more; it would encourage them to find better work. People without good work are more prepared to work less.

Care responsibilities generally remain unremunerated in the Netherlands; despite the high levels of workforce participation, opportunities for paid leave are limited. This means that especially female part-time workers pay a personal price for their commitment to care-giving. There is a social price as well, and the future may well see greater inequality between those who can negotiate (and afford) work arrangements that allow them to care for family and those who cannot. Control over working hours is crucial to control in life but is often limited or non-existent for low-skilled, temporary and on-call workers. While control in life is a cherished goal for most working people, it is certainly not something they all have.

5.6 Part 1 – Conclusion: Work Could Be better

People in the Netherlands are generally quite satisfied with their work. Nevertheless, there is substantial room for improvement across the three conditions necessary for work to be considered good: security of income, control over work and work-life balance. Based on Statistics Netherlands' *Monitor of Well-Being*, Fig. 5.5 places the quality of work in the Netherlands in European perspective (the slices) and in light of recent developments (the inner ring). As we see, the Netherlands does not consistently rank well (green) across the twelve indicators of good work. In some areas, the country lags behind other European nations or the quality of work has been deteriorating (red). In other areas, the Netherlands is mid-range or there have been few positive developments (grey).

5.6.1 Good Work in the Netherlands?

With the flexibilization of the labour market, more and more workers in the Netherlands have lost income security. If people have not experienced this uncertainty themselves, their partner, child or neighbour has. While the Dutch economy – even during the Covid-19 crisis – was generating a lot of jobs, many of these come with low (and further declining) job security. The social-security system itself has become a source of insecurity for many working people, especially the self-employed who are largely excluded from work-related social benefits.

While the Netherlands still scores better than many other European countries, workplace autonomy – necessary for shielding workers from excessive demands, for organizations to function effectively and for innovation – is declining. And although many Dutch workplaces offer social support, they can also be settings for

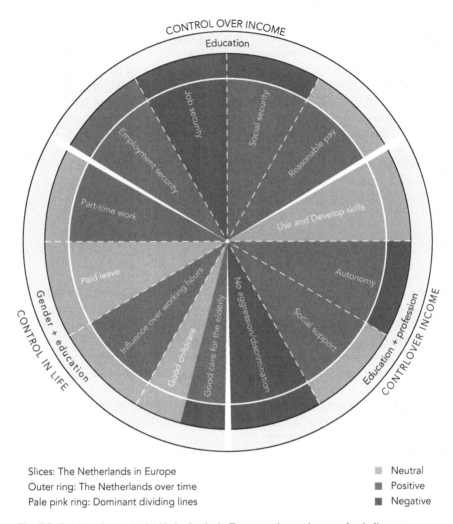

Fig. 5.5 Quality of work in the Netherlands, in Europe and over time: twelve indicators
Source: WRR, inspired by the *Monitor of Well-Being* (CBS)

aggressive behaviour; companies and institutions do not always bring out the best in people, especially for ethnic minorities and people with occupational disabilities. Nor has the kind of learning and professional development that would contribute to security of employment been widely embraced.

With widespread opportunities to work part-time, work and private life are easy to combine in the Netherlands. But the costs are borne by individuals, especially women. The country has limited paid leave arrangements to care for young children and the elderly although working people are increasingly likely to be assuming responsibilities for aging parents.

Publicly-funded child and elderly care make work possible. While quality child-care enables parents to work (more) – and encourages them to do so – the Netherlands does not excel in this area. Although care for the elderly is highly developed, there is scant emphasis on supporting working people who provide care outside of their working hours. The ability to determine when work starts and stops is important for work-life balance but not everyone has sufficient control over their working hours to allow taking on informal care responsibilities as well. In short, control in life is unevenly distributed.

5.6.2   Dividing Lines

The quality of work is under pressure for all working people in the Netherlands. Insecurity is increasing across the board and burnout is widespread. In this sense, there is no clear polarization between good and bad jobs, between "MacJobs" and "McJobs". There is no guarantee of good work, even for university graduates. That said, some people clearly have better work than others. People with modest educational qualifications on aggregate have less control over the three dimensions of good work. Women, too, generally earn less, are more insecure and enjoy less control over their work. The same applies to people with migration backgrounds.

New divisions are emerging in how much control people enjoy over their working lives. There are significant differences by level of education as well as between occupations, with public-sector professionals in healthcare and education as well as the police having the least control over their work. Alongside the classic gender divide, new divisions are emerging between workers who are able to combine their careers with informal care-giving and those who cannot because they have no say over the time and place of their shifts.

5.6.3   Three Core Developments

The three developments at the heart of this book – the automation, flexibilization and intensification of labour – may well have negative consequences for the quality of work in the coming years. One danger is that the wider use of robots and artificial intelligence will further limit workers' autonomy, reduce their wages and increase the flexibility expected *of* working people. But this need not happen; technology can also contribute towards good work.

While the intensification of work can exacerbate burnout and absenteeism, this need not happen if people retain sufficient control over their working lives. While the flexible labour market reduces people's control over their earnings, the risks are diminished if there is adequate social-security provision and if *all* workers enjoy greater opportunities for professional development.

5.6.4 Policy Choices

Whether or not work improves will depend primarily on decisions made by employers, who can support workplace learning and professional development and ensure that workers have adequate control over the organization of their tasks and the space they need to harmonize their lives at work and at home. This is also a matter for the government. Good work is supported by public policies for training and social security (Chap. 3), by legislation governing working conditions and its enforcement, and by protecting and promoting the rights of workers.

A Day at Work: The Retail Floor Manager

Although the shop does not open until 10 am, Cathelijn is there at 9. There is plenty to do, including cleaning up and checking the till. But first a cup of coffee. De Prael is a small brewery with a pub and shop in the heart of old Amsterdam. In addition to the 17 varieties of De Prael beer, the store also sells local or sustainable delicacies such as wine, liqueurs, cheese, nuts, chocolate and coffee to take away. Cathelijn, 49, works here as "floor manager" four days a week, between 9 am and 2 pm.

In the meantime, Atone (pronounced Ah-ton) has arrived as well, a cheerful 65-year-old man of Senegalese descent with a history of drug addiction. He works here one or two days a week on a voluntary basis. De Prael is a social enterprise employing dozens of people "distanced" from the labour market, either unpaid but with benefits or on subsidized wages. Some are making real progress. Cathelijn began here 5 years ago as a volunteer; for the past 2 years, she has been earning a regular salary through a sheltered employment scheme. For others, like Atone, it is enough that they have somewhere they are expected to be.

Cathelijn vacuums the store and Atone follows her with a mop. Sales were good yesterday, meaning there are empty spaces on the shelves to be replenished. At 10 am Cathelijn opens the door and Atone inserts the company banners into their holders outside. He used to attend an addiction clinic, he says, and was not the easiest of clients. "I didn't listen", he laughs out loud. "But now I do." He is full of praise for Cathelijn: "She has motivated me."

Cathelijn has a university degree and used to work as a researcher, but 10 years ago suffered a nervous breakdown. "For years I spent my days in bed." She finally realized she had to do something and ended up at De Prael after being referred there by the mental health service. First in administration, later in the shop. "The depression slowly subsided, and the work helped. Structure. Cycling to work in the morning, along with all the other people doing the same. Keeping busy, but at your own pace. You can do that here." Cathelijn no longer needs much supervision, although she did at the beginning. "That's not structured guidance – here, you get what you ask for."

(continued)

Two Asian tourists enter the store, look around and leave. A young woman comes in for a cappuccino. A couple, clearly in love, pick out a selection of beers. Cathelijn takes their money. Atone jumps in to help, wrapping each bottle in a sheet of newspaper. Otherwise they will clink in the bag, he explains.

Two years ago, Cathelijn's case manager asked if she would like to convert her volunteer position into a paid job under the sheltered work scheme. She jumped at the chance. Before she could make the move, the Employee Insurance Agency had to assess her fitness for work. That was "very confrontational". De Prael now pays her in line with the results of the assessment, with the city council topping it up so that she is earning the statutory minimum wage. She loves not being on benefits anymore. "They're just hassle and stress. They can try to make you work somewhere, and maybe I wouldn't be able to handle that."

The pressure at De Prael is lower than elsewhere but the laws of economics still apply. The shop is not bringing in enough money. Because its future is uncertain, Cathelijn has been looking around for other work. She has made three applications, for both regular and sheltered jobs, and two have been accepted. But she is not sure what to do. "Change is hard. I know what I have here, and I don't know what I might get."

Cathelijn has lunch at 12:30 pm. What she calls "the canteen" is a good-sized kitchen with dining tables laid with bread, milk, boxes of chocolate sprinkles and family jars of peanut butter. Two quiet older ladies keep them topped up, clear away the used dishes and wash up. A dozen or so workers from the brewery are eating. Cathelijn does not know them all, or how they came to work here. "That's not important." She thinks everyone deserves a paid job. "Not everyone is productive enough, but it's important that you have opportunities to grow. There has to be hope that you can make progress."

Atone leaves just before 2 pm. He gives Cathelijn a hug. A little later she puts on her coat as well. Five years ago, she would come home exhausted after half a day at work. Now she has energy to spare.

Sheltered employment is meant for people who need extra guidance and a suitable workplace due to an occupational disability. They have a contract and are paid at least the statutory minimum wage. There were approximately 3000 sheltered positions in the Netherlands as of mid-2019, a number which should eventually increase to 30,000 under agreements between the central government and local authorities who are responsible for managing the schemes. Sheltered employment is one of many participation-enhancing interventions consistently shown by research to strengthen self-reliance and enhance social participation. But very few sheltered employees move into regular work.

Part II
Work for All

Chapter 6
Everyone into Work

Despite successive Dutch governments emphasizing "jobs, jobs, jobs", thousands of people who want to work have no jobs at all, never mind good jobs. More than 1.6 million people in the Netherlands live entirely on benefits. In 2017, some 810,000 were claiming benefits for disability and another 378,000 for unemployment, while 442,000 were receiving a basic subsistence benefit. One million individuals in 2018 possessed "unused labour potential", including approximately 600,000 unemployed who would like to work and 400,000 underemployed eager to work more. These numbers will only increase with the Covid-19 crisis.

Are the automation, flexibilization and intensification of work leading to more or fewer people finding and retaining jobs? Who is benefiting or suffering the most from these developments? According to the OECD,[1] the Achilles' heel of the Dutch labour market is its lack of inclusiveness; although the vast majority of the population is working, specific groups are marginalized in the labour market. Are new technologies, flexible contracts and the intensification of work helping or hindering vulnerable groups to stay in work – in good work in particular? Is the changing labour market opening new opportunities? What are the prospects for the future? Are new vulnerable groups emerging?

This chapter seeks to answer these questions while analysing what is already being done to provide good work for all. We address, in turn, the automation (Sect. 6.1), flexibilization (Sect. 6.2) and intensification of work (Sect. 6.3) before discussing the need for active labour-market policies (Sect. 6.4) and presenting our conclusions (Sect. 6.5).

---

[1] OECD (2018a).

© The Author(s) 2021
M. Kremer et al., *Better Work*, Research for Policy,
https://doi.org/10.1007/978-3-030-78682-3_6

6.1   Technological Developments

The end of paid work and the working class has been a recurring prophecy in modern western history.[2] But despite the introduction of the factory assembly line in the nineteenth century, the personal computer and the global internet in the twentieth century, and mobile phones, robots and artificial intelligence in our own era, both dreams and nightmares about the coming end of human labour have come to naught.

Although a much-discussed 2013 study by Frey and Osborne[3] provoked fears that robots would eliminate 47% of jobs in the United States over the next two decades, little remains of the doom and gloom just a few years later. Some studies even warn that there will be too *few* people for all the new jobs created by AI, robots and cobots.[4] But these latter studies, too, remain speculation; many are based on the subjective expectations of CEOs and technical experts, which we need to take with a grain of salt.

> **Box 6.1 Robots Sacked**
> We have all heard predictions of the impending robot apocalypse which could cost up to half of all workers their jobs in the near future.[5] But the revolution is not proceeding as quickly as some expected. A hotel in Japan put hundreds of robots to work in 2015; half of them, due to malfunctions, were "sacked" in 2019.[6]
>
> Treatises on machines replacing people have recently become more nuanced and realistic. Approaching jobs as bundles of tasks, they focus on which *sub*-tasks are amenable to automation. This does not mean that the machines are taking over as all kinds of other considerations, power relationships and preferences remain.[7] Human beings do not only work to make money but to structure their days, gain self-esteem, enhance their identities and feel a part of society.[8]
>
> Although technology can take over specific tasks, this is less the case for entire jobs; no profession can be reduced to a set of tasks that can be done by machines alone. Much depends on the specific applications of the technology and the choices made about their implementation.

---

[2] Keynes (1932), Gorz (1994), Rifkin (1995).

[3] Frey & Osborne (2013).

[4] See, for example, Nakamura & Zeira (2018).

[5] See also Smulders & Oeij (2019).

[6] Tates (2019, January 17).

[7] Hueck (2018, April 3).

[8] See also Valenduc & Vendramin (2019).

Few people perform only a single task at work.[9] Although it may be possible to automate certain subtasks, whether this actually happens depends not only on the (often overestimated) capabilities of the new technology but on the structure of specific firms and sectors, and on the economic, social and political stakes involved. Studies by the Dutch government's three largest employment-related executive agencies for the *National Labour Market Analysis 2018–2025*[10] show that the time freed by partial task automation can be used to increase production, ease workloads, improve production quality, undertake other activities or use fewer people to produce the same amount – or some combination of the above.

As many firms have discovered, not all work can be done by computers and robots. Hal Varian, chief economist at Google, notes that many jobs are more complicated and much harder to automate than is often believed.[11] Although many driving jobs may seem obvious candidates for automation, anyone who regularly rides a bus or talks to a trucker knows better.[12] It is also doubtful whether we want to rid ourselves of the humans in our midst; bus drivers, tram conductors and train guards also attend to passenger safety.

Governments, employers and trade unions all have influence over how new technologies are implemented in the workplace.[13] While millions of workers have indeed seen their tasks change under the influence of new technology – a trend that will continue into the future – we need to focus on human-machine complementarity within specific applications of technology and on restructuring the labour market, both to increase productivity and to improve the quality of work.

Box 6.2 Robots in Cleaning?

The 2017 collective agreement for the Dutch cleaning sector included provisions for a pilot project in which employers and trade unions study the possibilities of developing robot technology which is good for both cleaners and companies. Although we do not yet know what will come of it, this initiative – based on the principles of complementarity, co-creation and co-ownership – suggests a way forward for other sectors wishing to take full advantage of the possibilities offered by robots, cobots and artificial intelligence.

---

[9] Nedelkosta & Quintini (2018).

[10] Brennenraedts et al. (2019).

[11] Snyder (2019, March 11).

[12] Broussard (2019, April 3).

[13] ter Weel (2018); Went et al. (2015).

6.1.1   Job Polarization

Which jobs are particularly vulnerable to automation? Although unemployment is highest among people who only have high-school diplomas, their prospects have not declined. Fig. 6.1 shows that unemployment among this group declined from 7.3% in 2003 to 6.6% in 2018.[14]

Scholars have predicted that automation will lead to "job polarization" – the disappearance of jobs such as routine administration in the middle segment of the labour market.[15] The phenomenon has affected the Netherlands less than many other countries (Fig. 6.2).[16] The proportion of Dutch jobs requiring only low skills – or conversely, high skills – has risen by about 5 percentage points over the past two decades, whereas jobs requiring post-secondary vocational education has declined by around 10 percentage points. According to the Netherlands Bureau for Economic

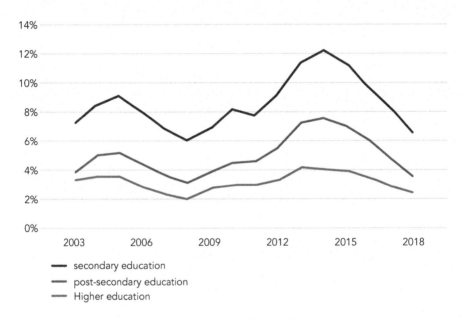

Fig. 6.1 Unemployment rate by level of education, 2003–2018
Source: CBS   StatLine.   (https://opendata.cbs.nl/statline/#/cbs/nl/dataset/82922NED/table?from statweb)

---

[14] See also de Beer (2018a).
[15] Goos et al. (2009), Graetz & Michaels (2015).
[16] Smits & de Vries (2015).

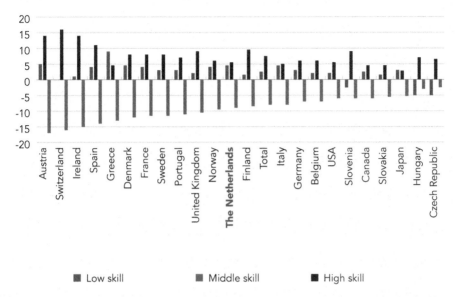

Fig. 6.2 Employment shares by skill content of occupations (percentage points), 1995–2015, OECD countries
Source: OECD (2018a)

Policy Analysis, this is creating a new divide among workers with post-secondary vocational qualifications[17]: some have moved down in the labour market, working jobs below their nominal skill levels, while others have moved up into jobs for which they are not formally qualified. The biggest changes are taking place *within* sectors and professions. Secretaries who previously used to type and distribute faxes are now involved in planning and project management.

It is not a foregone conclusion that technological changes will hollow out the middle class. Many routine white-collar tasks have already been automated, while it is conceivable – and at times already apparent – that tasks traditionally performed by university graduates can be done more effectively by, or together with, smart machines; consider how radiologists, accountants and lawyers are aided by algorithms in their work.[18] What this means for existing professions – and what new jobs may appear in the manufacture and maintenance of new machines or due to entirely new possibilities – is impossible to predict in advance (see also sect. 6.2).

---

[17] van den Berge & ter Weel (2015b).
[18] Ford (2015).

6.1.2 Switching Between Jobs

Good work allows people to adjust to advances in technology. Everyone needs to be able to learn on the job as emergent technologies may alter or eliminate their current tasks or create new ones. Having the space and support to cope with these changes – "learn while you earn" as *The Economist* calls it – is crucial for preserving work or, if necessary, for switching careers. The independent think tank DenkWerk estimates that Dutch employers will have to invest €4–7 billion a year in on-the-job retraining and refresher courses if the country is to make the most of the opportunities offered by new technology.[19]

Technological change within companies does not take place overnight. Supporting people into new lines of work cannot wait until they are declared redundant; the Employee Insurance Agency and its partners must get involved before lay-offs occur.[20] Workers need to be protected during such transitions, not least by the social-security system.[21]

6.1.3 Technology for Inclusivity

New technologies can aid current workers to learn new tasks, help people with occupational disabilities to find work, and to make the labour market more inclusive.[22] Technologies such as virtual reality can help workers learn new tasks in fields such as manufacturing, maintenance and medicine (e.g. wound care), while several organizations in the Netherlands are dedicated to using technology to help people with occupational disabilities find and retain work. Higher wages for low-paid workers in the United States has led some companies to automate their jobs out of existence, while other firms have turned to new technologies to make their workers more productive, thus justifying higher pay.[23]

New technologies will change the demand for labour and the nature of work. But how their application will affect the quality of work is neither a foregone conclusion nor a process we can leave to the market alone. As firms, institutions and governments often make decisions that undermine good work, these choices must be monitored. Machines can be deployed to replace people but also to help them work better, collaborate more effectively and to be more productive. New technologies can be

---

[19] Think tank Denkwerk (2019) calculates that 3 million people need their digital skills upgraded, at an estimated cost of €4–4.5 billion. Moreover, 400,000 specialists in the front line of digital innovation are seeing their skills rendered obsolete due to technological advances. Bringing their knowledge up to date will cost an estimated €2–2.5 billion.

[20] One example is the Mobility Centre launched in 2019 by trade-union federation FNV and the Employee Insurance Agency to guide redundant workers into new jobs following the announced closure of the coal-fired Hemweg Power Station in Amsterdam.

[21] Borghouts-van de Pas et al. (2019).

[22] OECD (2018b).

[23] Kopf (2019, January 18).

used to offer people currently marginalized in the labour market new prospects as well as to give lower skilled workers new tasks and opportunities.

6.2   Flexible Labour Market

It is often claimed that the flexibilization of the Dutch labour market has created jobs and allowed more people to keep working. It enables employers to remain agile, to lay off staff when necessary and recruit more readily in good times. But it could also be argued that flexible work undermines workers' incentives to innovate,[24] creates costs for companies through staff turnover, and exerts downwards pressure on wages, consumer spending and thus economic growth.[25] According to the Netherlands Bureau for Economic Policy Analysis (CPB), the question of whether flexible work creates jobs or simply replaces permanent jobs with more insecure ones cannot be answered with certainty: "From an economic perspective, it cannot be said which type of employment relationship is preferable or what proportion of flexible relationships within the working population is ideal."[26] In other words, this is a decision society has to make. How much do we value everyone having access to good work? As the CPB points out, the flexible labour market differentially affects segments of the workforce. Fully 45% of people with a low level of education had flexible jobs in 2018 (Fig. 6.3).

6.2.1   Permanently Temporary

At first sight, flexible labour markets may seem to favour people with occupational disabilities and outsiders such as migrants. Employers are disinclined to take risks and temporary contracts entail few obligations – certainly in the Netherlands. The OECD[27] credits temporary contracts and the flexible labour market for the comparatively high proportion of individuals with severe mental disorders working in the Netherlands. Others argue that employers will be more inclined to give refugees a chance if they can do so without longer term obligations.

Finding work is not the same as keeping it, as more and more people find themselves trapped in the labour market's ever-expanding "flexible shell". High-school graduates, ethnic minorities, migrant workers from Eastern Europe and people with chronic medical problems are more likely than others to have temporary jobs, which

---

[24] de Spiegelaere (2017).

[25] OECD (2018a).

[26] Euwals et al. (2016: 13).

[27] OECD (2015a).

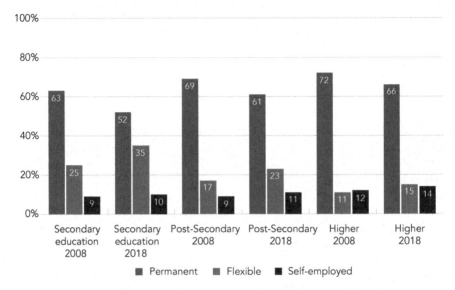

Fig. 6.3 Working people by type of contract and level of education, 2008 and 2018
Source: Statistics Netherlands

are now spreading among other segments of the population, most notably the over 25s and people with post-secondary qualifications.[28]

A temporary contract is now rarely a stepping stone to a permanent position, especially for on-call and casual staff.[29] Very few people hired on a temporary basis in the period 2010–2019 had a permanent position 1 year later; despite economic growth, this percentage has been falling since 2010, down to 14% in 2019.[30] It is common for temporary contracts to be strung together so that a worker is effectively employed on a "permanently temporary" basis.

6.2.2   A Revolving Door in Social Security

Labour market flexibility has opened a revolving door in the social-security system as people alternate between temporary work and unemployment. The proportion of flexible workers still working after 2 years is 10% lower than for employees with permanent contracts.[31] As shown in Fig. 6.4, temporary workers are far more likely to claim unemployment or subsistence benefits. Due to the high rate of economic inactivity caused by intermittent periods of unemployment, these workers place a

---

[28] van Echtelt et al. (2016).

[29] Euwals et al. (2016).

[30] CBS (2019f, 2019g, October 24).

[31] van Echtelt et al. (2016).

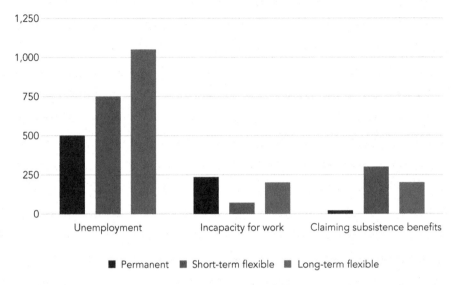

Fig. 6.4 Benefit claims by type of contract previously held, 2014
Source: Van der Werff et al. (2016)

heavy burden on the social-security system. Most jobs found by benefit claimants are temporary,[32] meaning their reintegration into the labour force is also only temporary.[33] Finding a job rarely means a job one can keep.

While even temporary work is generally better than no work at all, repeated bouts of short-term employment interspersed by applications to the benefits office mean a succession of demotivating disappointments, attacks on one's self-esteem, stress and financial uncertainty ("If my contract expires this month, will I receive money from the benefits agency next month?"). Research from the UK shows that people who can only find a succession of insecure jobs suffer deteriorating health.[34] The flexible labour market questions the very concept of "reintegration".

6.2.3   Less Training

Employers invest less in workers with temporary contracts.[35] This applies especially to formal training courses, from which temporary personnel are generally excluded. The difference is most marked for workers with post-secondary qualifications or university degrees, while high-school graduates have fewer learning opportunities,

---

[32] UWV (2015).

[33] Bannink (2018), Ruitenbeek et al. (2019).

[34] Chandola & Zhang (2017).

[35] Dekker (2017).

formal or informal, across the board.[36] Although training is crucial for people to be able to stay in work and to change jobs when necessary, the weaker responsibility relationships between employers and employees in the flexible economy renders it unusual.

Our era demands that everyone – regardless of their form of employment – has access to additional training or retraining to stay in work. Flexible workers should be able to make use of the sectoral training and development funds and the personal learning budgets from which they are now largely excluded. While individual learning accounts can increase participation in training, their use needs to be encouraged among groups that currently make scant use of such opportunities.[37] Such individual funds should be part of a contract-neutral social-security system (see sect. 3.1 and Chap. 8).

6.2.4 Protection

The flexible labour market poses additional problems for people with chronic health problems. The "flexicurity model" of the Netherlands and Denmark, which combines flexibility with good social-security provision, offers them few job opportunities.[38] Since the mid-1980s, the gap between less skilled workers with and without health problems has grown enormously in both the Netherlands and Denmark; Sweden has performed better, especially when protections against dismissal were more robust. A European comparative study likewise concludes that stronger contract protection leads to more people with occupational disabilities working.[39] Permanent contracts protect vulnerable workers more effectively as employers are legally obliged to take responsibility for them. The flexibilization of employment relationships thus contributes to the long-term marginalization of the "least productive" workers.

Both employers and employees would benefit from permanent staff having greater opportunities to switch tasks and positions, either in their current company or elsewhere in a pool of collaborating firms. This "internal flexibility" can to some extent replace "external flexibility". Both the trade-union movement and one of the main Dutch employers' organizations, the AWVN, advocate making greater use of such arrangements.

---

[36] Boermans et al. (2017).

[37] OECD (2019b).

[38] McAllister et al. (2015).

[39] van der Zwan & de Beer (2019).

6.2.5 Opportunities Through the Hybridization of Work

Other forms of flexible labour such as self-employment or working through online platforms can offer vulnerable people an alternative into the world of work. "Hybridization" – the concurrent pursuit of different activities under different types of contract – can also increase opportunities in the labour market. More than half a million multi-jobbers in the Netherlands already combine two or more (generally part-time) positions; some of them would be unable to make ends meet otherwise. Some multi-jobbers choose hybridization as a way to transition into other work, either because they want to or they must.[40]

For some groups, self-employment may be the answer. People with physical or mental disabilities may find it easier to work from home and to adapt their daily schedule to their own needs, gaining the control in life which comes from being their own boss. Ethnic and religious minorities sometimes choose – or are more or less forced into – self-employment because no-one will hire them or because they would rather work for themselves than in an unwelcoming organizational environment where they face discriminatory or aggressive behaviour from colleagues and managers.[41] Such discrimination often takes subtle forms such as "jokes" about terrorism, religion or crime, alienating them from the workplace.[42] To gain greater control over their work, some choose entrepreneurship.

Nevertheless, self-employment is no panacea for an inclusive labour market. Problems arise when people claiming benefits try to make money with freelance activities on the side; it is also much more complicated to be self-employed than on a payroll. The chances of success are often limited. Those working for online platforms or in the arts struggle more than most to pick up assignments. Combined with structurally low rates of pay, this often exposes them to poverty (see Chap. 3). Turnover is high in individual self-employment; while many register with the Chamber of Commerce as freelance workers each year, the number of deregistrations is considerable.[43] Those who move successfully from benefits into self-employment are indeed a select group; they tend to be young, with post-secondary or higher education or past freelance experience.[44]

In sum, the flexibilization of the labour market has led to more people in the Netherlands working, but not always in good jobs – especially for people with chronic health conditions, for many first, second and third generation immigrants, and people with no more than secondary education. This is not only detrimental to them; it also strains the social-security system (see sect. 3.1). Flexible workers have fewer opportunities for professional development and training and are less

---

[40] Dorenbosch (2017).
[41] Hooftman & Houtman (2017).
[42] Waldring (2018).
[43] KVK (2019). In 2018, 128,021 people registered and 70,300 deregistered as self-employed.
[44] Mevissen et al. (2013); Kok et al. (2018).

protected. To counter these adverse effects, employers and the government should invest more in these workers and in the more flexible apportioning of tasks within firms and organizations. Although juggling several part-time positions may allow workers to spread the risks and possibly provide stepping stones to other work, this is often wishful thinking for the most vulnerable groups.

6.3   Intensification of Work

Is the intensification of work creating new labour market vulnerabilities? Both the faster tempo and greater mental and emotional demands on the job can make work more challenging and interesting. But they are also linked to increased stress, emotional exhaustion and burnout.[45] The intensification of work can effectively push people out of the workforce and make it harder for specific groups to remain in or return to work.[46]

6.3.1   New Vulnerabilities

Workers who must deal with constant emotional pressure – for example because they interface with clients, customers and patients – are at higher than average risk of burnout. The same applies to those with heavy workloads or who work under severe time pressure (see Fig. 4.2). While many people can handle short periods of intensive work, long-term exposure to stress is unhealthy in many ways.[47]

The number of Dutch workers suffering symptoms of burnout is on the rise. Between 2007 and 2018, the proportion saying they are emotionally exhausted at least once a month rose from 11.3 to 17.5% .[48] Highly educated individuals, women and young people aged 25–35 suffer the most; the self-employed fare better. Experiencing some of its symptoms does not necessarily mean that a worker is suffering from full-blown burnout. Nevertheless, more and more reports to the Netherlands Centre for Occupational Diseases mention excessive strain and burnout, which now outnumber reports of work-related physical illnesses.[49] The intensification of work is accompanied by new forms of absenteeism. Almost half (46%)

---

[45] Korunka & Kubicek (2017).

[46] German sociologist Hartmut Rosa (2016) argues that societal acceleration leads to depression and burnout, and highlights the structural exclusion of workers unable to keep up with the flexibility and speed demanded by modern economic systems.

[47] van den Broeck et al. (2010), Bierings & Mol (2012); Schaufeli & Bakker (2013a), Smulders et al. (2013).

[48] Houtman et al. (2020), TNO (2019).

[49] NCVB (2018).

of all sick leave in the Netherlands is now due to conditions at work, the highest since 2007. The majority of affected workers (60%) attribute their problems to psychosocial workload – excessive stress or emotional pressure, problems with managers, customers and so on.[50] Workers are also suffering from higher levels of mental illness. It is precisely such problems that cause longer-term withdrawal from the labour market; over half of disability benefit claimants receive them for psychological conditions.[51]

Intensive working need not lead to emotional exhaustion and absenteeism (see also Chap. 2).[52] Sufficient autonomy and consultation in the workplace, alongside support from managers and colleagues, can ease the burden. If homecare workers, for example, were allowed to schedule their own shifts and to work to their own standards, they would be better able to cope with the tempo, workload and demanding clients. Whether the intensification of work leads to new vulnerabilities thus depends on whether the work is good. Especially young people and women experience less autonomy at work than their older and male counterparts; their work is also on average faster-paced and more emotionally demanding. These trends explain why young people and women are more likely to fall victim to burnout.[53]

Workers' domestic circumstances are crucial. Children with problems, financial worries or the lack of a supportive partner means there is no respite. Single people are more likely to report symptoms of burnout[54] as many are unable to unwind and recover at home.[55] Workers can also better cope with more exacting demands if they can keep their professional and personal lives separate.[56] The Social and Economic Council of the Netherlands[57] finds that intensive domestic care duties, especially looking after young children, makes it more difficult for employees to cope with demands at work.

The intensification of work is placing more people at risk, including groups who were previously not particularly vulnerable such as single and highly educated persons. While unceasing pressure or emotional strain is hard on anyone, it helps to have a degree of autonomy at work and support at home. Good work makes the intensification of work more manageable.

---

[50] TNO (2019).

[51] van Echtelt (2020).

[52] Houtman et al. (2020).

[53] TNO (2018), see Chapter 3.

[54] TNO (2018).

[55] Chandola (2010), Meijman & Zijlstra (2006), van Echtelt (2014).

[56] Korunka & Kubicek (2017).

[57] SER (2016a).

6.3.2 Exacerbating Existing Vulnerabilities

A demanding labour market makes it more difficult for workers limited by health conditions or occupational disabilities – any form of physical, visual, mental or psychological condition that affects the individual's ability to work. This definition extends well beyond the traditional notion of a disability as a visible impairment to include for instance people struggling with depression or the aftermath of cancer. Everyone – young or old and whatever their level of education – can experience an occupational disability at some point in their life.

The Netherlands lags behind many European countries in keeping people with occupational disabilities in work.[58] Despite the policy focus, their workforce participation has declined (Fig. 6.4). Many lost their jobs or found it difficult to work in the wake of the 2008 financial crisis; only after the 2013 Jobs Accord between employers' organizations, trade unions and the government did the number of employed persons with disabilities tick slightly upwards. Under this social contract, 125,000 jobs will be created for people with occupational disabilities by 2026, including 25,000 jobs in the public sector. Before the Covid-19 crisis, their workforce participation had not returned to pre-crisis levels; the disparities between this group and the rest of the population remain substantial.

People with physical disabilities have slightly better access to the labour market than people with mental disabilities[59] – the category of people most excluded from the labour market. Only one in five persons with a severe mental condition are currently working,[60] while the intensification of work poses particular challenges for people already struggling psychologically. For people with chronic illnesses or occupational disabilities, intensive activity or complicated, emotionally demanding work with a lot of human contact can generate unbearable stress (Fig. 6.5).

The intensification of work poses particular difficulties for people with mild intellectual disabilities. An estimated 1.4 million persons in the Netherlands – many of whom receive benefits[61] – have an IQ between 50 and 85 and experience problems with self-reliance. While low-skilled work certainly exists in the Netherlands (see Table 6.1), much of this work is now out of reach as requirements have changed: the pace has quickened while workers need to be able to work independently or in tight-knit teams, whereas persons with a mild intellectual disability typically benefit from a calmer tempo, less complexity, plenty of security and continuous guidance.[62] The intensification of work is increasingly distancing even basic work from the needs and capabilities of this group.

---

[58] Versantvoort & van Echtelt (2016), van der Zwan & de Beer (2019), OECD (2018a).

[59] Nivel (2018, 2019).

[60] Schaafsma et al. (2015).

[61] van den Berg et al. (2013).

[62] Woittiez & Putnam (2016), Woittiez et al. (2014), Sebrechts (2018).

There is thus a widening gulf between the labour market and workers with mental, psychological or medical disabilities (see Table 6.1). Many researchers have concluded that this gulf can only be narrowed if jobs are more individually tailored. Many vulnerable people simply do not fit available vacancies. It would be better to focus less on the requirements of the work organization and look more at the skills, working speed and qualities of the aspiring worker.[63]

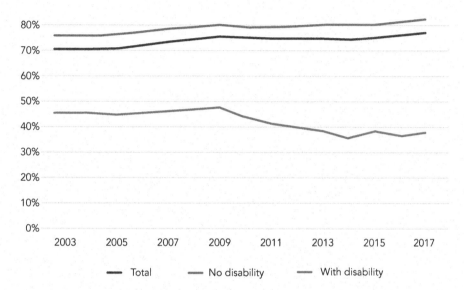

Fig. 6.5 Labour-market participation of people with and without disabilities, 2003–2017 Source: Statistics Netherlands (With thanks to Paul de Beer)

Table 6.1 Work requirements and the needs of people with an intellectual disability

Work requirements	Needs of people with an intellectual disability
Demand	**Supply**
Faster pace	Slower pace
Emotional workload	Few stimuli
Self-reliance	Supervision
Multi-tasking	Simple work
Intensive social interaction	Limited social interaction
Learning	Routine

Sources: Van den Berg et al. (2018), Woittiez et al. (2014), Beukema and Kuijpers (2018)

---

[63] See, for example, Adelmeijer et al. (2015, 2017).

6.3.3   Reintegration Is More Difficult

The intensification of work can make reintegration into the labour force more difficult for people who have taken time off. Because people are now working into old age and illnesses such as cancer are often recurrent, their reintegration in the workplace has become a pressing issue. While staying in work or returning to the same job works well in many cases, reintegration rarely unfolds smoothly and is often accompanied by complaints such as fatigue and concentration problems.[64] If the pace of the job has accelerated or old know-how has become obsolete, this only raises the barriers to a successful return.

Box 6.3 Working with an Occupational Disability

Ms. O, with rheumatism, osteoarthritis and deafness in her right ear, says that she is happy working at retailer X. "The nice thing is that there is no time pressure. The work I do is facing, making sure that the shop looks good by placing the different products in the right place. From time to time I can take the moments of rest I need, and I set my own working pace. That's important to me because it's what enables me to keep going."[65]

Many people who have been away from work for a long time have or develop complex problems. Half of all subsistence benefit claimants report that they are "sick"[66] – a catch-all term for a variety of ailments and issues. An estimated 40% of people on unemployment or subsistence benefits must deal with a multiplicity of problems in their lives.[67] Joblessness is rarely the sole problem; it goes hand in hand with debt, health complaints, family issues, language deficiencies and lack of social support. These problems also hinder their search for work, especially now that it has intensified.

Employers are reluctant to recruit people who are distanced from the labour market. Long-term unemployment in the Netherlands is higher than in many other countries; once workers have been side-lined, especially older and less skilled people tend to remain out of work for long periods.[68] For many employers, long-term unemployment is in itself a red flag for a person best avoided.[69] Having an occupational disability is an invitation to have doors slammed in one's face. Only one in

---

[64] See also Polder (2017).

[65] Beukema & Kuijpers (2018): 7.

[66] CBS (2017a, October 7).

[67] Bosselaar et al. (2010).

[68] de Graaf-Zijl et al. (2015).

[69] de Hek et al. (2018).

five employers claim they are willing to hire people with a (preferably physical) disability; an even smaller proportion actually do.[70] Although support from colleagues and managers is crucial during reintegration, productivity targets get in the way. Not everyone has the time to explain yet again how the computer system works, or to jump in when a returning colleague is unable to complete a task.

6.3.4 Limits to the Intensification of Work

There is a human limit to the intensification of work: "Just as an extension of the length of the working day is bounded by the number of hours in the day, so human physical and mental capacities do not allow an endless expansion to effort."[71] The question is whether the Netherlands has reached this limit. Absenteeism due to psychosocial complaints is increasing; people who were not previously vulnerable are falling ill – highly educated young women, for instance, who are reporting symptoms of burnout in ever-higher numbers. The intensification of work has placed many people who were already vulnerable at an even greater distance from the world of work. Clearly, people are better able to cope with intensive work if they have some autonomy in the workplace and control in their private lives. Again, the quality of work is crucial.

6.4 Policies to Help People into Work

"Work, work, work" has been a key policy objective in the Netherlands for decades. But is enough being done to ensure that everyone can find and keep a good job? To combat many thousands of people dropping out of the workforce, prevention is more effective than any cure. This section asks whether the Netherlands' labour-market policies are sufficiently active to help people find and retain work in the age of its automation, flexibilization and intensification.

---

[70] Adelmeijer et al. (2015, 2017). The Netherlands Institute for Social Research notes only 11% of employers expect to hire (more) people with occupational disabilities in the next 2 years, the same as in 2015/2016 (Van Echtelt et al. 2019a, b).

[71] Green (2004): 615.

Box 6.4 Starting Points for a Preventive Labour-Market Policy
Figure 6.6 summarizes how we can keep the automation, flexibilization and intensification of work from exacerbating existing vulnerabilities and creating new ones. There are a number of starting points to achieve positive change.

The use of new technologies in the workplace can benefit working people, even vulnerable ones, if it focuses on complementarity: encouraging co-operation between humans and machines, both in the development of applications and in their implementation.

Flexible labour markets require responsible employers who actively invest in their employees. So long as "permanently temporary" employment does not become the norm, temporary contracts need not be a problem. But the employer must invest in its temporary staff, including those with disabilities.

To mitigate the negative effects of the intensification of work, greater worker autonomy is essential. When people have a real say over what they do and when and where they do it, they are better able to be highly productive and to deal with emotionally challenging situations. Being able to co-ordinate the professional and the personal helps.

All of these aspects of good work offer greater protections against jobless-ness and are crucial ingredients within actively preventative labour-market policy.

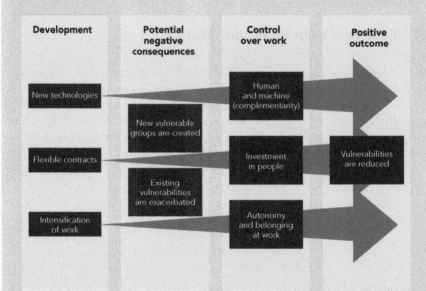

Fig. 6.6 How labour-market developments can reduce vulnerabilities

6.4.1 Limited Investments

Recent attention has focused on containing costs in the Dutch social-security system and on imposing obligations on its beneficiaries.[72] In contrast, little has been invested in people who have left the labour market. At the beginning of this century, the Netherlands was second only to Denmark in its investments in active labour-market policy (Fig. 6.7). In the past decade, spending in this area has nearly halved, dropping to 0.6% of GDP in 2017.[73] This is the same as in Germany, less than in France and Belgium (0.9%), and much less than in Sweden (1.3%) and Denmark (2.0%). While Denmark maintained and Sweden increased support for the unemployed during the 2008 economic crisis, the Netherlands cut back – although research shows that active policies have the greatest effect and are most needed during crises.[74]

OECD statistics provide an overview of the various components of active labour-market policy. Compared to other European countries, investments in vocational education and training are particularly low in the Netherlands, amounting to just

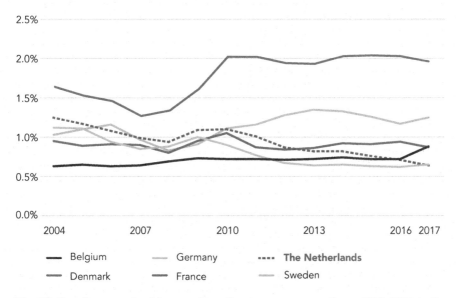

Fig. 6.7 Spending on active labour-market policy as a percentage of GDP, 2004–2017, in the Netherlands and other European countries
Source: OECD database. (https://stats.oecd.org/index.aspx?DataSetCode=lmpexp#)

---

[72] Vrooman et al. (2017).

[73] Eurostat figures show a similar pattern. See also Koning et al. (2017), CPB (2015).

[74] Kluve (2010), Card et al. (2017).

0.07% of GDP in 2017 – far less than in Denmark (0.46%) or France (0.28%).[75] This limited attention to training is striking, especially in light of the technological developments affecting the workplace and the intensification of work – the more so when we see that the majority of people claiming subsistence benefits in the Netherlands lack even a basic educational qualification. The Netherlands also commits less resources to job search assistance than the Scandinavian countries, France and the United Kingdom. Many unemployed persons thus fall through the cracks.[76] A significant proportion of those without work rarely see a case manager or anyone from the Employee Insurance Agency.[77] In contrast to the 1990s, virtually nothing is now spent on directly creating work.

Why has the Netherlands not maintained the active labour-market policies it initiated in the 1990s? There are three explanations. First, the focus of government policy, particularly labour-market policy, has shifted away from public provision towards individual self-reliance.[78] In the 1990s, the emphasis was on enforcing social-security rules and sanctioning non-compliance; now, the unemployed are expected to find the shortest route into work. Unlike the "human-capital" or "train-first" approach, this "work-first" approach best serves people who find it relatively easy to move into work. In other words, the policy primarily targets those who least need it.[79]

A second explanation is administrative decentralization and the Participation Act of 2015, which transferred responsibilities for the labour market reintegration of subsistence benefit recipients to local authorities. At the same time, supporting budgets were cut dramatically.[80] Local governments had little expertise in guiding people into work and were slow in taking up their new tasks. An evaluation of the Participation Act found that it led, at best, to a slight increase in workforce participation. In some respects it has had no effect or even reduced participation, most notably among people previously in sheltered employment who are now more likely to be at home than in work.[81] For "classic" social-security claimants, the chances of finding a job have risen by just 1 percentage point. Young adults with occupational disabilities are now more likely to be working, but their jobs are often poor, part-time and/or temporary; they can barely make ends meet, let alone build a meaningful life.[82] The Netherlands Institute for Social Research, which conducted the

---

[75] OECD database.
[76] OECD (2017).
[77] Inspectie SZW (2014).
[78] See Veldheer et al. (2012).
[79] Martin (2014).
[80] Berenschot (2018).
[81] For people previously qualifying for sheltered work, the chances of finding regular employment have fallen from 50% prior to the law's enactment to 30% (Sadiraj et al. 2018).
[82] Kok et al. (2019).

evaluation, concludes that the objectives of the Participation Act have not been achieved.[83]

Finally, academic research has contributed to the weakening of active labour-market policy.[84] Doubts have been raised, especially by economists, about the effectiveness of active labour-market policies, often due to contradictory findings.[85] This is often due to limitations in the research itself; it is difficult to gauge the effectiveness of interventions as conditions in the real world of work are hard to keep constant. There is often a degree of partiality in participant selection (or self-selection), while the interventions – a training course or a conversation with a case manager – differ.[86] If we look at the evidence in more detail, some instruments work better than others; it also matters who the intended beneficiaries are. For example, active policies are more effective for those with the fewest opportunities such as the less skilled, the long-term unemployed and people with occupational disabilities.[87] We also know little about whether interventions help people feel healthier or more valued, even when they do not directly lead to finding a job.

6.4.2   What We Know

Meta-analyses of research on hundreds of programmes[88] suggests that imposing obligations on benefit claimants and penalizing them for non-compliance has some effect on people who are not already distanced from the labour market. Education and training have less immediate success, but achieve modest results after 2 or 3 years.[89] The most effective form of intervention is instruction in specific skills currently in high demand, especially in the private sector[90] – preferably in the form of learning on the job. Temporary wage subsidies tailored to the individual beneficiary also have some positive effect.[91] Although digitization has penetrated the Dutch

---

[83] van Echtelt et al. (2019a).

[84] Kluve (2010), Koning et al. (2017).

[85] Martin and Grubb (2001) find that paying bonuses works better than imposing penalties. This is not apparent for Van der Klaauw and Van Ours (2013). See Card et al. (2010).

[86] See CPB (2016). Policy experiments in the Netherlands and elsewhere have sought to measure the effectiveness of interventions; see for example Knoef and Van Ours (2016) and Groot et al. (2019). Koning (2011) argues that it remains difficult to measure and stabilize the factors determining effectiveness.

[87] Card et al. (2017).

[88] Card et al. (2010, 2017), Martin (2014), Kluve (2010); see also CPB (2016).

[89] Lammers & Kok (2017). This applies more to people with lower educational levels.

[90] See also Martin & Grubb (2001).

[91] Card et al. (2010).

job-placement sector,[92] face-to-face meetings with a professional adviser helps to find a paid job sooner; even one conversation can make a big difference.[93]

Instruments are best tailored to the type of jobseeker.[94] While exhortations and penalties may suffice for people who are ready to work, they are pointless for people with very limited employment potential, chronic health problems or some other form of occupational disability. They need a different approach, one that is personal, intensive and long-term.[95] This is at long last being recognized in the Netherlands, as can be seen in the additional resources channelled to the Employee Insurance Agency following successive cutbacks, and by local authorities again focusing on personal contact with subsistence benefit recipients.[96] In 2016, the City of Amsterdam introduced a programme for refugees involving specialist case managers who focus on understanding their problems, building personal relationships, civic integration courses and labour-market guidance. The result has been higher workforce participation than in the city's past and in the rest of the country – although Amsterdam's thriving pre-pandemic economy has helped as well.[97]

The intensive approach means more personal contact with qualified professionals and a process attuned to the jobseeker's potential rather than to the brute fact that he or she is claiming benefits. Good work means work tailored to the individual in such a way that they gain greater control in life. People with limited work prospects often face a web of problems, at home and/or with their health; case managers need to look beyond the boundaries of labour-market guidance and work with, for instance, debt-counsellors and healthcare professionals. Although it has long been known that the unemployed are more likely to be ill and vice-versa, "care cannot be used for reintegration and reintegration cannot be used for care".[98] Academic studies furnish evidence to develop more personalized interventions.

6.4.3   What About Employers?

Most employers are reluctant to hire if applicants do not fit the profiles for available vacancies.[99] They are afraid to incur additional costs due to job and workplace adaptations, greater needs for supervision, sickness and absenteeism.[100] Research shows that potential health issues play a larger role in hiring and retention than age.[101]

---

[92] Martin (2014).

[93] Koning (2006), Koning et al. (2017), Heyma & van der Werff (2014), Lammers et al. (2015). For research in Denmark, see Van den Berg et al. (2012). For research in Switzerland, see Schiprowski (in press). For research on contact with benefit recipients, see Van der Valk and Fenger (2019).

[94] CPB (2016), Kok & Houkes (2011).

[95] See also CPB (2016), Lub (2017).

[96] Kremer et al. (2017b).

[97] Oostveen et al. (2019).

[98] Einerhand & Ravesteijn (2017); see also OECD (2014).

[99] See, for example, van Berkel et al. (2017).

[100] Adelmeijer et al. (2015, 2017), van Echtelt et al. (2019b).

[101] Houtman et al. (2013).

Predictable, stable finances are a prerequisite for employers. Targeted wage subsidies are more effective for enrolling vulnerable workers than general wage subsidies, which also benefit people who would have found work anyway.[102] The Netherlands, like most European countries, makes scant use of these instruments.[103] Other schemes to help people into work include wage dispensation and the appointment of a jobs coach. Different financial and legal regulations apply to each category of benefit recipient; many employers claim they are unaware of the regulations.[104]

The job-placement landscape in the Netherlands is fragmented and opaque. Figure 6.8 shows just how complicated the current system is. The roles played by the local authorities and the Employee Insurance Agency, employers' organizations

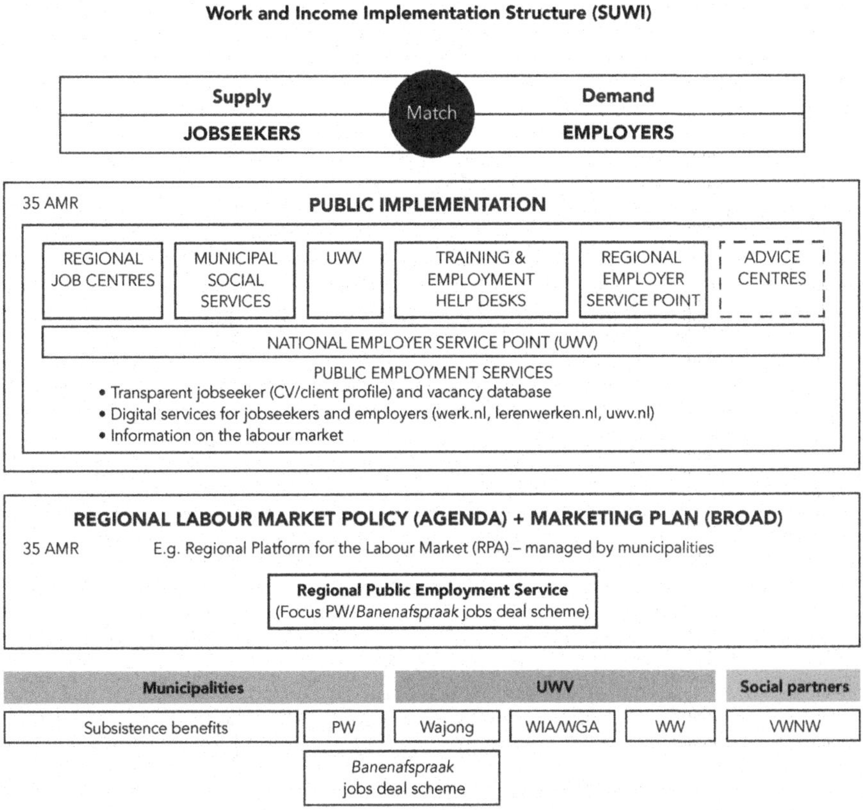

Work and Income Implementation Structure (SUWI)

Fig. 6.8 Organization of job-placement services
Source: Employee Insurance Agency (UWV)

---

[102] Card et al. (2017).
[103] See also CPB (2016).
[104] CPB (2015).

and trade unions differ across situations. Many jobseekers and employers have no idea where to turn.

Financial incentives do not suffice to persuade employers to hire as organizations must often change to accommodate different types of workers. Those that have made "diversity" part of their mission recruit more people from vulnerable groups; so do large firms (with over 100 employees), firms that already employ less skilled staff and the government.[105] Things are often more challenging for small and medium-sized firms. Active public labour-market policies must back employers' own HR. policies[106] to guide and support individual jobseekers while making the necessary adjustments within the organization to create space for them. Tailoring jobs for vulnerable workers often requires the involvement of the entire organization.[107] Effective activation requires long-term commitment from both sides.[108] The challenge is to innovate in such a way that more vulnerable workers are able to join the workforce.[109]

Box 6.5 Individual Placement and Support

An approach known as Individual Placement and Support is often used for people with severe mental impairments. Together with the jobseeker, a jobs coach determines what kind of work and tasks the person can handle. A suitable position is then created in a regular work organization, a process known as "jobcrafting". The new employee receives work, care and guidance for an extended period – sometimes even permanently. Shown to be effective, the approach is now being tried more widely among subsistence benefit recipients. The key is close attention to "the whole person" as well as to the work environment, where they are likely to need intensive internal supervision. Not only workers need coaches; so do their employers, managers and colleagues.

6.4.4   Good Basic Jobs

While active labour-market policies need to target both potential employers and employees, it does not suffice for people without realistic prospects of finding paid work. This is why "basic jobs" are back on the agenda, now championed by many

---

[105] In the "100,000 Jobs Plan" for people with disabilities, supported by employers' organizations VNO-NCW and MKB-Nederland, private sector employers are ahead of those in the public sector; TNO (2015).

[106] van Berkel et al. (2017).

[107] A Danish scheme using Public Employment Service funds allows paying colleagues to act as job coaches.

[108] See also OECD (2018a), Froyland et al. (2019).

[109] Blonk (2018), Nijhuis & Zijlstra (2015).

sociologists, lawyers, economists and several Dutch political parties.[110] The same discussion is taking place in other European countries. Basic jobs are a response to the changing face of work, to the "demanding and uncertain labour market" which offers insufficient opportunities for one million people in the country.[111] "The reintegration into work of the unemployed no longer offers any guarantee of a sustainable, fully-fledged job."[112] To some extent, basic jobs are also an answer to the campaign for a basic income. If work is so important to people mentally and socially, society should, instead of providing them with income, offer good work.[113]

Dutch cities such as Amsterdam and The Hague have been experimenting with basic jobs for people on subsistence benefits for some time.[114] Sweden has its own variants such as the 1000 "Stockholm Jobbs" its capital city is hoping to create. Similarly, "one-euro jobs" in Germany entail work in the social sector with the retention of benefits plus a bonus of 1 euro per hour.[115] The idea is that there is a lot of socially useful work to be done and that the financing of benefits may as well be converted into wage subsidization to create paid work.[116] Although these schemes incur organizational and supervision costs as well as additional social insurance contributions, the local authorities believe that general well-being is enhanced, that healthcare spending will fall and that community cohesion will benefit when everyone is able to be part of the workforce (see also Chap. 2).

The Netherlands has previous experience with subsidized jobs. The best known are the 40,000 "Melkert jobs" created in 1994 by the then Minister of Social Affairs and Employment, Ad Melkert. To avoid competing with regular work, these positions – paid 120% of the statutory minimum wage – had to be complementary; the idea was that the "Melketeers" would eventually move into "real" work. Half of these jobs were with private firms; the other half were in the public sector, where city wardens and school caretakers were supposed to improve the quality of

---

[110] Klosse & Muyskens (2011, November 4); Schippers et al. (2016). de Beer (2015) sees potential benefits but is more sceptical. The research unit of the co-governing Christian Democratic party (Siegmann 2018), the opposition Labour Party leader Lodewijk Asscher (Asscher 2019), and the economists Dankbaar and Muysken (2019) all advocate basic jobs, while Verhoeven and Wilthagen (in Wilthagen 2019) call for a "parallel labour market" in which money earmarked for benefits is used to fund workers. The proposals differ in how they organize the scheme. Most involve local authorities (which administer subsistence benefits) employing people and if necessary, seconding them to other workplaces. Verhoeven and Wilthagen favour public-private mixes.

[111] Wilthagen (2019).

[112] Klosse & Muyskens (2011, November 4).

[113] This does not alter the fact that customization is necessary and that the well-being of people entitled to subsistence benefits is bolstered by the security these payments provide. The "trust experiments" under way in several towns and cities give them the space they need (Groot et al. 2019). Some people gain more from doing voluntary work while retaining their entitlement to benefits. In other cases, the quid pro quo for payments from the public purse is best converted into a basic job.

[114] van Dodeweerd (2016).

[115] van der Meer & Kremer (2018, January 17).

[116] Schippers et al. (2016) calculate that an extra €8000 is needed to close the gap between subsistence benefits and wages. This excludes such factors as guidance supervision costs.

society.[117] The Melkert scheme was replaced in 1999 with "ID jobs" (from the Dutch abbreviation for "entry-level and step-up"). The central government abolished these positions with the decentralization of subsistence support in 2003. Many local authorities were unwilling or unable to make the investments necessary to maintain them and all subsidised labour eventually disappeared. Secretary of State Jette Kleinsma saw this as a positive development "because the ultimate goal of reintegration is to obtain regular, non-subsidized work".[118]

The basic jobs being proposed now are not meant as a path to regular work, although this may at times happen.[119] They are primarily for individuals lacking realistic prospects in the mainstream labour market who would otherwise remain dependent on benefits for extended periods. According to the alderman of The Hague who first tabled the idea, the main purpose of basic jobs is to prevent "people entering a downward spiral, at high cost to them individually but also to society."[120] The jobs should provide good work – and so not be temporary – thereby shielding their holders from the vagaries of the labour market and giving them some modicum of control over their work and in their lives.

In sum, the Netherlands is suffering from a qualitative mismatch between employers and jobseekers. People who have been out of work for a long time simply do not fit the available vacancies. Overcoming this predicament requires change, commitment and support from all sides. But even as the automation, flexibilization and intensification of work make this urgent, there is scant public investment in active labour-market policy. Renewed policies in this area should focus on good work for all, with tailored strategies for different groups of jobseekers and good basic jobs as the final piece of the puzzle.

6.5   Conclusion: New Vulnerabilities, New Policy Challenges

Dutch policy jargon includes the frequently heard term "people distanced from the labour market". But in many cases it is the market that has distanced itself from the people. How will the three developments at the heart of this book – the automation, flexibilization and intensification of work – affect those looking for and trying to stay in paid work?

---

[117] Laid down in the 1995 Regulations on Additional Work Opportunities for the Long-Term Unemployed.

[118] Aanhangsel Handelingen II 2009/2010, No. 664.

[119] Meta-analyses (e.g. Card et al. 2017) invariably show job creation schemes to be ineffective. This is due to the "lock-in effect" – additional subsidized work does not lead to regular employment because the taught skills do not match those required in the rest of the labour market. Like the trust experiments with benefit recipients, we need to study the long-term effects of basic jobs on health and well-being.

[120] Baldewsingh (2016).

All three developments have the potential to make all workers more vulnerable, not only those already on the margins. In this respect, the dividing lines between social groups are becoming less clear-cut. Automation, robots and artificial intelligence have already increased insecurity for some white-collar workers. The intensification of work likewise affects society more broadly; although burnout still affects more women and university graduates, it can happen to anyone. Temporary employment, too, is no longer reserved for classic vulnerable groups as the "flexible shell" has penetrated to the core of the labour market.

Vulnerable groups including high-school graduates and people with occupational disabilities may encounter even higher obstacles to labour-market participation. Once a person has been out of work for some time, it is harder to re-enter the workforce; in the jargon, one's distance from the labour market has increased. Here, the automation, flexibilization and intensification of work are largely exacerbating the divide between highly educated, healthy and productive workers and less productive, less confident people. For specific vulnerable groups, the gulf between the demands of the labour market and their own needs is widening; the long-term unemployed find it almost impossible to keep up with the changing world of work. As a hectic working environment is no place to attempt a gentle re-entry into active life, this puts the whole notion of reintegration to the test.

Prevention is better than cure, but the question is whether Dutch labour-market policy is preventive enough.[121] Keeping everyone in work is an important aspect of the quality of work; focusing on good work is the best preventive labour-market policy of all.

Technology can serve vulnerable groups and help their members to find and retain work. Economist Tony Atkinson[122] in *Inequality, What Can Be Done?* argues that the "direction of technological change should be an explicit concern of policy makers, encouraging innovation in a form that increases the employability of workers". This does not happen automatically; focusing on complementarity – on people working with machines – is crucial. For their own protection, workers need to be involved in transitions and to be able to prepare for them.

Elements of the flexible labour market such as self-employment can offer some people opportunities to find and stay in work. Temporary contracts can in theory offer flexible workers stepping stones towards greater security – although in practice revolving-door unemployment is more common. Flexible working offers scant protection for people with health issues or occupational disabilities. Investing in greater "internal flexibility" – the ability to move into different work within the same firm or within a pool of firms – may be a reasonable response to eroded corporate responsibility.

---

[121] OECD (2018a).
[122] Atkinson (2015).

The intensification of work is more manageable when people have sufficient autonomy and support at work. The high rate of work-related absenteeism and burn-out would be mitigated to some extent if people enjoyed more control over their work and a healthy work-life balance.

Although new technologies and the flexibilization and intensification of work open new possibilities for active labour-market policy, the Netherlands in recent decades has halved its budget in this area. As a result, the country now lags behind the rest of Europe. To reverse the tide, active labour-market policies should focus not only on personal training but on the entire work organization. Basic jobs can be a solution for people who are still unable to find work.

The three key developments we analyse in this book do not have predestined effects on working people; there is no question of technological or economic determinism in their outcomes. The automation, flexibilization and intensification of work can be influenced, adjusted, stimulated, inhibited and offset. The next chapter looks at how much scope the government, companies and institutions have to invest in better work: good quality work for people who are already working and for the unemployed who want to work.

A Day at Work: The Chartered Accountant
David is a chartered accountant at one of the major accounting firms in the Netherlands. Its office block is tall with lots of glass; the entrance is elegant and access is limited. One needs a pass to open the building's many gates.

David shares a room on the sixth floor with a colleague. He starts his day with coffee as he browses his e-mails. An accountant's core task, he explains, is to provide certainty about the client's financial situation. Companies and organizations are legally obliged to have their annual financial statements and other regular reports audited by accountants as a true representation of their situation so that other parties – investors, suppliers, the tax authorities and so on – trust them. "Accountants have a social function," David says, "because without trust every transaction would fall through."

David is a partner in the firm and thus a co-owner. Partners receive a share of the profits instead of a salary. They are personally responsible for the quality of their own work and that of the junior accountants under them. If something goes wrong, they can face disciplinary proceedings with legal force.

David's first task today is to consult a colleague for advice about a client with overseas subsidiaries in a complex ownership structure. They outline the situation on a whiteboard, discuss the options and decide which is most realistic. He then dashes to his next appointment. Five minutes late, David storms into a meeting room where 12 people are sitting around a large table with a speaker for teleconferences in the middle and a screen on the wall. They are all partners – predominantly male, white and between 40 and 50 years old – each sitting behind a laptop and a stack of papers. The atmosphere is relaxed,

(continued)

the tempo punishing, the language impenetrable with acronyms and English jargon. Someone explains the items on the agenda; much of the meeting concerns quality improvement. One topic is how to respond to the firm's forthcoming inspection report by the Financial Markets Authority. The session goes on for 3 h with a short toilet and telephone break half-way through. Lunch is set out and eaten while talking.

At 1:30 pm the meeting is still not over but David has to leave. In his own room, he has a Skype chat with a client about a quote for an annual audit. When the client tries to negotiate a lower rate, David is willing to think about it, although it has already been adjusted once. After half an hour he has to break off and go to another appointment in yet another meeting room. He discusses a quality problem with four partners. One of the firm's main competitors is ahead on this point, they note jealously. They at least need to reach the same level.

At 3 pm, David is back at his desk. Only now does he find out that his scheduled call has been postponed. He uses the spare time to check his e-mails again – 15 new messages since this morning, which is not so bad – to listen to his voicemail and to fill in his timesheet. He quickly scans the latest financial news on his phone.

At 3:30 pm he calls a fellow partner who will be leaving the firm shortly about the handover of his clients and projects. This is followed by another scheduled call, this time with someone from his own team. David finds the solution being proposed acceptable but warns his colleague not to take on too much work.

At about 5 pm, David sinks back into his chair. It has been a hectic day but not a stressful one. There are also days when he must check reports compiled by his junior accountants, which means spending hours on end behind his computer. The dynamism is why he likes his work – alongside accountancy's social function, which makes it a difficult profession. After a number of recent scandals, supervision by the Financial Markets Authority has become stricter; the bar for audits has been raised. This has increased costs for clients and the competition between accountancy firms is fierce. "We try to compensate by working smarter", says David. Ultimately, the pressure falls on the auditing accountants who must deliver high quality in as few billable hours as possible. While software to review standard financial data is advancing, everything else needs to be done by people, including the communication with clients.

At 5:15 pm, a colleague offers David a lift home. Once there, he will spend another half an hour answering e-mails.

Accountant, like notary and lawyer, is a regulated profession in the Netherlands. Practitioners must be registered with the Royal Netherlands Institute of Chartered Accountants. There are currently more than 21,000 active accountants, 80 per cent of them men. Most hold university degrees

(continued)

(chartered accountants), a smaller number higher vocational qualifications (certified accountants), in both cases followed by practical training. The remuneration varies according to their qualifications, workplace and experience, in the range of €3000–9000 gross per month. As co-owners of their firms and thus entrepreneurs, partners are in a separate category and sometimes earn many hundreds of thousands of euros a year. The average (modal) income in the Netherlands in 2020 will be just over €2800 per month, excluding holiday pay. Accountants are in great demand and there are high rates of turnover in the large firms. Recent research by Nyenrode Business University points to heavy workloads in the profession, especially for young accountants, both in terms of hours (an average of eight hours of overtime a week) and quality requirements. New technologies including automated data analysis are expected to change the profession, rendering some human tasks unnecessary.

Part III
The New Societal Mission

Chapter 7
Room to Choose Good Work

Economic globalization and technological development are often presented as inevitable trends to which people and nations can only adapt. By this reasoning, national governments no longer have the room to make choices and companies cannot provide good jobs due to the pressures of international competition. But is this really true? Is it realistic to pursue good work for everyone who can and wants to work?

The economist Anna Salomons argues that the digital revolution will not make existing work organizations superfluous. We should instead reflect on how we can develop ourselves, our institutions and our machines in such a way that human work remains human: "if employees are treated like robots, that hinders the productivity gains to be achieved by introducing *real* robots."[1]

David Weil concludes *The Fissured Workplace* by analysing what the fragmentation and outsourcing of work has meant for employees: greater insecurity, worse terms of employment, fewer on-the-job training opportunities and restricted opportunities for advancement. Yet he is hopeful. We are emerging from a long period during which pay, conditions and standards of *fairness* in the workplace did not improve. But by taking advantage of new ways of organizing production, better work can be had for all.[2]

Other experts have argued along similar lines. But is their optimism realistic? Are companies and governments really still able to prioritise creating good work for everyone? This chapter first addresses globalization (Sect. 7.1) and technological developments (Sect. 7.2) before turning to the choices open to companies (Sect. 7.3) and the government (Sect. 7.4).

---

[1] Salomons (2015).
[2] Weil (2014).

© The Author(s) 2021
M. Kremer et al., *Better Work*, Research for Policy,
https://doi.org/10.1007/978-3-030-78682-3_7

7.1   Globalization with Policy Space

Economic globalization has transformed the world since the late 1970s. There is now greater process interdependence across national borders; the international trade in goods and services has blossomed while financial flows have become faster and more extensive. Companies are now more likely to operate internationally, producing and assembling goods and delivering services through cross-border value and production chains. Many firms have subsidiaries, affiliates and production units abroad; about 15,000 Dutch businesses have a foreign parent company.[3] The Netherlands, a medium-sized nation with an open economy, now earns approximately 34% of its GDP abroad[4] – a proportion which has remained stable for many years. Domestic economic activity thus still accounts for almost twice as much income as the international trade on which the country prides itself.[5]

7.1.1   Winners and Losers

Globalization has long been presented as a development over which we have no control. But recent years have shown that its rules can and do change.[6] The International Monetary Fund has become less doctrinaire about controls on capital movements; many international organizations have published reports on the need to make globalization more inclusive. In any case, the world economy is nowhere as globalized as it could theoretically be,[7] and there is scant likelihood that economic globalization will receive renewed impetus in the near future. New technologies may well make it more attractive to organize aspects of production closer by, while some in the affluent world have high hopes for "reshoring" – the return of production previously outsourced to emerging economies.

Ever since the Brexit referendum in the UK and Donald Trump's election in the USA, analysts have been warning about the backlash to globalization – perhaps the end of the phenomenon as we know it.[8] No-one any longer denies that globalization

---

[3] Boorsma (2018).

[4] CBS (2019d).

[5] Hueck and Went (2016, January 9); WRR (2013a).

[6] Rodrik (2017).

[7] Ghemawat and Altman (2016).

[8] van Bergeijk (2019); Bremmer (2018); King (2017); Rodrik (2017).

has losers as well as winners – although they are not always easy to identify.[9] The obvious candidates are people who lose their jobs when production moves abroad and workers who find their pay and conditions undermined by foreign competition. Entire communities can suffer losses in income and well-being when a local company closes its doors and shifts its activities to a cheaper location.[10]

For people, work is much more than a source of income; not even generous benefit payments can offset its loss. How does one measure and compensate for the impact on families and communities of a company closure or relocation?[11] According to researchers at the Netherlands Bureau for Economic Policy Analysis, the Dutch losers of globalization are better off than in many other countries. In a recent policy briefing on inclusive globalization, they observe that "we are seeing shifts in employment across sectors, but unemployment remains low and the levelling effects of the tax system, along with the social-security safety net, are mitigating the sometimes painful transition effects of globalization."[12] This is of course not the case everywhere, which is one of the reasons why alarming analyses of how robots will devastate the future landscape of work in the United States are often used to justify calls for a basic income there.[13]

7.1.2   The Political Trilemma of the World Economy

Concerns about the workings and future of globalization and the revival of nationalism have fuelled debate on more inclusive ways of organizing the international economy, national economies and the welfare state.[14] "The question today is what type of globalization there will be," writes Angel Gurría, Secretary-General of the OECD. "It doesn't have to be the one we've had. We must return people's well-being to the centre of our focus, and ensure that the benefits derived from further interconnectedness of our economies, societies, institutions and cultures are more equally shared."[15] At issue is whether and how the policy space available to national governments should be expanded so that they are better able to pursue domestic priorities. Small emerging economies have been hamstrung by globalization much more than large, rich economies like the United States or even advanced medium-sized economies like the Netherlands.

---

[9] Nolan (2018, August 3); Rodrik (1997); Rodrik (2011); Stiglitz (2002); Went (2017).

[10] Collier (2018); Rajan (2019).

[11] Cass (2018); Goldstein (2017); Rodrik (2018, November 9).

[12] Euwals and Meijerink (2018).

[13] Ford (2015).

[14] See, for example: Block (2018); Collier (2018); Corneo (2017); IPPR Commission on Economic Justice (2018); Mazzucato (2018); Rajan (2019); Raworth (2017); Rodrik (2017); Went (2018).

[15] Gurría (2017, June 6).

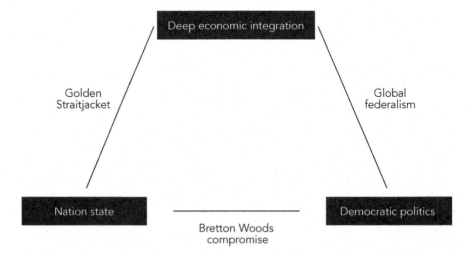

Fig. 7.1 The political trilemma of the world economy
Source: Rodrik, 2007

Dani Rodrik's "political trilemma" posits that it is impossible for far-reaching globalization *and* democracy *and* nation states to co-exist (see Fig. 7.1); we must choose which two of the three we consider more important. In the post-war Bretton Woods era, international trade was promoted but brakes were placed on the globalization of capital movements (see the lower axis in Fig. 7.1). The idea was that national priorities, such as lowering central-bank interest rates to boost employment, should not be hindered by (the threat of) capital flight. Since the 1980s, greater efforts have been made to achieve far-reaching globalization (the left-hand axis). As globalization limits the options and policy space available to individual nations, Thomas Friedman calls this "the golden straitjacket".[16] The third choice (the right-hand axis) is technically possible but implies something like a world government and global democracy that go far beyond the many forms of "global governance" we know today. In practice, these choices involve gradations.[17]

National governments largely retain the ability to make their own policy decisions.[18] Torben Iversen and David Soskice even argue that "the autonomy of the advanced nation-state has increased even as globalization and mutual dependence have risen."[19] The Social and Economic Council of the Netherlands argued in 2008 that states should use this policy space to help companies and workers losing out from globalization.[20] Countries, conclude IMF researchers, are in a position to choose to make economic growth more inclusive and less uneven.[21]

---

[16] Friedman (1999).

[17] Rodrik (2007, June 27); Rodrik (2011); Derbyshire (2017, July 28).

[18] See, for example: Rodrik (1997); Rodrik (2011); Rodrik (2017); SER (2008); Went (2018).

[19] Iversen and Soskice (2019): XII.

[20] SER (2008).

[21] Ostry et al. (2019).

7.1.3 Lasting Differences Between Countries

Researchers of the "varieties of capitalism"[22] have analysed the differences between so-called "liberal" market economies like the US, the UK and Australia and "co-ordinated" economies like Germany, the Scandinavian countries and the Netherlands. What is striking is that all of these countries have continued to develop without converging towards an average or lowest common denominator. Despite the steady advance of globalization, there remain significant institutional differences between nations in areas such as social protection and the taxation of labour. Even a cursory glance at the statistics for OECD or EU member states shows that they remain as dissimilar as ever on numerous indicators, despite – or perhaps in part because of – globalization.[23]

While Sweden and Japan both have highly open economic borders, "it is difficult to maintain that these countries have made identical political choices when it comes to issues such as taxes, distribution of income, education or social security".[24] In the realm of work, Germany, Belgium and France proportionally have fewer flexible and self-employed workers than the Netherlands. These enduring differences between countries facing similar pressures from globalization are the result of their histories, traditions and preferences – in other words, of path dependencies, institutions and policy choices.[25]

7.1.4 The Same Picture in the Globalization of Production...

One important difference between the current wave of globalization and the previous one, between about 1870 and the First World War, is that the production of goods and services has now also gone global – at least in part. Firms have divided their activities into tasks and subtasks which are then organized into production or value chains. This gives them choices. According to Stoker and Garretsen, globalization has enlarged the decision space available to CEOs: "In a world of open borders in which markets have largely been liberalized compared with the first few decades after the Second World, CEOs and corporate boards have huge strategic discretion."[26]

---

[22] Hall and Soskice (2001).

[23] "Although corporations are now organized with greater flexibility and are more decentralized ... [r]edistribution and welfare states, while they have changed over time, remain different across advanced capitalist democracies" (Iversen & Soskice, 2019: 39).

[24] Stoker and Garretsen (2018).

[25] Admiraal (2018, October 16); de Beer and Verhulp (2017); Kremer et al. (2017d).

[26] Stoker and Garretsen (2018).

Most jobs in the Netherlands are with companies and institutions serving the domestic market; pay levels and the quality of work are generally determined nationally, not internationally. But local autonomy may be limited by foreign owners or shareholders demanding returns on investment, and by firms favouring an international strategy or division of labour as they compete.[27] For the 15,000 foreign-owned businesses in the Netherlands, the Dutch employers' organization AWVN finds that it matters where the parent company is based: "A Japanese firm is very different from an American or a French one. French companies often allow a fair degree of local freedom: as long as you pay your own way and keep the money coming in, you can do pretty much as you like. Japanese companies tend to be characterized by strict conventions and a methodical way of working, with plenty of protocols."[28] Statistics Netherlands and the Netherlands Organization for Applied Scientific Research report that Dutch local employees of US multinationals work more overtime and experience higher workloads and greater levels of mental fatigue than staff at non-multinationals.[29]

7.1.5   ...and of Labour

The globalization of labour also has its limits. Immigration to the Netherlands over the past decade has largely been due to agreements made within the European Union, whose member states have decided that people, like goods and services, should be able to move freely across the continent's internal borders. While only a small percentage of Europeans (2.5% in 2010) use this right, Eastern Europeans do so far more than others. The largest group of recent immigrants to the Netherlands comes from Poland, currently totalling an estimated 370,000 people.[30]

We again see significant differences between European countries, with some drawing many more migrant workers than others. In the Netherlands, labour migration is encouraged by active temporary employment agencies[31] and constrained by collective labour agreements, high (minimum) wages, and barriers to temporary working and self-employment – especially the enforcement of existing rules and regulations.[32] Under European agreements about working conditions, wages and

---

[27] See also Koster (2020).

[28] Boorsma (2018).

[29] CBS (2019b, March 31).

[30] Heyma et al. (2018).

[31] McCollum and Findlay (2015).

[32] Ruhs (2012); Holtslag et al. (eds.). (2012).

training, employers and member states have great latitude in determining what work is offered, and to whom; the institutions regulating national labour markets have replaced the customs posts of yesterday.

Research shows that labour migrants rarely steal jobs from native populations. Migrant workers mostly arrive in times of economic growth. There is in effect a dual labour market, with newcomers doing the work locals are unable or unwilling to do.[33] In economically precarious sectors or work organizations, this may lead to less investment in training, downwards pressure on wages and fewer opportunities for collective action (Box 7.1).[34]

Box 7.1 What About Flexibility?

Globalization and technological advances allow the monitoring and adjusting of production and stock levels in real time and the breaking up of manufacturing processes so that they can be organized as efficiently as possible. But these developments, which have encouraged the growth of the flexible labour market, do not on their own explain the rapid rise in Dutch self-employment. The OECD in its report for the Netherlands Independent Commission on the Regulation of Work agrees.[35] If globalization and technology were the sole drivers of flexible work, there would be fewer differences between countries. Can flexible working then be tied to cultural trends? People increasingly value having say over their work; the growing number of working women means that more people want to combine work with care, while the rise of self-employment can in part be explained by freelance workers wanting more freedom and control over their own time. The flexible labour market does not only emanate from the top down – pushed by globalization and new technologies – but from the bottom up. That said, Dutch self-employment is not always a free choice; nor is the Netherlands so different culturally from places like Germany and the Scandinavian countries where self-employment is much less common. The number of flexible jobs and self-employed individuals in the Netherlands is then primarily the result of domestic political decisions, regulations and policies: everything from dismissal law and collective agreements to the system of taxation and social security. These are summarized in Fig. 7.2.

While economic integration can indeed set limits on countries trying to avoid capital flight in a crisis, economic globalization does not eliminate the ability of countries to define preferences and to act on them. Politicians in many parts of the world have become more aware of this in recent years. With the downsides of

---

[33] van den Berge et al. (2018); Berkhout et al. (2014); Portes (2018, April 6).
[34] Ruhs and Anderson (2010); Ruhs (2012).
[35] OECD (2019a).

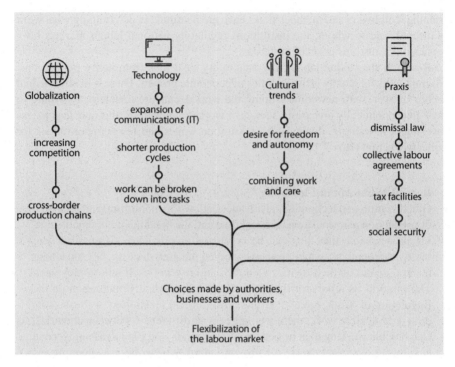

Fig. 7.2 Causes of flexibilization in the Dutch labour market
Source: Kremer et al., 2017d

economic globalization becoming more readily apparent, there is growing international interest in how the policy space available to nation-states can be utilized more effectively.

7.2   Technology Does Not Just Happen

Like globalization, technological development is often seen as a force we can only prepare for and adapt to, not shape. Although its momentum may seem unstoppable to individuals, as the many bank staff who have lost their jobs to computers can testify, the bulldozer effect does not apply across the board. Politicians, governments, companies, engineers, technology workers, stakeholder organizations, social movements and others all help define how technology is developed and applied. "The future is not something we arrive at so much as something we create through our actions in the present" (Box 7.2).[36]

---

[36] Rushkoff (2019).

Box 7.2 Technological Revolutions
We know from previous technological revolutions that the rollout and application of general-purpose technologies is a lengthy process of trial and error, correction, adjustment and adaptation.[37] While these technologies have great potential, realizing them requires a great deal of investment and, often, organizational change. Processes must be developed, management must gain experience, employees must be trained, software must be adapted and so on.

There is nothing inevitable about how new technologies are applied; it is not something society must simply accept. Over time, we have seen changes in the (initially mostly positive) attitude towards disruptive online platforms such as Uber and Airbnb. Around the world, platforms are now being challenged by new interest groups, networks and co-operatives formed by their workers. Cities such as New York and Barcelona and states such as California have begun subjecting platforms to stricter requirements, for example by limiting the number of vehicles allowed to operate on behalf of Uber, Lyft and similar companies, or by imposing requirements for drivers' pay, safety and working conditions.

Many communities are now responding to protect local residents and hoteliers from Airbnb's explosive growth. Amsterdam is working with other major tourist destinations such as Paris and Barcelona to limit the number of days homes can be rented out and to obtain more data from Airbnb about tenants and landlords. Governments are not powerless against platforms: it is possible to regulate them and to respond to their unwanted effects and side-effects through policy and enforcement.

7.2.1   Humanizing Work

New technologies were already threatening the quality of work in 1776 when Adam Smith wrote that the government should act to prevent the occupations of the working poor from being reduced to simple, monotonous operations which make people "as stupid and ignorant as it is possible for a human creature to become".[38] While new technologies can give workers more autonomy and control over the organization of their tasks, all too often the opposite happens.[39]

Digital technology need not lead to the surveillance or control of workers through machine-generated feedback.[40] There are many examples of robots and "cobots" in

---

[37] Freeman and Louçã (2001).

[38] Best (2018).

[39] de Stefano (2018).

[40] Head (2018, May 24).

construction and the automobile industry making work for humans safer, more varied and less physically grinding. There are also inspiring initiatives to help people
with physical or mental disabilities to find work or to function better in their current
jobs; many expect such possibilities involving technology to increase in the future.
Fred Block[41] argues that, in principle, the ability to automate repetitive tasks creates
more room for work requiring human judgement, creativity, problem-solving, interaction and contact in fields such as healthcare and care for the elderly.[42]

Economists similarly argue that algorithms will make forecasting cheaper and
thus increase the importance and value of human judgement.[43] Paul Daugherty and
James Wilson at the consultancy Accenture point out that while humans have long
had to adapt to the rhythm of machines, artificial intelligence now offers opportunities to rehumanize work and to alter the nature of human-machine interactions to
increase both workers' productivity and well-being; in the coming age of AI, they
anticipate huge demand for creative workers with people-skills able make decisions
within new, fully thought-out work processes.[44] This will not be the case everywhere, and it may have to be fought for, but it is one of the possibilities offered by
new technology.

7.2.2   The Economics of Robots and AI

Whether and how robots and algorithms enter the workplace – and what impact they
will have on the quantity and quality of work – will depend on numerous factors and
decisions. To successfully introduce robots to automate routine subtasks, companies
will need both adequate financial resources and employees able to assess the available technologies. When a company decides to adopt robots or cobots, it is often not
clear in advance what this will mean for the number of jobs. In theory:

- capital (robots and cobots) can replace human labour;
- the use of technology can increase productivity (and therefore wages);
- the use of robots can create new human tasks and functions.

In practice, the balance between the above mechanisms will determine whether
the demand for human labour increases or decreases.[45]

The story is similar for AI, with parallel predictions for how its entry into the
workplace will affect functions and subtasks. Again there are many factors at play
and decisions to be made: about what is or seems technically possible, about what
actually works and about what is pursued in practice. Although how AI will affect
the quantity and quality of work has been the subject of intense speculation,[46] so far

---

[41] Block (2018).

[42] See also: Colvin (2015); Davenport and Kirby (2016); Dekker and Freese (2018).

[43] Agrawal et al. (2018).

[44] Daugherty and Wilson (2018).

[45] ter Weel (2018).

[46] See: Agrawal et al. (eds.). (2019b); Mateos-Garcia (2019, October 7).

there is scant hard evidence. In theory, the use of algorithms can have many possible consequences[47]:

- algorithms can substitute capital for human labour;
- algorithms can increase the relative return on capital, compared with the return on labour (for example, as a result of full automation);
- algorithms can increase the productivity of labour (and therefore wages);
- algorithms can reduce uncertainty and so create new tasks for human labour and/ or capital;
- algorithms can create new human work upstream or downstream.

In practice, the overall balance between the above mechanisms will determine their consequences for both the quantity and quality of work.[48]

Just as the introduction of robots is happening more slowly than enthusiasts once hoped, the widespread application of AI is not going to happen overnight; practical problems need to be solved and adjustments will take time.[49] A 2018 report on robot-based process automation in *The New York Times* described how "companies are eager to promote the bots as helpful assistants instead of job killers. The technology, they say, will get smarter and more useful, liberating workers rather than replacing them".[50] Others warn that AI is no panacea: "To a certain type of technocrat, innovations offer an irresistible opportunity to do a lot more talking at the expense of doing."[51] If the culture, people and working practices of an institution are not ready for AI, the chances of success are small; time and space will be needed for trial and error.

7.2.3 Co-creation

Many experts argue that companies and institutions will benefit most when humans and machines complement each other and work as allies. One example is the robot *Moxi*, developed to make the lives of nurses easier after first carefully studying what nurses actually do on the job.[52] By focusing on machine-human collaboration, it is possible to take advantage of their "complementary strengths".[53] As a Japanese

---

[47] Agrawal et al. (2018).

[48] See: Daugherty and Wilson (2018); Bughin and Manyika (2019, July 25).

[49] Cass (2018).

[50] Lohr (2018, August 5).

[51] Greenway et al. (2018).

[52] Schwab (2019, August 7).

[53] Daugherty and Wilson (2018).

saying has it, people give wisdom to machines.[54] It is about encouraging co-operation with machines in a way that is good for people, society and the economy.

Technological applications should aim to make people function better; for this
reason, they should be developed through "co-creation" wherever possible. The
Social and Economic Council of the Netherlands underlines the importance of firms
first consulting with the workers who will be using the applications.[55] Without their
input – as well as that of clients and consumers – firms may end up with technologies no-one wants or which undermine people's control over their working and
personal lives.[56] Jacques Bughin and James Manyika of the consultancy McKinsey
argue that efforts with AI "won't succeed unless they benefit employees" (Box 7.3).[57]

Box 7.3 The Human Factor
Anna Salomons argues that "new technologies are not being introduced in a
vacuum. A company which installs a computer or a robot in a workplace does
not see automatic increases in productivity: that also requires a change in its
way of working. For example, the division of labour amongst staff or teams
may change. Or the physical layout of the workspace may have to be adjusted.
Or the technology may enable the introduction of new products or services,
which first need to be invented. Changes of this kind to the production process
require adaptability and risk-taking, because finding the best new working
method and developing novel or improved services do not happen of their
own accord."

The academic literature on how new technology impels adjustments in the
workplace "shows that the human factor is indeed of vital importance.
Employees' involvement and the way in which their work within a company
is organized determine the extent to which new technology generates improved
productivity."[58]

How technology is used and the measures taken to reduce its social costs will
ultimately depend on decisions made by employers and politicians.[59] It is up to policymakers to ensure that new technology leads to more prosperity for everyone, as
this will not happen on its own. "Economists tend to place great trust in the market's
ability to allocate resources in the most efficient way. But most experts recognise
that the market's star does not shine as brightly when it comes to innovation. There
are several reasons for market failures in innovation in general, as well as some
specific reasons that are important in the context of AI."[60] One is that the market does

---

[54] Kochan and Dyer (2017).
[55] SER (2016b).
[56] Melis (2019, February 13).
[57] Bughin and Manyika (2019, July 25).
[58] Salomons (2015).
[59] Gallie (2017).
[60] Acemoglu and Restrepo (2019a).

not price in the social benefits of work, for instance that "employed people are happier and become better citizens".[61]

In sum, we need to recognize that technology does not just happen to us. Robots and AI will not determine how humans organize work in the future, how working people will interact with machines and algorithms, or whether workers will have more or less freedom of movement or control over their work. Ultimately, it is people who decide how technology is used and what it means for the quality of our work. If we want everyone to benefit from technology, engineers, entrepreneurs, employers, trade unions, civil society organizations and governments all have a role to play.[62]

7.3 Investing in Good Work

The responsibility for investing in good work rests primarily with the management boards of companies and institutions.[63] Firms make strategic choices within their sectors,[64] about terms of employment and about whether and how to automate (by replacing human labour or by increasing its productivity). Investing in workers by paying them well and giving them more room to organize their own tasks should result in higher engagement[65] and productivity as well as less workplace friction and spending on the recruitment and training of new staff[66] (see also Chap. 2).

In the Netherlands, a case study of 19 companies providing low-skilled work in labour-intensive agriculture found both "precarious" employers treating their staff as disposable and "socially responsible" firms investing in their workers and trying to keep them for longer. There were significant differences in personnel and remuneration policies and in employer-staff relationships, which could only be the result of deliberate choices by management as the economic environment in which these

---

[61] Acemoglu and Restrepo (2019b, March 29).

[62] Markoff (2015); ter Weel (2018); Went et al. (2015).

[63] "Going beyond formal rules governing the labour market, the future of work and the actual quality of jobs depends on the working environment at the firm level. Hence creating 'good' and healthy jobs depends on employers' initiatives to organize work in a sustainable and productive way. While standards can be set by legislation and collective agreements, and while this can be supported by incentives given to firms, the ultimate responsibility lies with individual employers and management in day-to-day activities. Using different forms of effective employee representation and participation can help develop good working environments" (Eichhorst et al. in press).

[64] One Dutch example is the retail chain Mediamarkt, which for years competed on price. In late 2018 it implemented a "complete change of culture" to focus on quality (van der Velden & Polman, 2018).

[65] Economists also call this an "efficiency wage". See for example the explanation at https://en.wikipedia.org/wiki/Efficiency_wage

[66] Research by economists at banking group ABN-AMRO on staff turnover in the Dutch hospitality industry shows that replacing a full-time cook costs almost €30,000 and a full-time server over €15,000. The costs incurred due to staff turnover equal 6% of the sector's entire sales income (Driessen, 2019).

companies operate is more or less the same.[67] In another Dutch example, Frank Pot studied the position of workers in short-cycle labour, typical in sectors such as cleaning, agriculture and horticulture, meat and fish processing, and in production lines and distribution centres. This kind of work generally "involves repetitive movements and its pace is often machine-led, with all the risks of RSI [repetitive strain injury] and stress that entails". Although the 1989 Working Conditions Act encourages employers to reduce short-cycle labour, few firms have made appreciable progress; some "seem to prefer class struggle over the co-creation to which the Dutch employers' association AWVN is committed".[68]

Ferry Koster[69] concludes from his review of the literature on labour deployment that "financialization and competition may well put pressure on the labour factor" but that this competition can be met "by choosing the 'high road' rather than reducing labour to a simple cost item to be cut back as far as possible". A lot of research has addressed the "low-road" versus "high-road" choices companies face in their employment relationships, with those choosing the high road offering their staff better pay, terms and conditions than are strictly necessary.[70] Jeffrey Pfeffer concludes that employers who implement practices good for the well-being of their personnel reduce "their own costs from employee medical expenses, absenteeism, workers' compensation insurance costs and the productivity loss from having employees who are physically at work but not 'really there'". These employers also reduce "the costs to society from people's poor physical and mental health and the harm done to individuals".[71]

Zeynep Ton's study of how US retail chains in highly competitive sectors treat their employees concludes that certain practices "allow retailers to break the presumed trade-off between investing in employees and maintaining low prices".[72] Successful chains like QuikTrip, Mercadona and Trader Joe's invest heavily in their staff but still have the lowest prices, achieve solid financial results and offer better customer service than their competitors. Such companies show that, even in segments where the lowest price is king, "bad jobs are not a cost-driven necessity but a choice". Ton chose to focus on these firms because they employ millions, because they have a reputation for paying low wages and because many people who value good work believe it is impossible in such companies. To managers, company directors and entrepreneurs who want to offer good work but are deterred by the costs, Ton points out that "offering good jobs can in fact reduce costs and increase profits, as long as it is combined with operational excellence".[73]

Paul Osterman,[74] who has written extensively on the high and low-road approaches to industrial relations, similarly concludes that "companies can do well

[67] Kroon and Paauwe (2014).
[68] Pot (2018a).
[69] Koster (2020).
[70] See Koster (2020).
[71] Pfeffer (2018).
[72] Ton (2012, January–February).
[73] Ton (2014).
[74] Osterman (2018).

if they do good". Nevertheless, evidence for the profitability of the high road alternative is thinner than one hopes. While virtuous employment policies may be possible in many low-wage industries, there is scant evidence "that the 'high road' is generalizable or that it will be a viable alternative for any randomly chosen company". Osterman argues that the government should use regulations and tenders to prod employers down the high road. Former US President Barack Obama deliberately visited companies with better working conditions to boost their business while ordering federal contractors to adhere to "high-road practices".[75] Osterman further advocates empowering stakeholders and trade unions to make it more difficult for financial markets to insist on profit maximization.

7.4 A Task for Government

If creating good work is in the interests of employers, why do so many fail to do so? Many researchers struggle with this question.[76] The business literature points to numerous instances of management being unaware of the problems, of not knowing what to do, or trying but failing to transform the organization accordingly.[77] In contrast, economists Dani Rodrik and Charles Sabel trace the shortage of good work to systemic failures of the market: the benefits of good work accrue more to society as a whole than to individual employers, for whom providing good work may be costly.[78] In other words, good work has positive externalities and the government has a clear role to play.[79]

Laws and regulations to safeguard better work are advocated by the research institute affiliated to the Dutch Christian Democratic Party. Its report on bringing greater certainty to the labour market claims that making flexible work more expensive – which the third Rutte government, in power since October 2017, has already done to some extent – might even find broad support among employers. The report refers to the "hockey helmet" mechanism, described by Thomas Schelling in 1973, who observed that most ice-hockey players at the time did not wear helmets during matches but nevertheless favoured their mandatory introduction: "They did not want to play in them voluntarily, because their peripheral vision was obstructed. But with a requirement, everyone would suffer the same disadvantage and the risk of

---

[75] Osterman (2018).

[76] See, for example, Pfeffer (2018).

[77] Presentation sheet by Steven Dhondt in 2018, based on Gibbons and Henderson (2013).

[78] Rodrik and Sabel (2019).

[79] "If the labor market settles on an efficient outcome in which large segments of the population lack meaningful work, our response can't be to say 'thanks, understood' and then to wait for those displaced people suddenly to transform themselves into something else, or simply to give them government aid. Our response must be 'that needs to change'" (Cass, 2018: 53).

head injuries would also be limited." This may also apply to the labour market: "Employers themselves want better, fairer regulations for permanent and flexible staff. So that those who are already socially aware do not suffer any disadvantage."[80] The government can ensure that firms that do the right thing are not undercut by firms that do not.

But laws and regulations to improve the quality of work are not enough; more is possible and necessary. So-called soft regulation encourages companies and institutions to focus on better work. "Economically non-optimum management styles are often tenacious in their survival", observes Frank Pot in an article on how the Dutch government, employers' organizations and trade unions previously sought to influence technological and organizational change. The government's task is "to promote productivity, innovation and quality of life, and hence also quality of work" – which requires different forms of organization[81] (see Box 2.6).

Harry Garretsen[82] points out that "in view of all kinds of external effects", it is plausible that "markets left to themselves generate a suboptimum (= too low) level of innovation". Garretsen sees a role for government intervention, for "supporting companies, perhaps through pilot projects, to initiate or step up innovation aimed at achieving better, smarter management and work". To successfully apply new technologies in the life sciences, nanotechnology, AI and robotics, public policy must consider the "complementarity between hard and soft technologies; … between technological and social innovation".[83]

Tuomo Alasoini[84] has studied the conditions under which workplace development programmes actually lead to better work in ten European and East Asian countries, including 16 projects in Finland between 2004 and 2010. He concludes that innovations in the workplace are rarely achieved through hard regulation, let alone deregulation, but through soft regulation – policy frameworks and recommendations, information on best practices, the training and education of managers and employees, advisory and consulting services, benchmarking tools, and grants and

---

[80] Siegmann (2018). Lodewijk Asscher, leader of the Dutch Labour Party, also discusses the importance of new certainties in *Opstaan in het Lloyd Hotel* ("Awakening in the Lloyd Hotel"): "For decades we have heard that it is a good thing that citizens no longer rely upon a protective government. Of course everyone knows that not all the old certainties can survive. But is it not now time for new certainties, instead of always having to manage by yourself?" (Asscher, 2019: 140).

[81] Pot (2019b).

[82] Garretsen (2019, September 26).

[83] See also WRR (2013a).

[84] Alasoini (2016).

subsidies to companies.[85] The Finnish government, for instance, prioritizes new forms of workplace organization and better quality work, as do high-tech programmes in Germany.[86]

Better work does not come about automatically. Market failings, management styles, lack of information, insufficient knowledge and under-resourcing can all hinder its emergence. But because societal interests – general well-being and economic productivity – are at stake, the government is justified to step in through hard and soft regulation. For starters, this would entail working with employers' associations and trade unions to embrace the importance of good work.[87] The government can also create incentives for stakeholders to reach agreements and take initiative (see Box 7.4).[88] The state is also a major employer and can lead by example, prioritizing good work for its own personnel and ensuring through socially responsible procurement that public tenders are competitive not only in price, but in sustainability and compliance with quality-of-work requirements.[89]

[85] Innovation vouchers worth €7500 distributed by drawing lots among Dutch SMEs in 2004 and 2005 made "a structural contribution to the advanced innovation activities of small and medium-sized enterprises" (Lemmers et al., 2019).

[86] Pot (2019b).

[87] In *For the Sake of Security* (Kremer et al., 2017d), we highlighted Koen Caminada's suggestion that a moral appeal be made to individuals and businesses employing other people. He believes "that it is simply obvious that the Minister of Social Affairs and Employment should let the Netherlands know what a socially and morally acceptable minimum rate is. When making an agreement with a local contractor, if you then communicate that if they go below x you will enter into a contract with them, that is not OK and you are not acting morally. I think that will help" (Houweling & Sprengers, 2016: 404–405). Economist Samuel Bowles (2016) shows that standards and societal and moral preferences matter in the economy.

[88] See Mazzucato (2018) on the value of government and of mission-driven public policy.

[89] On www.pianoo.nl, a website featuring expertise on public procurement from the Ministry of Economic Affairs and Climate, we read: "Organisations that adhere to the principle of social return reach purchasing agreements with contractors concerning the creation of additional jobs, work-experience jobs or internships for people who are disadvantaged within the labour market. These include the long-term unemployed, people who are partially disabled or young people with a disability. By creating additional jobs in this way, the target group can participate according to their ability, making use of extra productivity that would otherwise remain unused. Social return is not intended to supplant existing jobs." The site provides further advice, examples and guidelines.

Box 7.4 The Importance of Standards, Laws and Regulations
What constitute normal, acceptable or just working conditions is less clear than what laws and enforcement protocols define. This is one of the reasons why workers and their representatives must be involved in decision-making about automation[90] and the organization of work.[91] These are also key issues for politicians, trade unions, employers' associations, and professional organizations in areas such as education and healthcare. Legislation and regulations, collective agreements and social contracts all define conditions and performance requirements, enforced as necessary by regulators and inspectors. What society wants to regulate and possibly restrict to guarantee the quality of work is constantly evolving, as are laws, regulations and standards.[92] We need ongoing dialogue at the company, sector and national levels.

In sum, firms and institutions choose how to treat their workers; their choices are not imposed by globalization, technology or existing labour-market institutions. While good work benefits workers, the economy and society as a whole, it does not always come about on its own. There is thus a role for government (see the recommendations in Chap. 8).

7.5 Conclusion: Room for Choice

"The future of work", concludes the OECD, "is in our hands and will largely depend on the policy decisions countries make.... With the right policies and institutions, the future of work can be one of more and better jobs for all."[93] The findings in this chapter support this assessment. Robots, algorithms and global competition have not eclipsed the Netherlands' ability to pursue its own priorities. Companies and institutions are able to focus on creating better work for more people.

The government can promote good-quality work both through "hard" regulation (and its enforcement) and "soft" regulation. It can create incentives for stakeholders to reach agreements and take initiative. As an employer and contracting body, the government can also lead by example, by providing better work for its own staff, by purchasing sustainably and by imposing quality-of-work requirements in its tenders.

---

[90] As long ago as 1968, the Social and Economic Council of the Netherlands spoke out in favour of involving employees in automation: "It is apparent from the hearings that, in most cases, the information was provided at the time of the decision or later, and that only a few companies had consulted in advance about the automation before a particular decision was made. [In those cases] staff were engaged and so encouraged to help think about the technical innovations and the means of their implementation. In principle, the Council regards this form of consultation as the most appropriate" (quoted in Pot, 2019b).
[91] de Stefano (2018); Federal Ministry of Labour and Social Affairs (2017); Oeij et al. (eds.). (2017).
[92] AWVN (2018); Kremer et al. (2017d).
[93] OECD (2019a).

A Day at Work: The Homecare Worker

"You shouldn't do it for the money", says 22-year-old Bouchra, wearing trainers, casual trousers and a Muslim headscarf. "It's for the heart. If I leave people happy, my day is complete." Bouchra has been a care worker for 2 years now. She ended up in the job by accident; being her mother's main care-giver, she was unable to complete her training as an administrative assistant. She started as a domestic help but is now a homecare worker.

She reaches her first client at 7.30 am. "Home care", she says through the intercom. The door swings open. Behind it is a man in his bathrobe, with a walking frame. Bouchra has come to wash and dress him and put on his support stockings.

The man is 93 and, much to his own delight, still has full control over his mind. Almost a century, he says, "but I hope I don't make it that far". Bouchra is taken aback: "But I'll miss you!" The elderly gentleman is very pleased with Bouchra. "Some people have problems with a headscarf. They say, 'Take that thing off your head.' Incomprehensible. She's very good." Within 35 min the man is clean, dressed and sitting in the armchair in his living room. "Is there anything else I can do for you?", asks Bouchra, a cup of tea in her hand. "She always asks that now", he says. "And I always say, 'No, Bouchra, everything's just fine.'" She then explains that she is not coming tomorrow; Marja will be here instead. She will be back again on Tuesday. It does not quite seem to get through.

Bouchra rushes to her next appointment. "Clients are always upset if you're in a hurry. You should never look at the clock if they can see it." On her phone she checks who is next on her round and what she has to do for them: support stockings 15 min, washing 20 min. Her tasks and time allocations are set out in the care plan drawn up by the district nurse – the insurance company is watching. Despite repeated attempts by successive health ministers to abolish minute-by-minute registration, home care is still all about time.

Later that morning she has some crackers for lunch at the door of her fourth client, a water bottle within reach. It is now noon. "This is a quiet day", she says. This man is her last client of the morning. She rings the doorbell, but nobody comes. So she calls the client's landline. No answer. She calls the office. No answer. She checks her phone to see if someone else has already called by. No. She looks to see if there is a contact person she can call. No-one in the system. "I'll have to report that to the office, it's useful to have." Bouchra often finds herself on her own in this job. Finally, a neighbour opens his door.

After much knocking at the door and ringing the bell, they finally hear noises inside the flat. The man opens up, confused and wearing only incontinence pants. "Hello sir", Bouchra says gently. She shakes his hand. "Were you in the shower?" She stays until he is sitting comfortably at his table, has found and taken his pills and is eating a bowl of cereal. "Someone else might have just left, but I wanted to make sure everything was OK. Otherwise I wouldn't feel at peace."

(continued)

This gentleman really belongs in a nursing home, says Bouchra, but there are no vacancies at the moment. Everyone is expected to live at home for as long as possible. "You have to have serious dementia to be admitted." As a result, many of her clients have multiple and complex problems. "And sometimes they're angry. Especially when I'm late. If I'm due at 9:30 but don't reach them until 10:30. Because of that they almost miss an appointment at the hospital, or their legs are completely swollen because they've been wearing their support stockings for too long." When people yell at her, Bouchra tries to stay calm. She understands their frustration. She has never been on a course on how to deal with angry clients, but she has taken one about time registration on her phone.

Bouchra's next call is not until 4.45 pm. She hates these split shifts, as do her colleagues. The rosters are tailored to the clients' wishes. It would be nice if her route suited her better and there was not such a long break in the middle of the day. But she is happy that she finally has a permanent contract. They had promised her one after the first year, but it never materialized. Earlier this year she asked again, and this time it came. Bouchra is very pleased about this because it gives her stability and security. It means she can finally dream about buying a house of her own.

About 400,000 people, mainly women, work in home care in the Netherlands. While a small proportion are qualified nurses with a professional degree or Level 4 vocational qualification, the great majority are classified as care workers, social assistance workers or domestic helps, mostly with lesser qualifications. Their gross monthly salary is generally between €1400 and €2750, or slightly higher – up to €3300 – for graduates. The average (modal) income in the Netherlands in 2020 will be just over €2800 per month, excluding holiday pay. Most homecare workers (80%) have a permanent contract and work part-time, although half take on extra shifts because the sector is now growing again following a period of contraction between 2012 and 2016. Absenteeism and perceived workloads are high.

Chapter 8
Better Work: Conclusions and Recommendations

Good work is crucial for our well-being but is under pressure from the application of new technologies, the use of flexible employment contracts and the intensification of work. In this book we have argued that achieving better work – good work for everyone who can and wants to work – is a crucial mission for policymakers, employers and labour organizations.

In this final chapter we advance recommendations for how the government and other stakeholders can promote better work for more people, including for those who would like to work, or work more, but are currently not doing so. We summarize our findings from the previous chapters (Sect. 8.1) before presenting our recommendations (Sects. 8.2, 8.3, 8.4 and 8.5).

8.1   Good Work Is Under Pressure

The Netherlands Scientific Council for Government Policy advised in 1981: "If work is to retain its central position in society, the option of improving the quality of work must always be available: one of the main lessons of the substantial rise in prosperity during the 1960s was that welfare is not just a matter of higher consumption levels."[1] Some four decades later, human labour remains central to the organization and performance of our economies and to our well-being as individuals and societies. The International Labour Organization[2] continues to champion a "human-centred agenda" that privileges investment in human development and workplace well-being. "Decent work for all" is now among the United Nations' Sustainable Development Goals, to which governments and companies worldwide are committed (see Chap. 1).

---

[1] WRR (1981): 159.
[2] ILO (2019).

© The Author(s) 2021
M. Kremer et al., *Better Work*, Research for Policy,
https://doi.org/10.1007/978-3-030-78682-3_8

Governments, academics, professional and employers' organizations, trade unions and citizens around the world have been discussing the changing world of work. Concerns often revolve around what technological advances in robotics and artificial intelligence will mean for the *quantity* of work available to humans, and what increasingly flexible labour arrangements mean for income security. This book has broadened this discussion by focusing on the *quality* of work.

Paying attention to the quality of work is crucial because good work benefits individuals, the economy and society as a whole. While work provides people with incomes to live on, it also provides satisfaction, social status and self-esteem, the feeling that we are contributing to society. But to truly benefit individuals and society, work must meet certain requirements (see Chap. 2). From the international scientific literature, we distilled three key criteria for work to be considered "good", which align well with the needs of the Dutch service and knowledge economy and with the stated wishes and expectations of the population:

1. *Control over income.* Good work provides fair wages and long-term financial security.
2. *Control over work.* Good work allows workers sufficient autonomy to make the best use of their abilities and provides an inclusive and supportive social environment.
3. *Control in life.* Good work allows sufficient time and space to combine work with care responsibilities and a private life.

These three criteria are the necessary preconditions for work to be considered "good". If they are not met, both workers and work organizations suffer, leading to social costs down the line (see Chap. 2). When work is not good, people are disinclined to stay in their jobs; they may also fall ill, which today increasingly means mental illness. Fully 17.5% of Dutch workers reported suffering from symptoms of burnout in 2018.[3] By European standards, this is far from exceptional. Almost half of all sick leave in the Netherlands is work-related – the result of workplace stress, emotional exhaustion, or problems with colleagues, managers and clients (see Chap. 6). The Dutch National Institute for Public Health and the Environment estimates that unfavourable working conditions are responsible for almost 5% of the total burden of disease in the country. The result is both higher healthcare costs and lower productivity.

Good work is important not only for the well-being of workers, but for the effective functioning of companies and institutions, and for social cohesion and the economy at large. Good physical and emotional health increases workers' productivity; committed and engaged workers means greater initiative, innovation and organizational performance.

---

[3] Schaufeli (2018).

8.1.1   We Could Do Better

According to recent research by the OECD[4] and Eurofound,[5] the Netherlands is often mid-table in international indices tracking the quality of work (see Chap. 1). This is partly because income security has declined, with 36% of Dutch workers now without permanent contracts. Opportunities for on-the-job learning have stalled, which does little to enhance security of employment over the life course (see Chap. 3). Almost half of all workers claim that they lack sufficient autonomy in the workplace, and their numbers are rising regardless of their level of education. Growing numbers are feeling perpetually rushed at work and/or that their jobs are emotionally draining. Firms and institutions in the Netherlands as they are currently organized are thus not always bringing out the best in people (see Chap. 4). A tenth of Dutch workers report an imbalance between their private and working lives (see Chap. 5).

Good work in the Netherlands is not evenly distributed, with stark differences along educational, occupational, gender, health and ethnic lines. Quality of work is thus an issue of distributive justice, one with the potential to undermine social cohesion should current trends continue (see Chap. 2). The most obvious division is level of education, which is clearly correlated to quality of work. There are also stark differences between occupations. Those suffering the most from the combination of increased workloads and a lack of control over their work includes public-sector professionals such as teachers, nurses and police officers.

Surveys of public opinion find that the Dutch have high expectations of their work: their jobs must provide income and security, cordial relationships, interesting tasks, opportunities to develop their abilities and to achieve something in life. At the same time, most do not want work to always come first and expect to have time and space for a private life as well (see Chap. 2). Although most people in the Netherlands claim to be satisfied with their work, things could clearly be much better.

8.1.2   Good Work is At Stake

The three macro-level trends we have addressed in this book – the automation, flexibilization and intensification of labour – clearly have the potential to affect the quality of work. They can make work good or better for some people, bad or worse for others, or have no impact at all. In some cases, they exacerbate existing divisions, such as between people with and without disabilities. In other cases, they give rise to new divisions, for instance between professions.

The introduction of new technologies such as robots and artificial intelligence can cost jobs; combined with the flexible labour market, new technological

---

[4] OECD (2016a).
[5] Eurofound (2017).

applications can push down wages. But technology can also have positive effects for workers; much depends on the efforts to support *human-machine complementarity* and whether workers in the face of changing tasks have opportunities to learn on the job. While technology can be used to ruthlessly monitor workers and turn them into mechanical appendages, it can also create opportunities for people to work more independently or to assist them into the workforce. Depending on how and why it is applied, technology can both improve or undermine work-life balance.

Flexible work is widespread in the Netherlands; more than a third of workers do not have a permanent contract. The consequences are becoming increasingly apparent as new dividing lines emerge. The self-employed professionals who enjoy autonomy in their working lives tend to be male, older and well-educated; the flexible, temporary workers whose income security often depends on the welfare state are more likely to be female, young and formally less educated.

The negative consequences of flexible work can be limited by welfare state arrangements as well as employer investment in workers. The self-employed in the Netherlands are largely excluded from the social-security system, denied access to everything from occupational disability benefits and labour-force reintegration schemes to training and leave. Temporary employees are generally denied meaningful say over their tasks and have limited opportunities for on-the-job learning and professional development; not knowing whether they will have a job in 6 months, they have few incentives to offer ideas on how to improve their work. Flexible workers with little control over their working hours often find that their jobs disrupt their personal lives. Workers with temporary contracts face greater difficulties building up decent lives with a home and family than employees with permanent positions.

The intensification of work can undermine the quality of work. The increasing pace of work and its emotional toll have been an issue in the Netherlands for some time, with almost 40% of workers claiming they frequently or always have to work hard and fast, and over 10% reporting that their work is emotionally draining (see Chaps. 1 and 4). Professionals in healthcare, education and the police who must deal directly with patients, clients and members of the public are affected most by the growing demands, while burnout disproportionately affects women and university graduates. The intensification of work also creates additional difficulties for people with occupational disabilities, those returning to the labour force after an absence, people with difficulties at home and those who have little control over their work (see Chap. 6). Whether the intensification of work is detrimental thus largely depends on whether workers have sufficient *autonomy* – freedom to shape their own activities in the workplace.

8.1.3 Room for Better Work

The negative scenario is not a fait accompli. Speaking at the launch of the Global Commission on the Future of Work, ILO Director-General Guy Ryder stated that "the future of work is not decided for us in advance. It is a future that we must make according to the values and the preferences that we choose as societies and through the policies that we design and implement."[6] In its report for the Netherlands Independent Commission on the Regulation of Work, the OECD likewise concluded: "the future of work will largely depend on the policy decisions countries make".[7]

The Borstlap Committee[8] in its 2019 advisory report to the Dutch government underlined that national actors can still give direction to the labour market. Despite facing similar pressures from globalization and new technologies, European countries continue to differ in their labour codes, tax regimes, and embrace of flexible work and self-employment – a product of their national institutions, histories, choices and preferences. What the labour market looks like – now and in the future – largely depends on our priorities and decisions.

8.1.4 Good Work for All

Knowledge and service economies rely on human capital. As the Netherlands Scientific Council for Government Policy argued in its 2013 report *Towards a Learning Economy*, the Netherlands, if it wants to invest in its earning power, needs to nurture, develop and mobilize all the human capital at its disposal. Especially in light of demographic change, this means *all* people: young and old, male and female, healthy and unhealthy, whatever their educational attainment.

We can manage the automation, flexibilization and intensification of work in such ways that more people will have good jobs. Algorithms and robots can take over routine and disagreeable tasks while good forms of flexible labour – greater flexibility *for* employees and *by* employers – can make it easier to cope with demanding jobs or to combine work with private life.

8.2 More Control over Income

The Netherlands has never had so many people in work. This at least was the case on the eve of the Covid-19 crisis. But although unemployment is low by European standards, too many people remain side-lined from the labour market. Given the loosening of relationships between employers and workers and the need to invest in human capital, the Netherlands needs to renew its social-security system and reintroduce an active labour-market policy attuned to contemporary realities. This section explains how this could be done.

---

[6] Ryder (2017, August 21).

[7] OECD (2019a).

[8] Commissie regulering van werk (2019).

8.2.1 Prevent Unfair Competition Between Workers

The flexible labour market has become synonymous with uncertainty. Any modern economy needs a degree of flexibility which can be useful, even necessary, to cope with peaks and troughs, absences from illness and the unique requirements of specific projects. When making a film, it makes sense to hire a temporary production assistant, a freelance screenwriter and catering staff through an agency. But at primary or nursery school, parents and children need familiar faces. Employers need to offer contracts appropriate to the nature of the work.

With temporary work now so widespread in the Netherlands, it is doubtful whether the benefits still outweigh the economic and social costs (see Chap. 3). But as these costs are borne primarily by flexible workers and by society, individual firms do not include them in their cost-benefit analyses when considering whether to create permanent jobs.

Working people on different types of contract should not be competing against each other. Eliminating such competition requires regulation; a start has been made with the 2019 Work in Balance Act which raises employers' social-insurance contributions for temporary workers and mandates transition payments after firms terminate or fail to renew a temporary contract. Higher costs for flexible work are also meant to encourage work organizations to enter into alliances to offer their employees greater security and to make permanent staff more widely deployable across a pool of organizations (see Chap. 6).

The principle of the level playing field should also apply to the self-employed. The Dutch government has proposed introducing minimum rates for freelance work and granting collective bargaining rights to the self-employed, both currently banned under competition law. The Authority for Consumers and Markets announced in 2019 that it will allow freelances to agree minimum rates between themselves and to enter into their own collective agreements.[9] What this means in practice remains to be seen.

Freelance workers can now leverage their benefits that accrue from the tax code to compete with regular employees.Current deductions are meant to enable freelances to take out insurance against occupational disability but the windfall for employer payroll costs has unintentionally swelled the number of the self-employed (Chap. 3). The Netherlands needs a model of social security that does not encourage such unfair competition but provides security for all workers.

---

[9] ACM (2019, July 23).

8.2.2   Develop a System of Contract-Neutral Basic Insurance and Benefits

The social-security system created in the Netherlands after the Second World War was tailored to members of the active workforce (then primarily men) either having permanent jobs or being unemployed and thus entitled to make claims on the system. This model no longer suffices. The flexibilization of the labour market means that today's workers are more likely to have a succession of employers or clients and to juggle learning, work and care responsibilities throughout their active lives. This requires collective guarantees for all workers regardless of the type of contract they have. Social insurance and benefits need to be linked more to individual citizens and less to their form of employment or to specific agreements between employers and employees. Everyone should be minimally insured against all risks from old age to incapacity to work; on top of these standard arrangements, people would be free to take out additional insurance. Such a system would be an answer to the flexible labour market, although the government must remain alert to any new inequalities arising between people who can and cannot take out additional cover.

With a system of basic insurance and benefits, people would invest more in themselves, would dare to take risks, would be able to start families earlier and would be healthier overall (see Chaps. 2 and 3). Provisions would go beyond traditional social-security benefits – the state pension, occupational disability benefit and so on – to include allowances for care, education, on-the-job learning and other combinations of education and work. Investment in personal and professional development is essential to any modern, universal system of social security. Working people must adapt to changes in the labour market and must be supported to do so.

It is in the public interest that everyone takes part in this new contract-neutral form of social security. Like employees with permanent contracts, the self-employed and flexible workers would be entitled to basic security and benefits, with the choice to insure themselves more comprehensively. There are many reasons why everyone needs to participate. It is impossible to predict whether freelancers doing booming business now will still be so lucky 10 years from now, or whether they will have enough of a cushion by then to support themselves in case of a setback. The Corona crisis offers a clear illustration. The self-employed are hit hard by the Covid-19 pandemic lockdowns. The course of a life rarely runs entirely to plan; a divorce or disability can quickly cause wealth to evaporate.

If self-employed individuals were free to opt out, unfair competition could persist. Those most likely to opt out would be self-employed professionals with high incomes and low occupational risks who have the least to gain from such a collective system. Allowing them to opt out would drive up premiums, raise the question of why only the self-employed can do so, and undermine public support for the system. The self-employed worry about both the consequences of occupational disability and the costs of compulsory insurance; any new system must be attractive for them. If everyone participates, economies of scale will keep the costs in check (see Chap. 3).

The post-war welfare state is no longer adequate for today's world of work. What is needed is a modern system of risk-sharing and protection for all categories of workers. This means that the responsibilities placed on employers, working people and the collective need to be reallocated. Some responsibilities such as paying for parental and care leave are more appropriately borne by the public purse. In other cases, employers should have more responsibility: who for instance is better placed to ensure that workers are adequately supported to reintegrate after long-term illness or have the time and resources for professional development? Employers should be less responsible for matters more logically arranged collectively, and more responsible for matters directly related to work.

8.2.3   Update Active Labour-Market Policy

The changing labour market is side-lining vulnerable workers. To improve income security, more needs to be invested in guiding people into work and from one job to another. Given current demographic projections and the predicted structural shortages of labour, any exclusion of people who can and want to work (more) must be combatted. This requires a renaissance of active labour-market policy (see Chap. 6).

First, guidance to job seekers needs to be more individually tailored. While financial incentives may suffice for those who are already employable, they are largely ineffective for people who have genuine difficulties finding work. Regardless of the benefits they receive, people without work need more opportunities for serious training. The long-term unemployed need more intensive personal coaching, which currently often takes place in a vacuum without enough attention to serious language training or healthcare. Guidance also needs to continue after the entitlement to benefits ends.

Second, getting as many people into work as possible requires intervening in the supply of jobs. While many jobs have been created in recent decades, many unemployed individuals do not fit the vacancies, and this cannot always be remedied through the right training or better matching. The intensification of work, which has pushed some people out of the labour force (see Chap. 6), requires investment in new approaches that transcend traditional supply and demand thinking. Work organizations can create tailor-made jobs – technology-assisted positions in which robots or other digital aids help integrate individuals into the workplace. Another promising approach is Individual Placement and Support (see Box 6.5), which focuses on both the individual and the workplace and involves continuous supervision from employers, managers and colleagues. Employers need certainty when hiring; they too need to be supported through clear guidance and simpler long-term financial compensation packages. To combat revolving-door unemployment, it is reasonable to make state support conditional on companies entering into long-term commitments rather than only offering temporary contracts.

Third, employers and the government should be more pro-active in helping people remain in work and, when necessary, to switch to new work. Workers must anticipate changes arising from new technologies; employers should help them through perpetual on-the-job training and retraining. The Employee Insurance Agency and local authorities should get involved earlier when people are at risk of unemployment or burnout, rather than – as currently – waiting until they have to pay out benefits.

Finally, active labour-market policies need adequate funding. The Dutch economy has the downside that it excludes those unable to satisfy its exacting requirements. Funding for active labour-market policies have been steadily declining over the past decades; far more should be allocated than the 0.7% of GDP spent in 2016. Denmark, for example, devotes 2% of its GDP to active labour-market policies (see Chap. 6).

8.2.4 Good Basic Jobs for People on Benefits with Few Opportunities

As work is vital to human well-being, the default safety net should not be benefits but the right to a basic job. Creating these jobs is the final element in the approach we propose so that all those currently "distanced" from the labour market can find a way into work. A wage imparts self-esteem and feelings of belonging to society much more than benefits ever can (see Chap. 2). Work is so important psychologically and socially that people who can work should no longer be side-lined with payments for doing nothing.

Local governments in the Netherlands, including those in The Hague and Amsterdam, have been creating basic jobs for some time. Similar schemes exist in Sweden and Germany, while debate over comparable forms of work creation has reappeared in other European countries such as Belgium and the UK. Basic jobs must offer vulnerable people the security they lack in the regular labour market and protect them from the "permanently temporary" employment trap. This means continuity and permanent contracts. People entering or re-entering the labour force after long periods on benefits typically need support in multiple areas of their lives. Basic jobs are not necessarily designed as paths into regular work. The framework for assessing their success should also consider other goals such as social contact, a sense of belonging, gains in health and self-esteem.

The ultimate question is what value society places on everyone being able to have better work. It will probably be necessary to rely on the public purse to keep some people working. While basic jobs may eventually pay for themselves through lower costs for healthcare and social security, they are, first and foremost, meant to contribute towards our well-being.

8.3   More Control Over Work

Ensuring that people gain greater control over their work is an often-neglected aspect of good work. Greater commitment is required from all sides to take advantage of the opportunities for innovation and productivity opened up by new technologies (see Sect. 7.3). At present, the responsibility for adjusting to change largely falls on individual workers. But better work requires companies and institutions to change as well, to organize work and allocate powers and responsibilities in different ways. This section explains how this could be done.

8.3.1   Develop a Programmatic Approach to Good Work

To realize the economic potential of emerging technologies, innovations in the workplace must complement innovations in technology. Better collaboration between workers – and between humans and machines – will lead to better work as well as productivity, which in the Netherlands has been stagnating.

This programmatic approach encompassing workers, technology, training and care will require coordination between multiple government ministries: the Ministries of Finance; Social Affairs and Employment; Economic Affairs; Education, Culture and Science; and Health, Welfare and Sport. Promoting good work will require all kinds of "soft regulation": publicity campaigns, setting goals and standards, establishing frameworks, making recommendations, disseminating information about best practices, education and training for managers and staff, accessible advice for employers and employees, benchmarking, making binding agreements (good work codes) initially on a voluntary basis, subsidizing companies to hire external expertise, and so on. The government, employers' associations and trade unions also need to pressure employers to report annually on the quality of work they offer, and what they are doing to improve it (see Sect. 7.3).[10]

Good work organizations are the key to improving the quality of work. Trade unions and employers need to focus more on social innovation in the workplace – on structuring work organizations in a way that brings out the best in people. In an economy that depends on "human capital", this is in everyone's interest. As companies and institutions come in all shapes and sizes, a programmatic approach to good work will have to be multifaceted, mobilizing professional organizations, academic institutions, industry bodies, local authorities and so on. Companies and institutions without the capacity and expertise to choose or develop suitable applications of technology should be able to turn to experts for help.

Any programmatic approach to better work must focus on creating "work communities" that support employee engagement. The introduction of robots,

---

[10] As suggested by Duncan Gallie. This would require developing standards; the 12 indicators in the "Good work wheel" in the interim conclusion to Part 1 (Fig. 5.5) are an example.

cobots and AI into the workplace makes collaboration, problem-solving, asking questions and other human skills all the more important. While this may make work more interesting, these are also the aspects of work that are the most psychologically demanding. As routine tasks are automated, it is important to guard against cognitive or mental exhaustion as the job now only consists of intensive duties.[11] Here again, it is important to have access to labour experts and other specialists who can help design new jobs and keep work functions practicable.

Because contemporary jobs can be subject to numerous far-reaching changes, it is important not to wait until they disappear before offering workers opportunities for professional development, training and retraining. The Netherlands' recently instituted individual learning rights do not go far enough as those most in need of further training are often the least likely to receive it (see Chap. 3). Both formal and informal on-the-job learning opportunities need to be better integrated within work organizations than is currently the case.

Initiatives in other countries can serve as inspiration. Finland formulated its own vision of good work early on: to have "the best working life in Europe in 2020, with the highest labour productivity and the greatest joy at work".[12] The Finnish Centre for the Advancement of Technology – now Business Finland – has been supporting socially innovative firms since 1983. In Belgium, the Social and Economic Council of Flanders has taken the lead in promoting good work.[13] With employers' associations and trade unions worried about intensifying work, the council launched a "feasibility index" to guide policy. A 2016 study found that "psychological fatigue", "well-being at work" and "work-life balance" had deteriorated since 2013; only "learning opportunities" were meeting expectations. The regional government and its partners agreed on a plan to turn the tide, focused on the "innovative work organization" (see also Box 2.6).

8.3.2 Strengthen the Position of Workers

Working people can shape and enforce better work. The more say workers have in their company's employment practices, the more likely they will have meaningful control over their work. The position of workers within companies, in collective bargaining and in corporate governance needs to be strengthened (see Chap. 4). One way is to strengthen the position of the trade unions in the collective-bargaining process. Good worker representation and organization is ultimately in employers' interests, as is recognized by the Dutch employers' association AWVN.

Workers can also gain power within structures of governance. Highly visible initiatives in France, the United States and the United Kingdom have sought to

---

[11] Metta et al. (2018).

[12] Tekes (2014).

[13] Houtman et al. (2020); Pot (2018b).

reserve more places on company boards for staff or trade union representatives (see Chap. 4). Such possibilities already exist in the Netherlands. The staff councils of firms of a certain size have an "enhanced right of recommendation" in one-third of appointments to the supervisory (non-executive) board; better use of this prerogative could be made in practice. As investors have recently amassed sway over corporate decision-making, the idea is to restore the balance between the interests of different stakeholders, with greater weight for the interests of workers.

Existing legal frameworks, such as the Staff Councils Act, should facilitate better work for all workers, including those on temporary contracts and the self-employed. Staff councils have a broad range of statutory duties including the exercise of advisory rights in reorganizations, mergers and acquisitions and a right of consent when decisions concern the quality of work. Their broad remit requires that staff councils be sufficiently resourced.

Finally, greater support should be given to existing and new forms of business and organization in which workers themselves hold the reins. These include self-organizing platforms for gig workers, freelance work communities, firms in which employees share in the profits and decision-making, social enterprises and co-operatives. Supporting such initiatives – particularly when they encounter legal or fiscal hurdles – will give workers more opportunities to shape better work for themselves.

8.4   More Control in Life

Workers need to be able to look after their children, while the ageing population means that parents and partners in need of care are becoming more common. The world of work is going to have to pay more attention to the world at home. Dutch policies have largely focused on the right to work part-time – an important criterion for good work. But working part-time must be a real choice, not a compulsion due to full-time jobs being unavailable or too demanding, or due to the lack of quality childcare or elderly care. Work-life balance in the Netherlands is still largely seen as a private matter which people must arrange for themselves. Given the coming structural shortage of labour, the country must invest in making work and care responsibilities easier to combine. This section explains how this could be done.

8.4.1   Invest in Good Care Facilities for Children and the Elderly

The Netherlands is caught in a "part-time trap" with care for young children and the elderly organized to facilitate part-time work. If the number of hours people work is to be a genuine choice, the government must invest in affordable, quality childcare accessible to all. While it has been known since the 1990s that early-years childcare is at least as important for child development as school, the quality of Dutch childcare is still not up to standard. It is expensive, especially for middle-income earners; the personnel are often poorly qualified and there is high staff turnover. Quality, development-oriented public childcare would help parents who want to work longer hours.[14]

There is an ever-greater need for accessible, quality care for the elderly and the chronically ill. Particularly in light of the ageing population, it is essential that the policy emphasis on informal care-giving does not come at the expense of professional care in the home. More and more working people are looking after partners or parents on a regular basis. If especially those with full-time positions are to remain working, the government will have to invest in social-care infrastructure that includes support for working informal care-givers so that their work is not adversely affected by the situation at home.

8.4.2   Make More Working Hours Easier to Secure

People sometimes work part-time because their jobs are so mentally or physically exhausting that a full-time position would leave them drained. Some employers such as homecare providers, cleaning firms and distribution centres no longer offer full-time work. Other workers, especially people with occupational disabilities, are denied extra hours even when they are keen to work them (see Chaps. 5 and 6). While the 2016 Flexible Working Act stipulates that workers can ask their employer for more as well as fewer hours, the right to work more is overshadowed both in policy and legal enforcement by the right to work less. Increasing one's formal hours should be made easier, not least as it can signal that a person is regularly working excessive overtime or that an employer is unnecessarily creating new part-time jobs when it has staff who would like to work more. The collective agreement for the disabled care sector stipulates that employers are obliged to offer their employees a contract with extended hours if, on average, they have worked in excess of 10% more than their agreed hours during the previous 12 months.[15] In general, work should be organized, arranged and supported in such a way that it can be undertaken on a full-time basis.

---

[14] WRR (2013a).

[15] See Bosschart (2019, September 25).

8.4.3   Provide Long-Term Paid Care Leave

People need financial certainty and control over their working lives to take care of ailing parents, young children or sick partners. Their numbers will only increase in the future. Working people today generally have other responsibilities – sometimes a range of more or less permanent, often unpredictable, care obligations (see Chap. 6). The Dutch solution – encouraging part-time work – means that informal care-givers do so on their own account. This means that those who work part-time and care for a chronically ill partner are at high risk of poverty. Long-term paid leave is part of the social-care infrastructure needed to ensure a future of better work.

If everyone is to have a chance to care for their loved ones, collectively-funded long-term paid leave arrangements are essential – certainly for new parents and informal care-givers. Here the Netherlands lags behind many other European countries (see Chap. 5). In Germany the period of government-funded parental leave is 14 months, which the parents can divide between them. In Sweden it is 16 months, with the government paying a basic allowance, topped up by employers. In both Sweden and Germany, the labour-force participation rate is at least as high as in the Netherlands. While arrangements for paid informal care leave across Europe leave much to be desired, the ageing workforce means they will soon be as necessary as parental leave.

Such collective schemes should be open to the self-employed, as they are in Sweden. At present, the self-employed in the Netherlands find it almost impossible to access provisions of this kind. Employers' organizations and trade unions need to negotiate more comprehensive arrangements for care in their collective agreements, including allowances for informal care-giving. Flexibility at work, including flexibility in working hours, is crucial to allow caring for sick parents or partners.[16] Fewer people doing more work in the future will only be possible if jobs are better tailored to workers' care-giving needs.

8.4.4   Provide More Control Over Working Hours

Employers are increasingly asking their staff to be flexible at work. New technologies often make these requests seem natural. Many employees work overtime, voluntarily or otherwise, because they cannot complete their tasks within the allotted time (see Chap. 6). Others are answering work e-mails from home, late at night after the children have gone to bed. Employers need to ensure that they allow their staff to lead uninterrupted private lives. Control over one's working hours is crucial, and

---

[16] Banking group ING's recently concluded collective agreement includes personalized flexibility "to increase happiness at work". It is now easier for people to take time off; nor will they face a backlog when they return. The idea is that a pool of "happiness providers" takes over the tasks of colleagues temporarily or suddenly called away.

the blurring of the boundaries between work and private life can keep employees from recovering properly. In the interests of both the work organization and workers' health, it is essential that overtime be limited and that a clear line be drawn between work and personal life. This line should be made clear in employment contracts and collective agreements,[17] especially for workers who lack individual bargaining power. The new collective agreement for the disability care sector stipulates that workers are entitled to be unreachable on their days off.[18]

8.5 Better Work as an Objective of Public Policy

Over the past century, the Dutch state has been involved in every period of major technological change by enacting legislation on social security and working conditions and by subsidizing research and small and medium enterprises.[19] This remains the case today. In the final analysis, the government – as legislator, enforcer, funding body and employer – has a responsibility to promote better work (see Sect. 7.3). Coordinated action by national and local authorities is necessary to ensure that good work becomes possible for everyone, including those currently on the margins of the labour market.

The government must keep good work high on the public policy agenda. By doing so, it will set a benchmark for the rest of society. An obvious first step would be to include progress towards better work in the national *Monitor of Well-Being*, published each year since 2018 on Accountability Day when the national government and its ministries present their annual reports to Parliament. Figure 5.5 shows how this data could be transparently presented. In the accountability debate in the House of Representatives in 2019, Prime Minister Mark Rutte promised that his Cabinet would "explore whether the Monitor could be more extensively used during the policy cycle itself".[20] Coverage of the three dimensions of good work – income security, control over work, and work-life balance – in the *Monitor of Well-Being* would ensure that good work for everyone receives the attention it deserves from policymakers and stakeholders.

The government is needed to enforce labour-market legislation and regulations (see Chap. 4). While the Social Affairs and Employment Inspectorate has previously focused on wage payments and compliance with flexible work regulations, the broader pursuit of good work requires a more intensive, wide-ranging role for regulatory and enforcement bodies. At present, the inspectorate still focuses mainly

---

[17] See the white paper by the German Federal Ministry of Labour and Social Affairs (2017).

[18] See Bosschart (2019, September 25).

[19] Pot (2019b).

[20] For the further development of the Dutch *Monitor of Well-Being*, see also the letter from the directors of the three national planning agencies to both houses of Parliament on 15 May 2019: www.scp.nl/Nieuws/ Brief_planbureau_over_Brede_welvaart.

on physical working conditions and the observance of health and safety regulations,[21] and pays scant attention to issues such as control over work and psychosocial complaints. Although the existing legislation on working conditions provides a starting point, it merits review for how the law could be modernised to better protect income security, workplace autonomy and work-life balance. As with the renewal of the social-security system and active labour-market policies, consideration should be given to how inspections and regulation can help improve the quality of work.

8.5.1 The Government Spends Public Money and Is an Employer

The government spends large sums of public money which it can use to indirectly support better work. What is the point of the government imposing temporary contracts on its security, cleaning and catering staff? The government does not close buildings or canteens overnight, or stop cleaning and guarding them. So why does it employ people on terms that imply it might?

When awarding contracts, the government can encourage or oblige suppliers to employ members of vulnerable groups. Sustainable or socially responsible procurement means attention not only to the price of goods and services, but to how their purchase affects society and the environment. The government can set an example by demanding that tenders be competitive not only in price, but in quality of work.

As an employer in its own right, the government should set an example in its personnel policies. Especially public-sector workers in education, the police, healthcare and social care combine relatively low pay with ballooning workloads and diminishing workplace autonomy (see Chap. 3). From general practitioners to primary-school teachers, university staff to homecare workers, many are struggling with symptoms of burnout (see Chap. 4). And it is not only the employees who are affected: the services and amenities they deliver are vital to us all. Publicly financed work needs to be valued, organized and funded differently, placing greater trust in workers and their collaborative abilities. The government should be the first to start using the programmatic approach proposed above to improve the quality of work for public-sector professionals.

---

[21] In its report *Supervising Public Interests: Towards a Broader Perspective on Government Supervision*, the WRR (2013b) counselled looking beyond the incidents of the day. Serving the public interest requires reflective, agenda-setting supervisory bodies that mirror and feed the public debate.

8.5.2 Finally: Better Work Is everyone's Concern

Providing good work for all is a social mission for everyone. While new technologies, flexible labour markets and the intensification of work threaten to undermine the quality of work, they also have the potential to create better work and enhance our well-being as workers and citizens. Employers, governments, industry organizations, trade unions and even individual citizens as workers, colleagues and consumers all have a role to play.

In this book we have analysed what good work is and why it is important, where the Netherlands currently stands and how improvements can be made. We hope that policymakers, researchers, employers, trade unionists and ordinary citizens everywhere may draw inspiration from this analysis.

Bibliography

Aanhangsel Handelingen II 2009/2010, No. 664.

Acemoglu, D. (2001). Good jobs versus bad jobs. *Journal of Labor Economics, 19*(1), 1–21.

Acemoglu, D., & Restrepo, P. (2019a). *The wrong kind of AI?* Artificial intelligence and the future of labor demand (Paper, version 5 March). Retrieved from https://economics.mit.edu/files/16819

Acemoglu, D., & Restrepo, P. (2019b, March 29). The revolution need not be automated. *Project Syndicate.* Retrieved from https://www.project-syndicate.org/commentary/ai-automation-laborproductivity-by-daron-acemoglu-and-pascual-restrepo-2019-03

Achterhuis, H. (1984). *Arbeid, een eigenaardig medicijn.* Ambo.

ACM [Authority for Consumers and Markets]. (2019, July 23). *ACM: Zzp'ers kunnen afspraken maken over minimuminkomen.* Retrieved from https://www.acm.nl/nl/publicaties/acm-zzpers-kunnen-afspraken-maken-over-minimuminkomen

Adelmeijer, M. H. M., Schenderling, P. J., Heekelaar, M. S., Oostveen, A., & Beerepoot, R. (2015). *Onderzoek Participatiewet bij werkgevers. Rapportage fase 1 (peiljaar 2015).* Berenschot.

Adelmeijer, M., Schenderling, P., van Urk, F., & ten Hoor, J. (2017). *Onderzoek Participatiewet bij werkgevers. Rapportage fase 2 (2017).* Berenschot.

Adler-Bell, S. (2019, August 3). Surviving Amazon. *Logic.* Retrieved from https://logicmag.io/bodies/surviving-amazon/

Admiraal, M. (2018, October 16). Sterke toename tijdelijke arbeidscontracten. *ESB.* Retrieved from https://esb.nu/kort/20045494/sterke-toename-tijdelijke-arbeidscontracten

Agrawal, A., Gans, J., & Goldfarb, A. (2018). *Prediction machines: The simple economics of artificial intelligence.* Harvard Business Review Press.

Agrawal, A., Gans, J., & Goldfarb, A. (2019a). Artificial intelligence: The ambiguous labor market impact of automating prediction. *Journal of Economic Perspectives, 33*(2), 31–50.

Agrawal, A., Gans, J., & Goldfarb, A. (Eds.). (2019b). *The economics of artificial intelligence: An agenda.* University of Chicago Press.

Akgunduz, Y. E., & Plantenga, J. (2013). Labour market effects of parental leave in Europe. *Cambridge Journal of Economics, 37*, 845–862.

Alasoini, T. (2016). *Workplace development programmes as institutional entrepreneurs: Why they produce change and why they do not.* Aalto University.

Algemene Onderwijsbond. (2017). *Tijdsbesteding leraren po en vo.* Retrieved from www.voion.nl/downloads/3c0fc381-20a4-4afd-875a-e421e857f903

Annink, S. M. (2017). *Busyness around the business: A cross-national comparative research of the work-life balance of self-employed workers.* Erasmus University Rotterdam.

Arbeidsmarktplatform PO. (2019). *Deeltijdwerk nader bekeken. Verkenning naar motieven voor deeltijdwerk in het primair onderwijs* [Factsheet]. Arbeidsmarktplatform Primair Onderwijs.

© The Author(s) 2021

M. Kremer et al., *Better Work*, Research for Policy,

https://doi.org/10.1007/978-3-030-78682-3

Arets, M. (2019, February 25). De coöperatie als vakbond 2.0? *ZiPconomy*. Retrieved from https://www.zipconomy.nl/2019/02/de-cooperatie-als-vakbond-2-0/

Arets, M., & Frenken, K. (2019). Zijn platformcoöperaties levensvatbaar? [PDF file]. *TPEdigitaal, 13*(2), 19–32. Retrieved from http://tpedigitaal.nl/sites/default/files/bestand/zijn-platformco%C3%B6peraties-levensvatbaar.pdf

Asscher, L. (2019). *Opstaan in het Lloyd Hotel*. Podium.

Atkinson, A. B. (2015). *Inequality: What can be done?* Harvard Business Press.

Aubenas, F. (2011). *De bodem van de pan. Undercover aan de onderkant van de samenleving*. Atlas-Contact.

AWVN [The General Employers' Association of the Netherlands]. (2018). *Wegwerkzaamheden. 10 ideeën voor de wereld van werk*. AWVN. Retrieved from www.awvn.nl/publicaties/brochure/wegwerkzaamheden-tien-ideeen-voor-de-wereld-van-werk/

Bakker, A. B., & Schaufeli, W. B. (2015). Work engagement. *Organizational behavior, 11*. https://doi.org/10.1002/9781118785317.weom110009

Baldewsingh, R. (2016). *Extra impuls werkgelegenheid* (Brief, June 30). Retrieved from https://denhaag.raadsinformatie.nl/document/3672436/3/ris294630%20Extra%20impuls%20werkgelegenheid 3-6-2018

Baldwin, R. (2019). *The globotics revolution: Globalization, robotics, and the future of work*. Weidenfeld & Nicolson.

Ballafkih, H., Zinsmeister, J., & Meerman, M. (2017). A job and a sufficient income is not enough: The needs of the Dutch precariat. *Journal of Workplace Rights, 7*(4), 1–12.

Bannink, D. (2018). Flexibiliseer de bijstand. *S&D*. Retrieved from https://www.wbs.nl/publicaties/

Béjean, S., & Sultan-Taïeb, H. (2005). Modeling the economic burden of diseases imputable to stress at work. *The European Journal of Health Economics, 6*(1), 16–23.

Benz, M., & Frey, B. S. (2008). Being independent is a great thing: Subjective evaluations of self-employment and hierarchy. *Economica, 75*(298), 362–383.

Berenschot. (2018). *Aantallen en financiën Participatiewet. Beschikbare en benodigde middelen*. Berenschot.

Berg, G. J., van den Kjærsgaard, L., & Rosholm, M. (2012). *To meet or not to meet (your case worker) – that is the question*. IZA.

Berkhout, E., & Euwals, R. (2016). *Zelfstandigen en arbeidsongeschiktheid*. Centraal Planbureau.

Berkhout, E., Bisschop, P., & Volkerink, M. (2014). *Grensoverschrijdend aanbod van personeel. Verschuivingen in nationaliteit en contractvormen op de Nederlandse arbeidsmarkt 2001–2011*. SEO Economisch Onderzoek.

Best, M. (2018). *How growth really happens. The making of economic miracles through production, governance, and skills*. Princeton University Press.

Beukema, L., & Kuijpers, I. (2018). *Stilzitten is niets voor mij. Onderzoek naar de ervaringen van mensen met een beperking met (duurzaam) werk*. Hanzehogeschool Groningen.

Bierings, H. (2017). *Beroep en werkdruk in Nederland. Sociaaleconomische trends*. Centraal Bureau voor de Statistiek.

Bierings, H., & Mol, M. (2012). Burn-out: de rol van werk en zorg. *Sociaaleconomische trends, 2012*(4), 26–35.

Block, F. (2018). *Capitalism: The future of an illusion*. University of California Press.

Blonk, R. W. B. (2018). *We zijn nog maar net begonnen*. Tilburg University.

Bloodworth, J. (2018). *Hired. Six months undercover in low-wage Britain*. Atlantic Books.

Blum, S., Koslowski, A., Macht, A., & Moss, P. (Eds.). (2018). *14th international review of Leave Policies and related research 2018* [PDF file]. Retrieved from https://www.leavenetwork.org/fileadmin/user_upload/k_leavenetwork/annual_reviews/Leave_Review_2018.pdf

Boermans, S., Kraan, K., & Sanders, J. (2017). Ongelijke kansen in leven lang leren. In CBS & TNO, *Dynamiek op de Nederlandse arbeidsmarkt. De focus op ongelijkheid* (pp. 241–276). CBS/TNO.

Bol, T. (2017). Beroepen en loongelijkheid in Nederland. In CBS & TNO, *Dynamiek op de Nederlandse arbeidsmarkt* (pp. 68–84). CBS/TNO.

Bolhaar, J., Brouwers, A., & Scheer, B. (2016). *De flexibele schil van de Nederlandse arbeids-markt: een analyse op basis van microdata.* Centraal Planbureau.

Boorsma, P. (2018). Help! Een buitenlandse moeder!. *De werkgever, 2018*(3). Retrieved from https://werkgeven.awvn.nl/werkgeven/59/help-een-buitenlandse-moeder/

Borghouts-van de Pas, I., Bosmans, M., Verschoor, J., & Wilthagen, T. (2019). *Overstappen op de arbeidsmarkt. Een onderzoek naar Van Werk Naar Werk-beleid en –trajecten.* Celsus juridische uitgeverij.

Bosschart, E. (2019, September 25). Recht op onbereikbaarheid vastgelegd cao Gehandicaptenzorg. *FNV.* Retrieved from https://www.fnv.nl/nieuwsbericht/sectornieuws/zorg-welzijn/2019/09/fnv-recht-op-onbereikbaarheid-vastgelegd-in-cao-ge

Bosselaar, J. H., Prins, R., Maurits, E., & Molenaar-Cox, P. (2010). *Multiproblematiek bij cliënten. Verslag van een verkenning in relatie tot (arbeids)participatie.* Ministerie van Sociale Zaken en Werkgelegenheid.

Bouter, S. (2019, July 25). Geld zat, maar bijscholen, ho maar. *NRC.* Retrieved from https://www.nrc.nl

Bowles, S. (2016). *The moral economy: Why good incentives are no substitute for good citizens.* Yale University Press.

Bredewold, F., Duyvendak, J. W., Kampen, T., Tonkens, E., & Verplanke, L. (2018). *De verhuizing van de verzorgingsstaat. Hoe de overheid nabij komt.* Van Gennep.

Bremmer, I. (2018). *Us vs. them: The failure of globalism.* Penguin Books.

Brennenraedts, R., Vankan, A., te Velde, R., Veldman, J., Groot Beumer, T., Bakker, H., & Wester, M. (2019). *Arbeidsmarktanalyse Rijk 2018–2025.* Dialogic & Ecorys.

Broeders, D., Das, D., Jennissen, R., Tiemeijer, W., & de Visser, M. (2018). *Van verschil naar potentieel. Een realistisch perspectief op de sociaal-economische gezondheidsverschillen* (WRR policy brief No. 7). Wetenschappelijke Raad voor het Regeringsbeleid.

Broussard, M. (2019, April 3). Self-Driving cars will be considered unthinkable 50 years from now: Removing drivers from our transportation system disrupts delicate social contract. *Vox.* Retrieved from https://www.vox.com/

Brummelkamp, G., de Ruig, L., & Roozendaal, W. (2014). *Prikkels en knelpunten. Hoe werk-gevers de loondoorbetalingsverplichting bij ziekte beleven.* Panteia.

Brynjolfsson, E., & McAfee, A. (2014). *The second machine age.* Norton.

Bughin, J., & Manyika, J. (2019, July 25). Your AI efforts won't succeed unless they ben-efit employees. *Harvard Business Review.* Retrieved from https://hbr.org/2019/07/your-ai-efforts-wont-succeed-unless-they-benefit-employees

Burri, S. (2020). Care and the workplace: The Dutch approach to part-time work, flexible work-ing arrangements and leave. In L. Gelsthorpe, P. Mody, & B. Sloan (Eds.), *Spaces for Care* (pp. 134–164). Hart Publishing.

Bus, A., de Vries, C., & van Zeele, S. (2017). *Effecten van de tegenprestatie in Rotterdam.* Onderzoek en Business Intelligence (OBI).

Card, D., Kluve, J., & Weber, A. (2010). Active labour market policy evaluations: A meta-analysis. *The Economic Journal, 120*(548), F452–F477.

Card, D., Kluve, J., & Weber, A. (2017). What works? A meta analysis of recent active labor market program evaluations. *Journal of the European Economic Association, 16*(3), 894–931.

Casiday, R. (2015). *Volunteering and health: What impact does it really have?* Retrieved from www.researchgate.net/publication/228628782_Volunteering_and_Health_What_Impact_Does_It_Really_Have

Cass, O. (2018). *The Once and future worker: A vision for the renewal of work in America.* Encounter Books.

Cazes, S., Hijzen, A., & Saint-Martin, A. (2015). *Measuring and assessing job quality: TheOECDjob quality framework* (OECD Social, Employment and Migration working paper No. 174). OECD Publishing. https://doi.org/10.1787/5jrp02kjw1mr-en

CBS [Statistics Netherlands]. (2016, January 19). Vooral jongeren werken onder hun niveau. Retrieved from https://www.cbs.nl/nl-nl/nieuws/2016/03/vooral-jongeren-werken-onder-hun-niveau

CBS [Statistics Netherlands]. (2017a, October 7). Helft niet-werkenden met uitkering kan/wil niet werken. Retrieved from https://www.cbs.nl/nl-nl/nieuws/2017/40/helft-niet-werkenden-met-uitkering-kan-wil-niet-werken

CBS [Statistics Netherlands]. (2017b, October 24). Zelfstandigen meest tevreden, uitzendkrachten minst. Retrieved from https://www.cbs.nl/nl-nl/nieuws/2017/43/zelfstandigen-meest-tevreden-uitzendkrachten-minst

CBS [Statistics Netherlands]. (2018a). *De arbeidsmarkt in cijfers 2017*. Centraal Bureau voor de Statistiek.

CBS [Statistics Netherlands]. (2018b, June 7). Inkomensverschillen onder laagopgeleiden het kleinst. Retrieved from https://www.cbs.nl/nl-nl/nieuws/2018/23/inkomensverschillen-onder-laagopgeleiden-het-kleinst

CBS [Statistics Netherlands]. (2018c). *Monitor Brede Welvaart 2018*. Centraal Bureau voor de Statistiek. Retrieved from https://www.cbs.nl/nl-nl/publicatie/2018/20/monitor-brede-welvaart-2018

CBS [Statistics Netherlands]. (2018d). *Monitor Brede Welvaart 2018: Een toelichting*. Centraal Bureau voor de Statistiek. Retrieved from https://www.cbs.nl/nl-nl/achter-grond/2018/20/toelichting-monitor-brede-welvaart

CBS [Statistics Netherlands]. (2018e, May 1). *In 2017 meeste stakingen sinds 1989*. Retrieved from https://www.cbs.nl/nl-nl/nieuws/2018/18/in-2017-meeste-stakingen-sinds-1989

CBS [Statistics Netherlands]. (2018f, February 19). *Weer meer vast werk maar flexwerk groeit harder*. Retrieved from https://www.cbs.nl/nl-nl/nieuws/2018/08/weer-meer-vast-werk-maar-flexwerk-groeit-harder

CBS [Statistics Netherlands]. (2018g). *Wie zijn de zzp'ers?* Retrieved from https://www.cbs.nl/nl-nl/faq/zzp/wie-zijn-de-zzp-ers-

CBS [Statistics Netherlands]. (2018h, July 24). *Meer dan de helft van de managers werkt regelmatig over*. Retrieved from https://www.cbs.nl/nl-nl/nieuws/2018/30/meer-dan-de-helft-van-de-managers-werkt-regelmatig-over

CBS [Statistics Netherlands]. (2019a). *De arbeidsmarkt in cijfers 2018*. Centraal Bureau voor de Statistiek.

CBS [Statistics Netherlands]. (2019b, March 31). *Meer loon en hogere werkdruk bij Amerikaanse bedrijven*. Retrieved from https://www.cbs.nl/nl-nl/nieuws/2019/12/meer-loon-en-hogere-werkdruk-bij-amerikaanse-bedrijven

CBS [Statistics Netherlands]. (2019c, May 29). *Hogeropgeleide flexwerker stroomt vaker door naar vast*. Retrieved from https://www.cbs.nl/nl-nl/nieuws/2017/22/hoogopgeleide-flexwerker-stroomt-vaker-door-naar-vast

CBS [Statistics Netherlands]. (2019d). *Nederland handelsland 2019. Export, investeringen & werkgelegenheid*. Centraal Bureau voor de Statistiek.

CBS [Statistics Netherlands]. (2019e, March 5). *Van werkenden loopt zzp'er meeste risico op armoede*. Retrieved from https://www.cbs.nl/nl-nl/nieuws/2019/10/van-werkenden-loopt-zzp-er-meeste-risico-op-armoede

CBS [Statistics Netherlands]. (2019f). *Hoe staat het met de werkzekerheid van flexwerkers*. Retrieved from https://www.cbs.nl/nl-nl/dossier/dossier-flexwerk/hoofdcategorieen/werkzekerheid-van-flexwerkers

CBS [Statistics Netherlands]. (2019g, October 24). *Ruim helft flexwerkers na jaar nog in flexibele schil*. Retrieved from https://www.cbs.nl/nl-nl/nieuws/2019/43/ruim-helft-flexwerkers-na-jaar-nog-in-flexibele-schil

CBS [Statistics Netherlands]. (n.d.). *Hoeveel verdienen zzp'ers en hoeveel vermogen hebben ze?* Retrieved from https://www.cbs.nl/nl-nl/faq/zzp/hoeveel-verdienen-zzp-ers-en-hoeveel-vermogen-hebben-ze-

Chandola, T. (2010). *Stress at work*. The British Academy.

Chandola, T., & Zhang, N. (2017). Re-employment, job quality, health and allostatic load biomarkers: prospective evidence from the UK Household Longitudinal Study. *International Journal of Epidemiology, 2018*, 47–57.

Chkalova, K., & van Gaalen, R. (2017). *Flexibele arbeid en de gevolgen voor relatie- en gezinsvorming. Eindrapportage*. Centraal Bureau voor de Statistiek.

Chkalova, K., & van Gaalen, R. (2019). *Eindreportage Flexhealth Project*. Centraal Bureau voor Statistiek.

Chung, H., & van der Horst, M. (2017). Women's employment patterns after childbirth and the perceived access to and use of flexitime and teleworking. *Human Relations, 71*(1), 47–72.

Clark, A., Flèche, S., Layard, R., Powdthavee, N., & Ward, G. (2018a). *The origins of well-being over the life course*. Princeton University Press.

Clark, A. E., Flèche, S., Layard, R., Powdthavee, N., & Ward, G. (2018b). *The origins of happiness: The science of well-being over the life course*. Princeton University Press.

CNV Zorg & Welzijn. (2018). *Veiligheid in de gehandicaptenzorg [PDFfile]*. Retrieved from https://zorgenwelzijn.cnvconnectief.nl/wp-content/uploads/2018/05/Veiligheid-gehandicaptenzorg-onderzoeksresultaten.pdf

Coates, D. (2009). *Advancing opportunity: The future of good work*. The Smith Institute.

Collier, P. (2018). *The future of capitalism: Facing the new anxieties*. Penguin Random House.

Colvin, G. (2015). *Humans are underrated: What high achievers know that brilliant machines never will do*. Portfolio/Penguin.

Commissie regulering van werk. (2019). *In wat voor land willen wij werken? Discussienota van de Commissie regulering van werk over toekomstbestendig arbeidsrecht, sociale zekerheid en fiscaliteit.* Ministerie van Sociale Zaken en Werkgelegenheid. Retrieved from https://www.rijksoverheid.nl/documenten/rapporten/2019/06/20/discussienota-in-wat-voorland-willen-wij-werken

Commissie Toekomstscenario's Herverdeling Onbetaalde Arbeid. (1995). *Onbetaalde zorg gelijk verdeeld*. VUGA.

Conen, W. (2018). Waarden van werk. *ESB, 103*(4760), 186–189.

Conen, W. (2020). *Waarde van werk in Nederland* (WRR working paper No. 38). Wetenschappelijke Raad voor het Regeringsbeleid.

Conen, W., & Debets, M. (2019). Precariousness and social risks among solo self-employed in Germany and the Netherlands. In W. Conen & J. Schippers (Eds.), *Self-employment as precarious work. A European perspective* (pp. 108–131). Edward Elgar Publishing Limited.

Corneo, G. (2017). *Is capitalism obsolete? A journey through alternative economic systems*. Harvard University Press.

Cottingham, M. D. (2016). Theorizing emotional capital. *Theory and Society, 45*(95), 451–470.

Coyle, D. (2014). *GDP: A brief but affectionate history*. Princeton University Press.

CPB [Netherlands Bureau for Economic Policy Analysis]. (2005). *Naar een toekomstbestendig stelsel voor arbeidsmarkt en sociale zekerheid* (CPB memorandum). Centraal Planbureau.

CPB [Netherlands Bureau for Economic Policy Analysis]. (2015). *Kansrijk arbeidsmarktbeleid, Deel 1*. Centraal Planbureau. Retrieved from https://www.cpb.nl/publicatie/kansrijk-arbeidsmarktbeleid

CPB [Netherlands Bureau for Economic Policy Analysis]. (2016). *Kansrijk arbeidsmarktbeleid. Deel 2*. Centraal Planbureau.

Crawford, E. R., Lepine, J. A., & Rich, B. L. (2010). Linking job demands and resources to employee engagement and burnout: A theoretical extension and meta-analytic test. *Journal of Applied Psychology, 95*(5), 834–848.

Crouch, C. (2018). Redefining labour relations and capital in the digital age. In M. Neufeind, J. O'Reilly, & F. Ranft (Eds.), *Work in the digital age: Challenges of the fourth industrial revolution* (pp. 187–197). Rowman & Littlefield International.

Dankbaar, B., & Muysken, J. (2019). Op weg naar een baangarantie voor iedereen. In M. Somers (Ed.), *Fundamenten. Sociale zekerheid in onzekere tijden* (pp. 262–276). Minerva. Retrieved from https://static1.squarespace.com/static/580dffc9f7e0ab87773fc653/t/5cc-1c76a0d92977b2f28cb07/1556203380036/Fundamenten_Ben_Dankbaar_en_Joan_Muysken.pdf

Datta, N. (2019, July 19). Willing to pay for security: Gig workers, freelancers, and the self-employed want steady jobs. *VoxEU*. Retrieved from https://voxeu.org

Daugherty, P., & Wilson, J. (2018). *Human + machine: Reimagining work in the age of AI*. Harvard University Press.

Davenport, T., & Kirby, J. (2016). *Only humans need apply: Winners and losers in the age of smart machines*. HarperCollins.

Davies, W. (2015). *The happiness industry: How the government and big business sold us well-being*. Verso.

de Beer, P. (2001). *Over werken in de postindustriële samenleving*. Sociaal en Cultureel Planbureau.

de Beer, P. (2015). Basisinkomen, basisbaan of gewoon armoede bestrijden? *S&D, 72*(3), 87–93.

de Beer, P.. (2018a). Laagopgeleiden vaker aan het werk, maar wel op laagbetaald en flexibele baan. *TPEdigitaal, 12*(2), 1–19. Retrieved from https://www.tpedigitaal.nl/sites/default/files/bestand/Laagopgeleiden%20   vaker%20aan%20het%20werk%2C%20maar%20wel%20op%20 laagbetaalde%20en%20flexibele%20baan.pdf

de Beer, P. (2018b). Waarom gebruiken werkgevers (steeds meer) flexibele arbeidskrachten? *Tijdschrift voor Arbeidsvraagstukken, 34*(1), 62–84.

de Beer, P., & Berntsen, L. (2019). Vakbondslidmaatschap onder druk in Nederland, maar niet in België. *Tijdschrift voor Arbeidsvraagstukken, 35*(3), 255–274.

de Beer, P., & Conen, W. (2019). De waarde van werk staat in Nederland onder druk. *Kort en bondig, 1*. AIAS.

de Beer, P., & Verhulp, E. (2017). *Dertig vragen en antwoorden over flexibel werk*. Amsterdams Instituut voor ArbeidsStudies. Retrieved from https://aias.s3-eu-central-1.amazonaws.com/website/uploads/1489737869934Dertig-vragen-en-antwoorden-over-flexibel-werk-def.pdf

de Boer, A., Plaisier, I., & de Klerk, M. (2019). *Werk en mantelzorg. Kwaliteit van leven en het gebruik van ondersteuning op het werk*. Sociaal en Cultureel Planbureau.

de Goede, P., Schrijvers, E., & de Visser, M. (Eds.). (2019). *Filantropie op de grens van overheid en markt*. Wetenschappelijke Raad voor het Regeringsbeleid.

de Graaf-Zijl, M., Josten, E., Boeters, S., Eggink, E., Bolhaar, J., Ooms, I., et al. (2015). *De onderkant van de arbeidsmarkt in 2025*. Centraal Planbureau/Sociaal en Cultureel Planbureau.

Grip, A. de. (2015, June). The importance of informal learning at work. *IZA World of Labor*. Retrieved from https://wol.iza.org

de Grip, A., Belfi, B., Fouarge, D., Kühn-Nelen, A., Peeters, T., & Poulissen, D. (2018). *Levenslang leren en competentieontwikkeling* (Policy report). ROA.

de Hek, P., de Koning, J., de Vleeschouwer, E., & Gabel, M. (2018). *Kwetsbaarheid over de levensloop. Een verkennend onderzoek in opdracht van het KWI*. SEOR.

de Jonge, J., Le Blanc, P., & Schaufeli, W. (2013). Theoretische modellen over werkstress. In W. Schaufeli & A. Bakker (Eds.), *De psychologie van arbeid en gezondheid* (pp. 23–46). Bohn Stafleu van Loghum.

de Klerk, M., de Boer, A., Plaisier, I., Schyns, P., & Kooiker, S. (2015). *Informele hulp: wie doet er wat? De omvang, aard en kenmerken van mantelzorg en vrijwilligerswerk in de zorg en ondersteuning*. Sociaal en Cultureel Planbureau.

de Klerk, M., de Boer, A., Plaisier, I., & Schyns, P. (2017). *Voor elkaar?* Sociaal en Cultureel Planbureau.

de Lange, R., & Jonker, U. (2018, December 10). Tjeenk Willink: "We zijn de publieke zaak structureel aan het uithollen". *Het Financieele Dagblad*. Retrieved from https://fd.nl

de Spiegelaere, S. (2017). Intermezzo: flexibel, maar ook innovatief? In M. Kremer, R. Went, & A. Knottnerus (Eds.), *Voor de zekerheid. De toekomst van flexibel werkenden en de moderne organisatie van arbeid* (pp. 145–147). Wetenschappelijke Raad voor het Regeringsbeleid.

de Stefano, V.. (2018). *"Negotiating the Algorithm": Automation, Artificial Intelligence and Labour Protection* (ILO employment working paper No. 246) [PDF file]. Retrieved from https://www.ilo.org/wcmsp5/groups/public/%2D%2D-ed_emp/%2D%2D-emp_policy/documents/publication/wcms_634157.pdf

Deci, E. L., & Ryan, R. M. (1985). *Intrinsic motivation and self-determination in human behaviour*. Plenum.

Deci, E. L., & Ryan, R. M. (2008). Self-determination theory: A macrotheory of human motivation, development, and health. *Canadian Psychology/Psychologie Canadienne, 49*(3), 182–185.

Deci, E. L., Olafsen, A. H., & Ryan, R. M. (2017). Self-determination theory in work organizational behaviour. *Annual Review of Organizational Psychology and Organizational Behavior, 4*, 19–43.

Deery, S., Kolar, D., & Walsh, J. (2019). Can dirty work be satisfying? A mixed method study of workers doing dirty jobs. *Work, Employment and Society, 33*(5), 631–647.

Dekker, F. (2017). Flexibilisering in Nederland: trends, kansen en risico's. In M. Kremer, R. Went, & A. Knottnerus (Eds.), *Voor de zekerheid. De toekomst van flexibel werkenden en de moderne organisatie van arbeid* (pp. 69–91). Wetenschappelijke Raad voor het Regeringsbeleid.

Dekker, F. (2018). In Nederland heeft niemand een bullshit job. *ESB, 103*(4758), 90–91.

Dekker, R., & Freese, C. (2018). *Samen werken met robots*. de Burcht. Retrieved from https://www.deburcht.nl/userfiles/file/Publicatie%2016%2C%20Samenwerken%20met%20robots.pdf

Dekker, W., & Vergeer, R. (2007). Soepel ontslag creëert onzekerheid. *ESB, 29*(4504), 116–118.

Demerouti, E., Bakker, A. B., Nachreiner, F., & Schaufeli, W. B. (2001). The job demands-resources model of burnout. *Journal of Applied Psychology, 86*(3), 499–512.

Denkwerk. (2019). *Arbeid in transitie. Hoe mens en technologie samen kunnen werken*. Retrieved from https://denkwerk.online/themas/arbeid-in-transitie/

Derbyshire, J. (2017, July 28). Why governments can't have it all. *Financial Times*. Retrieved from https://www.ft.com

Detollenaere, J., Willems, S., & Baert, S. (2017). Volunteering, income and health. *Plos One, 12*(3), e0173139. https://doi.org/10.1371/journal.pone.0173139

DNB. (2018, February 1). DNBulletin: Flexibilisering arbeidsmarkt gaat gepaard met daling arbeidsinkomensquote. *DNB*. Retrieved from https://www.dnb.nl/nieuws/nieuwsoverzicht-en-archief/DNBulletin2018/dnb372062.jsp

Dohmen, A. (2017, October 20). De dwang van de Nederlandse deeltijdcultuur. *NRC*. Retrieved from https://www.nrc.nl

Dorenbosch, L. (2017). Intermezzo: Samen (on)zeker? In M. Kremer, R. Went, & A. Knottnerus (Eds.), *Voor de zekerheid. De toekomst van flexibel werkenden en de moderne organisatie van arbeid* (pp. 93–96). Wetenschappelijke Raad voor het Regeringsbeleid.

Driessen, S. (2019). *Verloop personeel kost horeca jaarlijks 1,4 miljard*. ABN AMRO.

Duxbury, L., & Smart, R. (2011). The "Myth of Separate Worlds": An exploration of how mobile technology has redefined work-life balance. In S. Kaiser, M. J. Ringlstetter, D. R. Eikhof, & M. P. Cunha (Eds.), *Creating balance?* (pp. 269–284). Springer.

Edmondson, A. (2019). *The fearless organization: Creating psychological safety in the workplace for learning, innovation, and growth*. Wiley.

Eichhorst, W., Kalleberg, A., Portela de Souza, A., Siegrist, J., & Visser, J. (in press) [pdf file]. Designing good labour market institutions: Main findings from the IPSP chapter on employment. International Labour Review, (draft as of 15 January 2019). Retrieved from https://www.uva.nl/binaries/content/assets/subsites/amsterdam-centre-for-inequality-studies/final-ilr-paper-visser-etc_.pdf

Einerhand, M., & Ravesteijn, B. (2017). Psychische klachten en de arbeidsmarkt. *ESB, 102*(4754), 2–4.

Elshout, J. (2016). *Roep om respect. Ervaringen van werklozen in een meritocratiserende samenleving*. Stichting de Driehoek.

Engbersen, G., Schuyt, K., Timmer, J. S., & van Waarden, F. (1993). *Cultures of unemployment: A comparative look at long-term unemployment and urban poverty*. Westview Press.

Engbersen, G., Snel, E., & Kremer, M. (Eds.). (2017). *De val van de middenklasse? Het stabiele en kwetsbare midden*. Wetenschappelijke Raad voor het Regeringsbeleid.

Epstein, C. F., & Kalleberg, A. L. (2004). *Fighting for time: Shifting boundaries of work and social life*. Russell Sage.

ETUI. (2019). *Benchmarking Working Europe 2019*. European Trade Union Institute.

EU-OSHA. (2014). *Berekening van de kosten van werkgerelateerde stress en psychosociale risico's.* Europees Agentschap voor veiligheid en gezondheid op het werk.

Eurofound. (2013). *Work organisation and employee involvement in Europe.* Publications Office of the European Union.

Eurofound. (2017). *Sixth European working conditions survey – overview report.* Publications Office of the European Union.

Eurofound. (2018). *New tasks in old jobs: Drivers of change and implications for job quality.* Publications Office of the European Union.

Eurofound & ilo. (2017). *Working anytime, anywhere: The effects on the world of work.* Publications Office of the European Union/International Labour Office.

European Commission. (2017). *Thematic report on access to social protection of people working as self-employed or non-standard contracts.* European Commission.

Euwals, R., & Meijerink, G. (2018). *Inclusieve globalisering. Voordelen moeilijk herkenbaar, nadelen ongelijk verdeeld* (CPB policy brief 2018, No. 08). Centraal Planbureau. Retrieved from www.cpb.nl/sites/default/files/omnidownload/cpb-Policy-Brief-2018-08-Inclusieve- globalisering.pdf

Euwals, R., de Graaf-Zijl, M., & van Vuuren, D. (2016). *Flexibiliteit op de arbeidsmarkt. Lusten en lasten ongelijk verdeeld; verklein verschillen vast, flex en zzp.* Centraal Planbureau.

Falcke, S., Meng, C., & Nollen, R. (2017). Tweedegeneratieallochtonen hebben vaak een mismatch tussen opleiding en baan. *ESB, 102*(4749), 213–215.

Federal Ministry of Labour and Social Affairs. (2017). *Re-Imagining work: White paper, work 4.0.* Federal Ministry of Labour and Social Affairs.

Felstead, A., Gallie, D., Green, F., & Henseke, G. (2016). The determinants of skills use and work pressure: A longitudinal analysis. *Economic and Industrial Democracy, 40*(3), 730–754.

Ford, M. (2015). *Rise of the robots: Technology and the threat of a jobless future.* Basic Books.

Fouarge, D. J. A. G. (2017). *Veranderingen in werk en vaardigheden.* Maastricht University.

Freeman, C., & Louçã, F. (2001). *As time goes by: From the industrial revolutions to the information revolution.* Oxford University Press.

Freese, C. (2008). Zijn uw psychologische contracten nog houdbaar? *HR Strategie, 1*, 18–32.

Freese, C., Schalk, R., & Croon, M. (2008). De Tilburgse psychologisch contract vragenlijst. *Gedrag en Organisatie, 21*(3), 278–229.

Frenken, K., & van Slageren, J. (2018). Kluseconomie is meer dan Uber en Deliveroo. *ESB, 103*(4768S), 27–31.

Frey, C. (2019). *The technology trap: Capital, labor, and power in the age of automation.* Princeton University Press.

Frey, C., & Osborne, M. (2013). *The future of employment: How susceptible are jobs to computerisation?* Oxford Martin Programme on Technology & Employment.

Fried, J., & Heinemeier Hansson, D. (2018). *It doesn't have to be crazy at work.* HarperCollins.

Friedman, T. (1999). *The Lexus and the olive tree: Understanding globalization.* Farrar, Strauss and Giraux.

Frielink, N. (2017). *Motivation, well-being, and living with a mild intellectual disability: A self-determination theory perspective.* Prismaprint.

Froyland, K., Andreassen, T., & Innvaer, S. (2019). Contrasting supply-side, demand-side and combined approaches to labour market integration. *Journal of Social Policy, 48*(2), 311–328.

Fukkink, R. (Ed.). (2017). *De Nederlandse kinderopvang in wetenschappelijk perspectief.* Uitgeverij SWP.

Gallie, D. (2007a). *Employment regimes and quality of work.* Oxford University Press.

Gallie, D. (2007b). Production regimes and the quality of employment in Europe. *Annual Review of Sociology, 33*, 85–104.

Gallie, D. (2013). *Economic crisis, quality of work and social integration: The European experience.* Oxford University Press.

Gallie, D. (2017). The quality of work in a changing labour market. *Social Policy & Administration, 51*(2), 226–243.

Gallie, D., & Zhou, Y. (2013). Job control, work intensity and work stress. In D. Gallie (Ed.), *Economic crisis, quality of work and social integration* (pp. 115–141). Oxford University Press.

Garretsen, H. (2019, September 26). Een pleidooi voor indirect innovatiebeleid. *Me Judice*. Retrieved from https:/www.mejudice.nl/artikelen/detail/een-pleidooi-voor-indirect-innovatiebeleid

Geleijnse, L., Vrooman, J., & Muffels, R. (1993). *Tussen ministelsel en participatiemodel. Een verkennende studie naar stelselvarianten in de sociale zekerheid*. Sociaal en Cultureel Planbureau.

Gerschagen, M. (2018, June 6). Na het lezen van dit boek bestelt onze recensent niets meer bij Amazon. *NRC*. Retrieved from https://www.nrc.nl

Gezondheidsraad [The Health Council of the Netherlands]. (2017). *Gezondheidsrisico's door nachtwerk*. Gezondheidsraad. Retrieved from https://www.gezondheidsraad.nl/documenten/adviezen/2017/10/24/gezondheidsrisicos-door-nachtwerk

GGD Amsterdam & OIS. (2017). *Evaluatie trajecten Meedoen Werkt Amsterdam 2016*. GGD Amsterdam/Onderzoek, Informatie en Statistiek.

Ghemawat, P., & Altman, S. (2016). *The state of globalization in an age of ambiguity:DHLGlobal Connectedness Index 2016* [PDF file]. Retrieved from https://www.dhl.com/content/dam/downloads/g0/about_us/logistics_insights/gci_2016/dhl_gci_2016_full_study.pdf

Gibbons, R., & Henderson, R. (2013). What do managers do? Exploring persistent performance differences among seemingly similar enterprises. In R. Gibbons & J. Roberts (Eds.), *The handbook of organizational economics* (pp. 680–731). Princeton University Press.

Goldstein, A. (2017). *Janesville: An American story*. Simon & Schuster.

Goñalons-Pons, P., & Gangl, M. (2018). *Why does unemployment lead to divorce? Male-breadwinner norms and divorce risk in 30 countries*. Goethe University.

Goos, M., Manning, A., & Salomons, A. (2009). Job polarization in Europe. *American Economic Review, 99*(2), 58–63.

Gorz, A. (1994). *Capitalism, socialism, ecology*. Verso.

Goudswaard, K., & Caminada, K. (2017). Pensioenen voor zelfstandigen. In M. Kremer, R. Went, & A. Knottnerus (Eds.), *Voor de zekerheid. De toekomst van flexibel werkenden en de moderne organisatie van arbeid* (pp. 231–256). Wetenschappelijke Raad voor het Regeringsbeleid.

Graeber, D. (2018). *Bullshit jobs*. Simon & Schuster.

Graetz, G., & Michaels, G. (2015). *Robots at Work* (IZA discussion paper No. 8938). IZA.

Gray, M., & Suri, S. (2019). *Ghost work: How to stop Silicon Valley from building a new global underclass*. Houghton Mifflin Harcourt.

Graystone, R. (2019). Nurses on boards. A national imperative. *Journal of Nursing Administration, 49*(3), 111–112.

Green, F. (2004). Work intensification, discretion, and the decline in well-being at work. *Eastern Economic Journal, 30*(4), 615–625.

Greenway, A., Terrett, B., Bracken, M., & Loosemore, T. (2018). *Digital transformation at scale: Why the strategy is delivery*. London Publishing Partnership.

Gregg, M. (2011). *Work's intimacy*. Polity.

Groot, L., Muffels, R., & Verlaat, T. (2019). Welfare states' social investment strategies and the emergence of Dutch experiments on a minimum income guarantee. *Social Policy and Society, 18*(2), 277–287.

Gurría, A. (2017, June 6). Globalisation: Don't patch it up, shake it up. *OECD*. Retrieved from https:/www.oecd.org

Haas, de. (2010). The internal dynamics of migration processes: A theoretical inquiry. *Journal of Ethnic and Migration Studies, 36*(10), 1587–1617.

Halbesleben, J. R. (2006). Sources of social support and burnout. *Journal of Applied Psychology, 91*(5), 1134–1145.

Hall, P., & Soskice, D. (2001). *Varieties of capitalism: The institutional foundations of comparative advantage*. Oxford University Press.

Harbers, M. M., & Hoeymans, N. (Eds.). (2013). *Gezondheid en maatschappelijke participatie. Themarapport Volksgezondheid Toekomst Verkenning 2014*. RIVM.

Head, S. (2014). *Mindless: Why smarter machines are making humans dumber.* Basic Books.

Head, S. (2018, May 24). Big Brother goes digital. *The New York Review of Books.* Retrieved from https://www.nybooks.com

Heeger, S., & Koopmans, I. (2018). De facilitering en toerusting van de werkende mantelzorger in Nederland en Duitsland. In F. Pennings & J. Plantenga (Eds.), *Nieuwe vormen van arbeidsrelaties en van sociale bescherming* (pp. 143–162). Uitgeverij Paris.

Heidsma, V., & Zaal, I. (2019). Platformarbeid en medezeggenschap: is de WOR digiproof? *Arbeidsrecht, 27*(6/7), 11–15.

Henkens, K., & van Sollinge, H. (2017). Oudere werknemer komt met mantelzorg in het gedrang. *Demos, 33*(10), 4–6.

Heuts, P. (2017). DHL experiments with augmented reality. *HesaMag, 16,* 22–26.

Heuven, E. (2013). Emotionele arbeid. In W. Schaufeli & A. Bakker (Eds.), *De psychologie van arbeid en gezondheid* (pp. 251–262). Bohn Stafleu van Loghum.

Heyma, A., & van der Werff, S. (2014). *Een goed gesprek werkt.* SEO Economisch Onderzoek.

Heyma, A., Bisschop, P., & Biesenbeek, C. (2018). *De economische waarde van arbeidsmigranten uit Midden- en Oost-Europa voor Nederland.* SEO Economisch Onderzoek.

Hochschild, A. R. (1983). *The managed heart.* University of California Press.

Hodson, R. (2001). *Dignity at Work.* Cambridge University Press.

Hoekstra, R. (2019). *Replacing GDP by 2030: Towards a common language for the well-being and sustainability community.* Cambridge University Press.

Holtslag, J. W., Kremer, M., & Schrijvers, E. (Eds.). (2012). *In betere banen. De toekomst van arbeidsmigratie in de EU.* Wetenschappelijke Raad voor het Regeringsbeleid.

Honneth, A. (2001). Recognition or redistribution? *Theory, Culture & Society, 18*(1–2), 43–55.

Honneth, A. (2007). *Disrespect: The normative foundations of critical theory.* Polity.

Hooftman, W., & Houtman, I. (2017). Arbeidsomstandigheden van werknemers met een migratieachtergrond. In *Dynamiek op de Nederlandse arbeidsmarkt. De focus op ongelijkheid* (pp. 216–240). CBS/TNO.

Houtman, I., & van den Bossche, S. (2010). Trends in de kwaliteit van de arbeid in Nederland en Europa. *Tijdschrift voor Arbeidsvraagstukken, 26*(4), 432–450.

Houtman, I., Douwes, M., Jong, T. D., Meeuwsen, J. M., Jongen, M., Brekelmans, F., & Reinert, D. (2008). *New forms of physical and psychosocial health risks at work: Study.* European Parliament.

Houtman, I., Steenbeek, R., van Zwieten, M., & Andriessen, S. (2013). *Verklaring stijging WIA-instroom vanuit werkgeversperspectief. Een vignetten-studie.* TNO.

Houtman, I., Kraan, K., Bakhuys Roozeboom, M., & van den Bossche, S. (2017). Trends in arbeidsomstandigheden van werknemers in Nederland en Europa. *Tijdschrift voor Arbeidsomstandigheden, 33*(4), 404–428.

Houtman, I., Dhondt, S., Preenen, P., Kraan, K., & de Vroome, E. (2020). *Intensivering van werk in Nederland: wat is het, waar staan we en wat te doen?* (WRR working paper No. 36). Wetenschappelijke Raad voor het Regeringsbeleid.

Houweling, R., & Sprengers, L. (2016). *70 jaar VvA: Einde van het begin.* Wolters Kluwer.

Hueck, H. (2018, April 3). Nederland meer 'robotproof' dan gedacht. *Het Financieele Dagblad.* Retrieved from https://fd.nl

Hueck, H., & Went, R. (2015, January 25). Wij eisen geluk. *RTLZ.* Retrieved from https://www.rtlz.nl

Hueck, H., & Went, R. (2016, January 9). Vijf mythes over handel en de toekomst van Nederland als handelsland. *Follow the Money.* Retrieved from https://www.ftm.nl

Hupkens, C. (2005). Burn-out: de rol van psychische werkbelasting. *Sociaaleconomische trends, 2005*(3), 18–22.

ILO. (2019). *Work for a brighter future: Global commission on the future of work.* International Labour Organization. Retrieved from https://www.ilo.org/global/topics/future-of-work/publications/wcms_662410/lang%2D%2Den/index.html

Inspectie SZW [Inspectorate SZW; Ministry of Social Affairs and Employment]. (2014). *Ken uw klanten. Onderzoek naar het caseloadbeheer van uwv en gemeenten en hun kennis van de klant.* Inspectie SZW.

Inspectie SZW [Inspectorate SZW; Ministry of Social Affairs and Employment]. (2015). *Mannen en vrouwen in de sociale zekerheid.* Inspectie SZW.

Inspectie SZW [Inspectorate SZW; Ministry of Social Affairs and Employment]. (2016). *De aanpak van werkdruk: Hoe doen organisaties in Nederland dat? [Factsheet].* Inspectie SZW.

Inspectie SZW [Inspectorate SZW; Ministry of Social Affairs and Employment].(2018). *Aan het werk, voor hoe lang? Onderzoek naar de begeleiding van jongeren met een arbeidsbeperking naar duurzaam werk.* Inspectie SZW.

Inspectie SZW [Inspectorate SZW; Ministry of Social Affairs and Employment]. (2019). *Arbo in bedrijf 2018. Een onderzoek naar de naleving van arboverplichtingen, blootstelling aan risico's en genomen maatregelen in 2018.* Ministerie van Sociale Zaken en Werkgelegenheid.

IPPR Commission on Economic Justice. (2018). *Prosperity and justice: A plan for the new economy.* IPPR. Retrieved from https://www.ippr.org/files/2018-08/1535639099_prosperity-and-justice-ippr-2018.pdf

Iversen, T., & Soskice, D. (2019). *Democracy and prosperity: Reinventing capitalism through a turbulent century.* Princeton University Press.

Jahoda, M. (1982). *Employment and unemployment: A social-psychological analysis.* Cambridge University Press.

Jahoda, M., Lazarsfeld, P. F., & Zeisel, H. (1975). *Die arbeitslosen von Marienthal. Ein soziographischer versuch über die wirkungen langandauernder arbeitslosigkeit.* Suhrkamp.

Johnson, S., Robertson, I., & Cooper, C. (2018). *Well-being: Productivity and happiness at work.* Palgrave Macmillan.

Josten, E., & de Boer, A. (2015). *Concurrentie tussen mantelzorg en betaald werk.* Sociaal en Cultureel Planbureau.

Josten, E., & Vlasblom, D. (2017). Maakt zzp'er worden tevreden? *Tijdschrift voor Arbeidsvraagstukken, 33*(3), 269–283.

Kalleberg, A. L. (2011). *Good jobs, bad jobs: The rise of polarized and precarious employment systems in the United States, 1970s to 2000s.* Russell Sage Foundation.

Kalleberg, A. L. (2018). *Precarious lives: Job insecurity and well-being in rich democracies.* Polity.

Kalshoven, F. (2018, November 10). Overdreven flex is naar voor betrokken werkenden, maar ook nog eens schadelijk voor de economie. *De Volkskrant.* Retrieved from https://www.volkskrant.nl

Kamerstukken II [Parliamentary papers]. 2010/2011, 32 889, No. 3. Retrieved from https://zoek.officielebekendmakingen.nl/kst-32889-3.html

Kamerstukken II [Parliamentary papers]. 2015/2016, 34 298, No. 3. Retrieved from www.tweedekamer.nl/sites/default/files/atoms/files/34298-3.pdf

Kampen, T. (2014). *Verplicht vrijwilligerswerk: de ervaringen van bijstandscliënten met een tegenprestatie voor hun uitkering.* Van Gennep.

Karasek, R. A. (1979). Job demands, job decision latitude, and mental strain: Implications for job redesign. *Administrative Science Quarterly, 24*(2), 285–308.

Karasek, R. A., & Theorell, T. (1990). *Healthy work: Stress, productivity and the reconstruction of working life.* Basic Books.

Keizer, A., Tiemeijer, W., & Bovens, M. (2019). *Why knowing what to do is not enough. A realistic perspective on self-reliance.* Springer.

Kenniscentrum uwv. (2011). *uwvKennisverslag 2011-II.* Uitvoeringsinstituut Werknemersverzekeringen.

Keynes, J. M. (1932). Economic possibilities for our grandchildren. In *Essays in persuasion* (pp. 358–373). Harcourt, Brace & Company. Retrieved from https://www.hetwebsite.net/het/texts/keynes/keynes-1930grandchildren.html

King, S. (2017). *Grave new world: The end of globalization, the return of history.* Yale University Press.

Kleinknecht, A. (2014). Een erfenis van Schumpeter. Waarom arbeidsmarktrigiditeiten nuttig kunnen zijn voor innovatie [Farewell address, TU Delft]. *TPEdigitaal, 8*(3), 31–48.

Kleinknecht, R. (2018). *Organizational antecedents of managerial short-termism* (Doctoral dissertation). Amsterdam: Universiteit van Amsterdam.

Klosse, S., & Muyskens, J. (2011, November 4). Overheid moet geen uitkering maar werk aanbieden. *Me Judice*. Retrieved from https://www.mejudice.nl/artikelen/detail/overheid-moet-geen-uitkering-maar-werk-aanbieden

Kluve, J. (2010). The effectiveness of European active labor market programs. *Labour Economics, 17*(6), 904–918.

Knoef, M., & van Ours, J. (2016). How to stimulate single mothers on welfare to find a job: Evidence from a policy experiment. *Journal of Population Economics, 29*(4), 1025–1061.

Kochan, T., & Dyer, L. (2017). *Shaping the future of work: A handbook for action and a new social contract*. MIT Press.

Kok, L., & Houkes, A. (2011). *Gemeentelijk re-integratiebeleid vergeleken. Een literatuurstudie*. SEO Economisch Onderzoek.

Kok, L., Kroon, L., Scholte, R., & Tempelman, C. (2018). *Zelfstandig in en uit de bijstand: Kosten en baten Besluit Bijstandverlening Zelfstandigen*. SEO Economisch Onderzoek.

Kok, L., Kroon, L., Lammers, M., Oomkens, R., Geijsen, T., & Linssen, M. (2019). *Jonggehandicapten onder de Participatiewet. Tweede rapportage april 2019*. SEO/Pantheia/VU.

Koning, P. (2006). *Measuring effectiveness of public employment service (pes) workers; An empirical analysis based on the performance outcomes of regional employment offices*. Centraal Planbureau.

Koning, P. (2011). Experimenteren in de sociale zekerheid. *ESB, 96*(465), 150–153.

Koning, P., Vogels, E., & de Lange, M. (2017). De onderkant van de arbeidsmarkt en actief arbeidsmarktbeleid in internationaal perspectief. *TPEdigitaal, 11*(1), 1–16.

Kool, L., & van Est, R. (2015). Kansen en bedreigingen: Negen perspectieven op werken in de robotsamenleving. In R. Went, M. Kremer, & A. Knottnerus (Eds.), *De robot de baas: De toekomst van werk in het tweede machinetijdperk* (WRR-verkenning No. 31) (pp. 49–67). Amsterdam University Press.

Kopf, D. (2019, January 18). Wages for low-income workers are rising, so the fed says companies are looking to automation. *Quartz*. Retrieved from https://qz.com/work/1527260/the-fed-says-rising-wages-has-companies-looking-to-automation/

Kornelakis, A., Veliziotis, M., & Voskeritsian, H. (2018). *Improving productivity: The case for employee voice and inclusive workplace practices* (ETUI policy brief No. 1). Retrieved from www.etui.org/content/download/33501/310661/file/Productivity+Employee+voice+Kornelakis+et+al+ Policy+Brief+2018-01+Policy+Brief.pdf

Korunka, C., & Kubicek, B. (2017). *Job demands in a changing world of work: Impact on worker's health and performance and implications for research and practice*. Springer.

Koster, F. (2020). *Arbeidsrelaties in beweging. Een overzicht van de literatuur naar de inzet van de factor arbeid* (WRR working paper No. 40). Wetenschappelijke Raad voor het Regeringsbeleid.

Kowalsky, W. (2019). 'More democracy at work' or 'More power for big corporations' – Which is the new paradigm? In P. Scherrer, J. Bir, W. Kowalsky, R. Kuhlmann, & M. Méaulle (Eds.), *The future of Europe* (pp. 27–52). European Trade Union Institute.

Krekel, C., Ward, G., & de Neve, J. (2019). *Employee wellbeing, productivity, and firm performance* (Saïd Business School working paper 2019, No. 04). University of Oxford/Saïd Business School.

Kremer, M. (2007). *How welfare states care: culture, gender and parenting in Europe*. Amsterdam University Press.

Kremer, M. (2015, February 2). Bij Breman: meedelen en meebeslissen [Blog post]. Retrieved from wrrdenhaag.wordpress.com/2015/02/02/bij-breman-meedelen-en-meebeslissen/

Kremer, M. (2017). De verschillende gezichten van onzekerheid. Flexibel werkenden over werk, familie en sociale zekerheid. In M. Kremer, R. Went, & A. Knottnerus (Eds.), *Voor de zekerheid. De toekomst van flexibel werkenden en de moderne organisatie van arbeid* (pp. 97–122). Wetenschappelijke Raad voor het Regeringsbeleid.

Kremer, M., & Went, R. (2018). Mastering the digital transformation: An inclusive robotization agenda. In M. Neufeind, J. O'Reilly, & F. Ranft (Eds.), *Work in the digital age. Challenges of the fourth industrial revolution* (pp. 141–151). Rowman & Littlefield.

Kremer, M., Bovens, M., Schrijvers, E., & Went, R. (2014). *Hoe ongelijk is Nederland?* Amsterdam University Press.

Kremer, M., Das, D., & Schrijvers, E. (2017a). Onzeker in het midden. Over de verbroken beloften van de middenklasse. In G. Engbersen, E. Snel, & M. Kremer (Eds.), *De val van de middenklasse? Het stabiele en kwetsbare midden* (pp. 233–251). Wetenschappelijke Raad voor het Regeringsbeleid.

Kremer, M., van der Meer, J., & Ham, M. (2017b). Werkt de zachte hand in de bijstand? *Tijdschrift voor Sociale Vraagstukken, 4*, 4–9.

Kremer, M., Went, R., & Knottnerus, A. (2017c). *Voor de zekerheid. De toekomst van flexibel werkenden en de moderne organisatie van arbeid.* Wetenschappelijke Raad voor het Regeringsbeleid.

Kremer, M., Went, R., & Knottnerus, A. (2017d). *For the sake of security. The future of flexible workers and the modern organisation of labour.* Wetenschappelijke Raad voor het Regeringsbeleid.

Kroft, H., Engbersen, G., Schuyt, K., Timmer, J. S., Hoegen, S., Müller, H., & van der Sluis, J. (1989). *Een tijd zonder werk. Een onderzoek naar de levenswereld van langdurig werklozen.* Stenfert Kroese.

Kroon, B., & Paauwe, J. (2014). Structuration of precarious employment in economically constrained firms: The case of Dutch agriculture. *Human Resource Management Journal, 24*(1), 19–37.

Kubicek, B., Paskvan, M., & Bunner, J. (2017). The bright and dark sides of job autonomy. In C. Korunka & B. Kubicek (Eds.), *Job demands in a changing world of work: Impact on workers' health and performance and implications for research and practice* (pp. 45–63). Springer.

KVK [The Netherlands Chamber of Commerce]. (2019). *Data over de bedrijvendynamiek. Jaaroverzicht 2018.* Kamer van Koophandel.

Lammers, M., & Kok, L. (2017). *Long term effects of active labour market policies: UI benefit recipients and welfare recipients.* SEO Economisch Onderzoek.

Lammers, M., Imandt, M., & Heyma, A. (2015). *Wordt aan gewerkt.nl.* SEO Economisch Onderzoek.

Lamont, M. (2000). *The dignity of working men: Morality and the boundaries of race, and immigration.* Russell Sage Foundation.

Lemmers, O., Roelandt, T., Selp, M., & van der Wiel, H. (2019). Innovatievouchers zorgen structureel voor meer innovatieactiviteiten. *ESB, 104*(4779), 527–529.

Liebregts, W., & Stam, E. (2017). Ondernemende werkenden. In M. Kremer, R. Went, & A. Knottnerus (Eds.), *Voor de zekerheid. De toekomst van flexibel werkenden en de moderne organisatie van arbeid* (pp. 149–164). Wetenschappelijke Raad voor het Regeringsbeleid.

Lohr, S. (2018, August 5). "The beginning of a wave": AI tiptoes into the workplace. *New York Times.* Retrieved from https://www.nytimes.com

Lowry, A. (2018, May 11). A promise so big, democrats aren't sure how to keep it. Progressives are lining up behind a jobs guarantee—but leaving the details for later. *The Atlantic.* Retrieved from https://www.theatlantic.com

Lub, V. (2017). *Participatie in de bijstand: wat leert de wetenschap?* Bureau voor Sociale Argumentatie.

Lucas, A. (2016). Robotisering zonder achterblijvers [PDF file]. Retrieved from https://annewillucas.vvd.nl/uploaded/annewillucas.vvd.nl/files/5721ad587e292/robotisering-zonder-achterblijvers-1.pdf

Luebker, M. (2017). Poverty, employment and inequality in the SDGs: Heterodox discourse, orthodox policies? In P. van Bergeijk & R. van der Hoeven (Eds.), *Sustainable Development Goals and income inequality* (pp. 141–168). Edward Elgar.

Markoff, J. (2015). *Machines of loving grace: Between humans and robots.* HarperCollins.

Martin, J. P. (2014). *Activation and active labour market policies in* OECD *countries: Stylized facts and evidence on their effectiveness* (IZA policy paper No. 84). IZA.

Martin, J., & Grubb, D. (2001). What works and for whom: A review of OECD countries' experiences with active labour market policies. *Swedish Economic Policy Review, 8*(2), 9–60.

Mas, A., & Pallais, A. (2017). Valuing alternative work arrangements. *American Economic Review, 107*(12), 3722–3759.

Mateos-Garcia, J. (2019, October 7). *The economics of artificial intelligence today* [Blog post]. Retrieved from https://www.nesta.org.uk/blog/economics-artificial-intelligence-today/

Mazzucato, M. (2018). *The value of everything: making and taking in the global economy.* Allen Lane.

McAllister, A., Nylén, L., & Backhans, M. (2015). Do 'flexicurity' policies work for people with low education and health problems? A comparison of labour market policies and employment rates in Denmark, the Netherlands, Sweden, and the United Kingdom 1990–2010. *International Journal of Health Services, 45*(4), 679–705.

McCollum, D., & Findlay, A. (2015). Flexible workers for 'flexible' jobs? The labour market function of A8 migrant labour in the UK. *Work, Employment and Society, 29*(3), 427–443.

McKinsey Global Institute. (2018). *Het potentieel pakken. De waarde van meer gelijkheid tussen mannen en vrouwen op de Nederlandse arbeidsmarkt.* McKinsey & Company.

Meer, J., & Kremer, M. van der. (2018, January 17). Parkeren en investeren – Zweedse en Duitse bijstandspraktijken. Sociale Vraagstukken. Retrieved from https://www.socialevraagstukken.nl/

Meijman, T., & Zijlstra, F. (2006). Arbeid en mentale inspanning. In W. Schaufeli & A. Bakker (Eds.), *De psychologie van arbeid en gezondheid* (pp. 51–69). Bohn Stafleu van Loghum.

Melis, P. (2019, February 13). Ontwikkel geen zorg vóór, maar mét de gebruiker. *Waag.* Retrieved from https://waag.org/nl/article/ontwikkel-geen-zorg-voor-maar-met-de-gebruiker

Merens, A., & Bucx, F. (2018). *Werken aan de start.* Sociaal en Cultureel Planbureau.

Metta, G., Maresca, M., Attardi, G., Benhamou, S., & Vayatis, N. (2018). *Theme 4: The future of work: Skills for the modern economy* (Discussion paper). Presented on G7 Multistakeholder Conference on Artificial Intelligence, 6 December 2018.

Mevissen, J., Heuts, L., & van Leenen, H. (2013). *Grote dynamiek in kleinschalig ondernemerschap. De kansen van zzp-schap, in het bijzonder voor doelgroepen met afstand tot de arbeidsmarkt.* Boom Lemma.

Muller, J., Hooftmann, W., & Houtman, I. L. D. (2015). *Netherlands: Steady decline in job autonomy.* European Foundation for the Improvement of Living and Working Conditions (Eurofound).

Nakamura, H., & Zeira, J. (2018). *Automation and unemployment: help is on the way* (CEPR discussion paper No. 12974). Centre for Economic Policy Research.

NCVB [Netherlands Center for Occupational Diseases]. (2018). *Beroepsziekten in cijfers 2018.* Nederlands Centrum voor Beroepsziekten/Coronel Instituut voor Arbeid en Gezondheid, Amsterdam UMC.

Nedelkosta, L., & Quintini, G. (2018). *Automation, skills use and training* (OECD working paper). Retrieved from http://pmb.cereq.fr/doc_num.php?explnum_id=4268

Newport, C. (2016). *Deep work.* Grand Central Publishing.

NIBUD [The National Institute for Budget Information]. (2014). *Inkomenseffecten voor mantelzorgers. Wijzigingen in situatie en beleid en de effecten voor mantelzorgers.* Nibud.

Nijhuis, F., & Zijlstra, F. (2015). De arbeidsmarktpositie van mensen met een arbeidshandicap. *Tijdschrift voor Arbeidsvraagstukken, 31*(1), 81–87.

NIVEL [Netherlands Institute for Health Services Research]. (2018). *Participatiemonitor 2008–2016: Deelname aan de samenleving van mensen met een beperking en ouderen* [Tables enclosed in appendices]. Nivel.

NIVEL [Netherlands Institute for Health Services Research]. (2019). *Langer doorwerken, voor iedereen? Ontwikkelingen in de arbeidssituatie van 45- tot 75-jarigen met een chronische ziekte of lichamelijke beperking, monitor 2005–2017.* Nivel.

Nolan, B. (2018, August 3). Inequality and ordinary living standards in rich countries. *Vox*. Retrieved from https://voxeu.org

Noordegraaf, M., & Steijn, B. (2013). *Professionals under pressure: The reconfiguration of professional work in changing public services*. Amsterdam University Press.

Nordic Council of Ministers. (2018). *The Nordic future of work: Drivers, institutions, and politics*. Nordic Council of Ministers/Publication Unit.

NOS [Dutch Broadcasting Foundation]. (2016, September 22). CPB: Vaste banen verdwijnen door beleid. Retrieved from https://www.nos.nl

O'Connor, S. (2016, September 8). When your boss is an algorithm. *Financial Times*. Retrieved from https://www.ft.com

OECD. (2011). *Divided we stand: Why inequality keeps rising*. OECD Publishing.

OECD. (2014). *Mental health and work: Netherlands*. OECD Publishing.

OECD. (2015a). *Fit mind, fit job: From evidence to practice in mental health and work*. OECD Publishing.

OECD. (2015b). *Focus on minimum wages after the crisis: Making them pay*. OECD Publishing.

OECD. (2015c). Graph 4.6 - Net replacement rates of unemployment benefits in OECD countries: Net benefit relative to net income by duration of unemployment (percentages), 2012. In *Back to work: Canada: Improving the re-employment prospects of displaced workersn* (p. 117). OECD Publishing. https://doi.org/10.1787/9789264233454-graph34-en

OECD. (2015d). *In it together: Why less inequality benefits all*. OECD Publishing.

OECD. (2016a). *How good is your job? Measuring and assessing job quality*. OECD Publishing.

OECD. (2016b). *Society at a glance 2016*. OECD Publishing.

OECD. (2017). *OECD skills strategy diagnostic report: The Netherlands*. OECD Publishing.

OECD. (2018a). *Good jobs for all in a changing world of work: The OECD jobs strategy*. OECD Publishing.

OECD. (2018b). *OECD science, technology and innovation outlook 2018: Adapting to technological and societal disruption*. OECD Publishing.

OECD. (2019a). *OECD input to the Netherlands independent commission on the regulation of work*.OECD. Retrieved from https://www.rijksoverheid.nl/documenten/rapporten/2019/06/20/oecd-input-to-the-netherlands-independent-commission-on-the-regulation-of-work

OECD. (2019b). *Part-time and partly equal: Gender and work in the Netherlands*. OECD Publishing.

OECD. (2019c). *The future of work: OECD employment outlook 2019*. OECD Publishing.

OECD. (2019d). *Individual learning accounts: Panacea or Pandora's box?* OECD Publishing. https://doi.org/10.1787/203b21a8-en

Oeij, P., Rus, D., & Pot, F. (Eds.). (2017). *Workplace innovation: Theory, research and practice*. Springer.

Olivetti, C., & Petrongolo, B. (2017). The economic consequences of family policies: Lessons from a century of legislation in high-income countries. *Journal of Economic Perspectives, 31*(1), 205–230.

Oostveen, A., Klaver, A. J., & Born, M. (2019). *Versnelde participatie en integratie van vluchtelingen: de Amsterdamse aanpak* (Overarching report). Regioplan.

Osborne, S. P. (2010). The (new) public governance: A suitable case for treatment? In S. P. Osborne (Ed.), *The new public governance? Emerging perspectives on the theory and practice of public governance* (pp. 1–16). Taylor & Francis Ltd.

Osterman, P. (2018). In search of the high road: Meaning and evidence. *ILR Review, 71*(1), 3–34.

Ostry, J., Loungani, P., & Berg, A. (2019). *Confronting inequality: How societies can choose inclusive growth*. Columbia University Press.

Parent-Thirion, A., Biletta, I., Demetriades, S., Gallie, D., & Zhou, Y. (2020). *How does employee involvement in decision-making benefit organisations?* Eurofound.

Pfauth, E., Verkade, T., & Hofstede, B. (2016, April 12). Prestatiemaatschappij. Gelukkig zijn in een wereld die draait om succes. *De Correspondent*. Retrieved from https://www.decorrespondent.nl

Pfeffer, J. (2018). *Dying for a paycheck: How modern management harms employee health and company performance – and what we can do about it*. HarperCollins.

Piasna, A. (2018). Scheduled to work hard: The relationship between non-standard working hours and work intensity among European workers (2005–2015). *Human Resource Management Journal, 2018*(28), 167–181.

Pickett, K., & Wilkinson, R. (2018). *The inner level. How more equal societies reduce stress, restore sanity and improve everyone's well-being*. Penguin Books.

Pilling, D. (2018). *Growth delusion: Wealth, poverty, and the well-being of nations*. Tim Duggan Books.

Plantenga, J. (2017). Flexibel werken en de combineerbaarheid van werk en zorg. In M. Kremer, R. Went, & A. Knottnerus (Eds.), *Voor de zekerheid. De toekomst van flexibel werkenden en de moderne organisatie van arbeid* (pp. 257–273). Wetenschappelijke Raad voor het Regeringsbeleid.

Polder, J. (2017). Gezondheid werkt. *TPEdigitaal, 11*(1), 17–36.

Pollitt, C., & Bouckaert, G. (2004). *Public management reform: A comparative analysis*. Oxford University Press.

Ponce Del Castillo, A. (2017). *Artificial intelligence: A game changer for the world of work* (ETUI foresight brief No. 5). European Trade Union Institute.

Portegijs, W., & van den Brakel, M. (2016). *Emancipatiemonitor 2016*. Sociaal en Cultureel Planbureau.

Portegijs, W., & van den Brakel, M. (2018). *Emancipatiemonitor 2018*. Sociaal en Cultureel Planbureau.

Portegijs, W., Cloin, M., Roodsaz, R., & Oltshoorn, M. (2016). *Lekker vrij!? Vrije tijd, tijdsdruk en de relatie met de arbeidsduur van vrouwen*. Sociaal en Cultureel Planbureau.

Portes, J. (2018, April 6). The Economic Impacts of Immigration to the UK. *VoxEU*. Retrieved from https://voxeu.org

Pot, F. (2012). Sociale innovatie: historie en toekomstperspectief. *Tijdschrift voor Arbeidsvraagstukken, 28*(1), 6–21.

Pot, F. (2017a). Leid robotisering in goede banen. *Zeggenschap, 28*(4), 18–21.

Pot, F. (2017b). Workplace innovation and wellbeing at work. In P. Oeij, D. Rus, & F. Pot (Eds.), *Workplace innovation: Theory, research and practice* (pp. 95–110). Springer.

Pot, F. (2018a). Kortcyclische arbeid: maar sommigen zijn meer ongelijk dan anderen. *Tijdschrift voor Arbeidsvraagstukken, 34*(2), 187–199.

Pot, F. (2018b). Vlaamse sociale partners komen met actieplan: Kwaliteit van de arbeid moet omhoog. *Zeggenschap, 29*(1), 45–48.

Pot, F. (2019a). Ulbo de Sitter. Sociotechniek. In W. de Lange, P. de Prins, & B. van der Heijden (Eds.), *Canon vanHRM,. 50 theorieën over een vakgebied in ontwikkeling* (pp. 329–250). Vakmedianet.

Pot, F. (2019b). Zeggenschap over arbeid en technologie. *Tijdschrift voor Arbeidsvraagstukken, 35*(3), 236–254.

Pot, F. D., & Smulders, P. G. (2010). Kenniswerkers en kenniswerk. *ESB, 95*(4587), 365–366.

Pot, F., & Smulders, P. (2019). Arbeidskwaliteit moet een indicator voor brede welvaart zijn. *ESB, 104*(4772S), 42–54.

Pot, F., Kraan, K., & van den Bossche, S. (2009). De invloed van werk en organisatie op innovatief werkgedrag. *Tijdschrift voor Arbeidsvraagstukken, 25*(1), 44–62.

Pot, F., Totterdill, P., & Dhondt, S. (2017). European policy on workplace innovation. In P. Oeij, D. Rus, & F. Pot (Eds.), *Workplace innovation: Theory, research and practice* (pp. 11–26). Springer.

Poulissen, D., & Künn-Nelen, A. (2019, January 3). Werkgevers minder bereid tot investeren in tijdelijk personeel. *ESB*. Retrieved from https://esb.nu/kort/20047697/werkgevers-minder-bereid-tot-investeren-in-tijdelijk-personeel

Poulissen, D., Fernandez Beiro, L., Künn-Nelen, A., & Michiels, J. (2017). Arbeidsgehandicapten zijn relatief vaak onderbenut. *ESB, 102*(4749), 208–211.

Quart, A. (2018). *Squeezed: Why our families can't afford America*. HarperCollins.

Rajan, R. (2019). *The third pillar: How markets and the state leave the community behind*. Penguin Press.

Raworth, K. (2017). *Donuteconomie. In 7 stappen naar een economie voor de 21e eeuw*. Nieuw Amsterdam.

Rifkin. (1995). *The end of work: The decline of the global labor force and the dawn of the post-market era*. Putnam.

Rijksoverheid. (2015). *IBOZelfstandigen zonder personeel*. Ministerie van Financiën. Retrieved from https://www.rijksoverheid.nl/documenten/rapporten/2015/10/02/eindrapport-ibo-zelfstandigen-zonder-personeel

RIVM [The National Institute for Public Health and the Environment]. (2019). *Ziektelast in DALY's. Bijdrage risicofactoren*. Retrieved October, 2019, from https://www.volksgezondheidenzorg.info/onderwerp/ziektelast-dalys-0/bijdrage-risicofactoren

Rodrik, D. (1997). *Has globalization gone too far?* Institute for International Economics.

Rodrik, D. (2007, June 27). *The inescapable trilemma of the world economy* [Blog post]. Retrieved from https://rodrik.typepad.com/dani_rodriks_weblog/2007/06/the-inescapable.html

Rodrik, D. (2011). *The globalization paradox: Democracy and the future of the world economy*. W.W. Norton.

Rodrik, D. (2017). *Talking straight on trade: Ideas for a sane world economy*. Princeton University Press.

Rodrik, D. (2018, November 9). Reclaiming community. *Project Syndicate*. Retrieved from https://www.project-syndicate.org/commentary/economists-focus-on-markets-too-narrow-by-dani-rodrik-2018-11

Rodrik, R., & Sabel, C. (2019). Building a good jobs economy (Concept paper, version April 2019) [PDF File]. Retrieved from https://drodrik.scholar.harvard.edu/files/dani-rodrik/files/building_a_good_jobs_economy_april_2019_rev.pdf

Roeters, A. (Ed.). (2018). *Alle ballen in de lucht. Tijdsbesteding in Nederland en de samenhang met kwaliteit van leven*. Sociaal en Cultureel Planbureau.

Roeters, A., & Bucx, F. (2018). *Kijk op kinderopvang. Hoe ouders denken over de betaalbaarheid, toegankelijkheid en kwaliteit van kinderopvang*. Sociaal en Cultureel Planbureau.

Rosa, H. (2016). *Leven in tijden van versnelling. Een pleidooi voor resonantie*. Boom.

Rosenblat, A. (2018, October 12). When your boss is an algorithm. *New York Times*. Retrieved from https://www.nytimes.com

Rostgaard, T. (2014). *Family policies in Scandinavia*. Friedrich Ebert Stiftung.

Rousseau, D. M. (1990). New hire perceptions of their own and their employer's obligations: A study of psychological contracts. *Journal of Organizational Behavior, 11*, 389–400.

Rovny, A. (2011). Welfare state policy determinants of fertility level: A comparative analysis. *Journal of European Social Policy, 21*(4), 335–347.

RTL Nieuws. (2018, May 23). Bijenkorf stopt met 'gênante' beoordeling van personeel. Retrieved from https://www.rtlnieuws.nl

Ruhs, M. (2012). EU enlargement and labour migration: The UK experience. In K. Zelano (Ed.), *Labour migration: What's in it for us?* (pp. 63–120). European Liberal Forum.

Ruhs, M., & Anderson, B. (2010). *Who needs migrant workers? Labour shortages, immigration and public policy*. Oxford University Press.

Ruitenbeek, G., Mulders, H., & Zijlstra, F. (2019). Inclusief organiseren opent nieuwe perspectieven. *Sociaal Bestek, 81*(1), 46–48.

Rushkoff, D. (2019). *Team human*. W.W. Norton.

RVS [The Council of Public Health & Society]. (2019). *Blijk van vertrouwen. Anders verantwoorden van goede zorg*. Raad voor Volksgezondheid en Samenleving.

Ryder, G. (2017, August 21). Remarks by ILO Director-General Guy Ryder at the launch of the ILO Global Commission on the Future of Work [Statement]. Retrieved from https://www.ilo.org/global/about-the-ilo/how-the-ilo-works/ilo-director-general/statements-and-speeches/WCMS_570882/lang%2D%2Den/index.html

Sadiraj, K., Hoff, S., & Versantvoort, M. (2018). *Van sociale werkvoorziening naar Participatiewet.* Sociaal en Cultureel Planbureau.

Salomons, A. (2015). Hoe robots beter kunnen werken – en wij ook. In R. Went, M. Kremer, & A. Knottnerus (Eds.), *De robot de baas: de toekomst van werk in het tweede machinetijdperk* (WRR-verkenning No. 31) (pp. 131–133). Amsterdam University Press.

Schaafsma, F. G., Michon, H., Suijkerbuijk, Y., Verbeek, J. H., & Anema, J. R. (2015). *Eindrapportage kennissynthese arbeid en ernstige psychische aandoeningen.* Trimbos-Instituut.

Schaufeli, W. (2018). *Burnout in Europe. Relations with national economy, governance and culture* (Internal report). KU Leuven, Research Unit Occupational & Organizational Psychology and Professional Learning.

Schaufeli, W., & Bakker, A. (2013a). Burnout en bevlogenheid. In W. Schaufeli & A. Bakker (Eds.), *De psychologie van arbeid en gezondheid* (pp. 305–322). Bohn Stafleu van Loghum.

Schaufeli, W., & Bakker, A. (Eds.). (2013b). *De psychologie van arbeid en gezondheid.* Bohn Stafleu van Loghum.

Schaufeli, W., & Taris, T. (2013). Het Job Demands-Resources model: overzicht en kritische beschouwing. *Gedrag & Organisatie, 26*(2), 182–204.

Schaufeli, W. B., Bakker, A. B., & van Rhenen, W. (2009). How changes in job demands and resources predict burnout, work engagement, and sickness absenteeism. *Journal of Organizational Behavior, 30*(7), 893–917.

Schippers, J. (2015). De arbeidsmarkt van (over)morgen: kansen en bedreigingen. *Idee, 36*(1), 17–22.

Schippers, J. J., Kleinknecht, A., Kok, J., Ligteringen, B., & van Egmond, A. (2016). Een onvoorwaardelijk basisinkomen of een basisbaan? *Tijdschrift voor Arbeidsvraagstukken, 32*(4), 360–376.

Schiprowski, A. (2020). The role of caseworkers in unemployment insurance: Evidence from unplanned absences.. *Journal of Labor Economics.* Volume 38, no 4. Retrieved from https://www.journals.uchicago.edu/doi/pdfplus/10.1086/706092

Schmid, G. (2017). Transitional labour markets: Theoretical foundations and policy strategies. In MacMillan Publishers Ltd (Ed.), *The new Palgrave dictionary of economics* (pp. 1–15). Palgrave MacMillan.

Schuring, M., Mackenbach, J., Voorham, A. J., & Burdorf, A. (2011). The effect of re-employment on perceived health. *Journal of Epidemiology and Community Health, 65*(7), 639–644.

Schwab, K. (2019, August 7). A hospital introduced a robot to help nurses. They didn't expect it to be so popular. *Fast Company.* Retrieved from https://www.fastcompany.com

SCP [The Netherlands Institute for Social Research]. (2018, October 3). Aandeel werkende armen in Nederland gegroeid en overtreft dat van Denemarken en België. Retrieved from https://www.scp.nl/Nieuws/Aandeel_werkende_armen_in_Nederland_gegroeid_en_overtreft_dat_van_Denemarken_en_Belgie

Sebrechts, M. J. P. F. (2018). *When doing your best is not enough: Shaping recognition in sheltered workshops.* Libertas Pascal.

Sennett, R. (1986). *De flexibele mens. Psychogram van de moderne samenleving.* Byblos.

Sennett, R. (2003). *Respect, in an age of inequality.* Penguin.

Sennett, R. (2008). *The craftsman.* Penguin Books.

SEO Economisch Onderzoek [SEO Amsterdam Economics]. (2018). *The rise and growth of the gig economy in the Netherlands.* SEO Economisch Onderzoek.

SER [The Social and Economic Council of the Netherlands]. (2008). *Duurzame globalisering: een wereld te winnen.* Sociaal-Economische Raad. Retrieved from https://www.ser.nl/nl/publicaties/adviezen/2000-2009/2008/b26895.aspx

SER [The Social and Economic Council of the Netherlands]. (2016a). *Advies 16/08. Een werkende combinatie. Advies over het combineren van werken, leren en zorgen in de toekomst.* Sociaal-Economische Raad.

SER [The Social and Economic Council of the Netherlands]. (2016b). *Mens en technologie. Samen aan het werk.* Sociaal-Economische Raad.

SER [The Social and Economic Council of the Netherlands]. (2019a). *Diversiteit in de top. Tijd voor versnelling. Deel I Samenvatting & Visie raad op gender en culturele diversiteit.* Sociaal-Economische Raad.

SER [The Social and Economic Council of the Netherlands]. (2019b). *Hoge verwachtingen. Kansen en belemmeringen voor jongeren in 2019.* Sociaal-Economische Raad.

Shvartsman, E., & Beckmann, M. (2015). Stress and work Intensification: What is the influence of personnel policy? (Concept version) [PDF file]. Retrieved from http://conference.iza.org/conference_files/sums_2015/shvartsman_e21754.pdf

Siegmann, A. (2018). *De baan als basis. Een nieuwe aanpak om langdurige werkloosheid te voorkomen.* Wetenschappelijk Instituut voor het CDA.

Siegrist, J. (1996). Adverse health effects of high-effort/low-reward conditions. *Journal of Occupational Health Psychology, 1*(1), 27–41.

Silva, J. M. (2013). *Coming up short: Working-class adulthood in an age of uncertainty.* Oxford University Press.

Slot, P., Jepma, I. J., Muller, P., Romijn, B., & Leseman, P. (2017). *Landelijke kwaliteitsmonitor kinderopvang. Kwalitiet van de Nederlandse kinderdagopvang, peuteropvang, buitenschoolse opvang en gastouderopvang.* Universiteit Utrecht/Sardes.

Smits, W., & de Vries, J. (2015). Toenemende polarisatie op de Nederlandse arbeidsmarkt. *ESB. Arbeidsmarkt, 100*(4701), 24–25.

Smulders, P., & Oeij, P. (2019). Automatisering en robotisering gaan slechts beperkt samen. *ESB, 104*(4774), 267–269.

Smulders, P., & Pot, F. (2016). Aanwezigheid en effecten van medezeggenschap in Nederland. *Tijdschrift voor Arbeidsvraagstukken, 32*(2), 115–132.

Smulders, P. G. W., & van den Bossche, S. N. J. (2006). Werkdruk in Nederland en Vlaanderen vergeleken en verklaard. *Tijdschrift voor Arbeidsvraagstukken, 22*(4), 344–361.

Smulders, P., & Bossche, S. van den. (2017). 'Good & bad jobs' in Nederland. In CBS & TNO, *Dynamiek op de Nederlandse arbeidsmarkt: de focus op ongelijkheid* (pp. 197–215). CBS/TNO.

Smulders, P., Houtman, I., van Rijssen, J., & Mol, M. (2013). Burnout: trends, internationale verschillen, determinanten en effecten. *Tijdschrift voor Arbeidsvraagstukken, 29*(3), 258–278.

Snel, E. (2017). *Werkende armen in Nederland. Mens en Maatschappij, 92*(2), 175–201.

Snyder, B. (2019, March 11). Fears of job-stealing robots are misplaced, say experts. *The Robot Report.* Retrieved from https://www.therobotreport.com

Spasova, S., Baeten, R., Coster, S., Ghailani, D., Peña-Casas, R., & Vanhercke, B. (2018). *Challenges in long-term care in Europe. A study of national policies.* European Commission, European Social Policy Network.

Standing, G. (2011). *The Precariat: The new dangerous class.* Bloomsbury Academic.

Stavenuiter, M., & Oostrik, S. (2017). *Werknemerscoöperatie Schoongewoon. Resultaten enquête en groepsgesprekken.* Verwey-Jonker Instituut.

Stiglitz, J. (2002). *Globalization and its discontents.* W.W. Norton.

Stiglitz, J. (2018, December 3). GDP is not a good measure of wellbeing – it's too materialistic. *The Guardian.* Retrieved from https://www.theguardian.com

Stiglitz, J., Sen, A., & Fitoussi, J. P. (2009). *Mismeasuring our lives: Report by the Commission on Economic Performance and Social Progress.* The New York Press.

Stiglitz, J., Fitoussi, A., & Durand, M. (2018). *BeyondGDP: Measuring what counts for economic and social performance.* OECD Publishing. Retrieved from https://read.oecd-ilibrary.org/economics/beyond-gdp_9789264307292-en#page1

Stoker, J., & Garretsen, H. (2018). *Goede leiders zweven niet. De fundamenten van effectief leiderschap in organisaties en de maatschappij.* Business Contact.

Swierstra, T., & Tonkens, E. (Eds.). (2008). *De beste de baas? Prestatie, respect en solidariteit in een meritocratie.* Amsterdam University Press.

Taskforce Sociale Innovatie. (2005). *Sociale innovatie. De andere dimensie.* Ministerie van Economische Zaken.

Tates, T. (2019, January 17). Japans robothotel ontslaat helft androids wegens wanprestaties. *AD*. Retrieved from https//www.ad.nl

Taylor, M., Marsh, G., Nicol, D., & Broadbent, P. (2017). *Good Work: The Taylor Review of modern working practices* [PDF file]. Retrieved from https://www.gov.uk/government/uploads/system/uploads/attachment_data/file/627671/good-work-taylor-review-modern-working-practices-rg.pdf

Tekes. (2014). *Liideri – Business, productivity and joy at work (2012–18): Programme for the development of business through management and organisational renewal* [presentation]. Tekes.

Houte de Lange, S. ten. (2018, July 3). Broodfondsen zijn een succes, maar hoe komt dat dan?. *Sociale Vraagstukken*. Retrieved from https://www.socialevraagstukken.nl

Haar, B. ter. (2017, February 2). Sociale polarisatie, wat doen we er aan?. *Sociale vraagstukken*. Retrieved from https://www.socialevraagstukken.nl

ter Weel, B. (2018). Nieuwe technologie transformeert de vraag naar arbeid. *ESB, 103*(4766), 472–475.

The Economist. (2018, November 29). *Working for a purpose: An academic calls for an overhaul of the conventional company*. Retrieved from www.economist.com/business/2018/12/01/working-for-a-purpose

The Economist. (2019, August 10). Turn off and drop out. *The Economist*, p. 51.

Therborn, G. (2013). *The killing fields of inequality*. Polity.

Tinnemans, W. (2011). *Voor jou tien anderen. Uitbuiting aan de onderkant van de arbeidsmarkt*. Nieuw Amsterdam.

Tjeenk Willink, H. (2018). *Groter denken, kleiner doen. Een oproep*. Prometheus.

TNO. (2015). *QuickScan wetenschappelijke literatuur Gemeentelijke Uitvoeringspraktijk*. TNO.

TNO. (2016). *Arbobalans 2016. Kwaliteit van de arbeid, effecten en maatregelen in Nederland*. TNO.

TNO. (2017). *Technostress reikt verder dan alleen technologie*. TNO.

TNO. (2018). *Nationale enquête arbeidsomstandigheden*. TNO.

TNO. (2019). *Arbobalans 2018. Kwaliteit van de arbeid, effecten en maatregelen in Nederland*. TNO.

Ton, Z. (2012, January–February). Why 'good jobs' are good for retailers. *Harvard Business Review*. Retrieved from https://hbr.org

Ton, Z. (2014). *The good jobs strategy: How the smartest companies invest in employees to lower costs & boost profits*. Amazon Publishing.

Tros, F. H., Smit, E., van Houten-Pilkes, S., & van het Kaar, R. H. (2019). *Experimenteren in medezeggenschap: Evaluatie van vernieuwingsprojecten in medezeggenschap*. Amsterdams Instituut voor ArbeidsStudies.

Tummers, L., Bekkers, V., & Steijn, B. (2009). Beleidsvervreemding van publieke professionals: theoretisch raamwerk en een casus over verzekeringsartsen en arbeidsdeskundigen. *B en M, 36*(2), 104–116.

Tummers, L. G., Brunetto, Y., & Teo, S. T. T. (2016). Workplace aggression: Introduction to the special issue and future research directions for scholars. *International Journal of Public Sector Management, 29*(1), 2–10.

Tweede Kamer [The House of Representatives]. (2016). *Rapport Tijdelijke commissie Breed welvaartsbegrip* (Kamerstukken 34298, No. 3). Retrieved from https://zoek.officielebekendmakingen.nl/kst-34298-3.html

UKCES. (2014). *The future of work: Jobs and skills in 2030* (Evidence report No. 84). UK Commission for Employment and Skills.

UWV [Employee Insurance Agency]. (2015). *Flexwerk na de ww: gevolgen van flexibele arbeid voor werkzekerheid en herhalingswerkloosheid*. Uitvoeringsinstituut Werknemersverzekeringen.

V&VN [Professional Association of Nursing]. (2017). *Personeelstekorten in de zorg: oplossingen van de werkvloer*. V&VN.

Valenduc, G., & Vendramin, P. (2019). *The Mirage of the end of work* (ETUI foresight brief No. 6). Retrieved from https://www.etui.org/Publications2/Foresight-briefs/The-mirage-of-the-end-of-work

van Agteren, P.. (2017, October 26). Waarom vakbonden er nog steeds toe doen. AD. Retrieved from https://www.ad.nl

van Bergeijk, J. (2018). *Uberleven. Undercover als Uberchauffeur.* Ambo/Anthos.

van Bergeijk, P. (2019). *Deglobalization 2.0: Trade and openness during the Great Depression and the Great Recession.* Edward Elgar.

van Bergen, A. (2016). *De lessen van burn-out.* Uitgeverij Atlas Contact.

van Berkel, R., Ingold, J., McGurk, P., Boselie, P., & Bredgaard, T. (2017). Editorial introduction: An introduction to employer engagement in the field of HRM. Blending social policy and HRM research in promoting vulnerable groups' labour market participation. *Human Resource Management Journal, 27*(4), 503–513.

van den Berg, B., van den Heuts, L., van Horssen, C., & Kruis, G. (2013). *Ondersteuning van jongeren met een LVB: onderzoek naar doeltreffendere en goedkopere ondersteuning gericht op arbeidsparticipatie.* Regioplan.

van den Berg, E., van den Eldert, P., Fouarge, D., & ter Weel, B. (2018). *Taken en vaardigheden op het werk. Bevindingen uit de eerste en tweede Nederlandse skills survey.* ROA.

van den Berge, W., & ter Weel, B. (2015a). De impact van technologische verandering op de Nederlandse arbeidsmarkt, 1999–2014. In R. Went, M. Kremer, & A. Knottnerus (Eds.), *De robot de baas: de toekomst van werk in het tweede machinetijdperk* (WRR-verkenning No. 31) (pp. 89–112). Amsterdam University Press.

van den Berge, W., & ter Weel, B. (2015b). *Baanpolarisatie in Nederland* (CPB policy brief 2015, No.13). Centraal Planbureau.

van den Berge, W., Vlasblom, J. D., Ebregt, J., Putman, L., Zweerink, J., & de Graaf-Zijl, M. (2018). *Verdringing op de arbeidsmarkt. Beschrijving en beleving.* Centraal Planbureau/ Sociaal en Cultureel Planbureau.

van den Bossche, S., Muller, J., Smulders, P., & de Vroome, E. (2015). Dalende autonomie werknemers risico voor innovatiekracht. *ESB, 100*(4711), 348–350.

van den Brink, G., Jansen, T., & Pessers, D. (2005). *Beroepszeer. Waarom Nederland niet goed werkt.* Boom.

van den Broeck, A., de Cuyper, N., de Witte, H., & Vansteenkiste, M. (2010). Not all job demands are equal: Differentiating job hindrances and job challenges in the job Demands-Resources Model. *European Journal of Work and Organizational Psychology, 19*(6), 735–759.

van den Groenendaal, S. M., van Veldhoven, M., & Freese, C. (2020). *Werkintensivering van beroepen* (WRR working paper No. 37). Wetenschappelijke Raad voor het Regeringsbeleid.

van der Aa, P., Anschutz, J., & Jagmohansingh, S. (2014). *Bouwstenen voor evaluatie. Literatuurverkenning naar plausibele uitkomsten van het programma Maatschappelijke Inspanning.* Onderzoek en Business Intelligence.

van der Gaag, S. (2018). *Als je er wat op te zeggen hebt... Individuele en collectieve arbeidsrelaties van precair werkenden in beeld.* de Burcht.

van der Klaauw, B., & van Ours, J. C. (2013). Carrot and stick: How re-employment bonuses and benefit sanctions affect exit rates from welfare. *Journal of Applied Econometrics, 28*(2), 275–296.

van der Klein, M. (2017). Intermezzo: zoeken naar zekerheid, inkomen en eigen regie: de wensen van werkenden. In M. Kremer, R. Went, & A. Knottnerus (Eds.), *Voor de zekerheid. De toekomst van flexibel werkenden en de moderne organisatie* (pp. 123–130). Wetenschappelijke Raad voor het Regeringsbeleid.

van der Meer, J. (2017). De eenzame zzp'er staat niet alleen: over de nieuwe organisatie van de arbeid. In M. Kremer, R. Went, & A. Knottnerus (Eds.), *Voor de zekerheid. De toekomst van flexibel werkenden en de moderne organisatie van arbeid* (pp. 177–186). Wetenschappelijke Raad voor het Regeringsbeleid.

van der Torre, W., Lautenbach, H., van de Ven, H. A., Janssen, B. J. M., de Vroome, E. M. M., Janssen, B., et al. (2019). *Zelfstandigen Enquête Arbeid 2019. Methodologie en globale resultaten.* TNO/CBS.

202   Bibliography

Valk, S. van der, & Fenger, M. (2019, September 3). Intensief contact met bijstandsklanten: kleine stapjes naar de arbeidsmarkt. *Sociale Vraagstukken*. Retrieved from https://www.socialevraagstukken.nl

van der Veen, R. (2016). Sociale zekerheid in een open samenleving. In P. van Lieshout (Ed.), *Sociale (on)zekerheid. De voorziene toekomst* (pp. 89–112). Amsterdam University Press.

Velden, L. van der, & Polman, J. (2018, November 12). Mediamarkt gaat manieren leren. *Het Financieele Dagblad*. Retrieved from https://fd.nl

Zwan, R. van der, & Beer, P. de. (2019). Explaining the disability gap in European countries: The influence of labour market policies and public opinion towards people with disability [Paper]. Presented on the Nederlandse ArbeidsmarktDag, 10 October 2019.

van Dijk, B., van der Linde, D., van de Meerendonk, E., Buitenhuis, M., Steur, B., & van de Weijden, R. (2018). Maatschappelijk onbehagen te lijf met gedragswetenschappelijke inzichten. *ESB, 103*(4763), 314–317.

Dodeweerd, M. van. (2016). Asjemenou, de Melkertbaan is terug!. *Sprank, 9*, 20–21. Retrieved from https://www.divosa.nl/sites/default/files/sprank_bestanden/sprank-092016-asjemenou-de-melkertbaan-is-terug.pdf

van Echtelt, P. (Ed.). (2014). *Burn-out. Verbanden tussen emotionele uitputting, arbeidsmarktpositie en Het Nieuwe Werken*. Sociaal en Cultureel Planbureau.

van Echtelt, P. (2020). *Werk, zaligmakend of ziekmakend? De relatie tussen arbeid en gezondheid* (WRR working paper No. 39). Wetenschappelijke Raad voor het Regeringsbeleid.

van Echtelt, P., & de Voogd-Hamelink, M. (2017). *Arbeidsmarkt in kaart: werkgevers 2017*. Sociaal en Cultureel Planbureau.

van Echtelt, P., Croezen, S., Vlasblom, J. D., & de Voogd-Hamelink, M. (2016). *Aanbod van arbeid 2016*. Sociaal en Cultureel Planbureau.

van Echtelt, P., Sadiraj, K., Hoff, S., Muns, S., Karpinska, K., Das, D., et al. (2019a). *Eindevaluatie van de Participatiewet*. Sociaal en Cultureel Planbureau.

van Echtelt, P., Putman, L., & de Voogd-Hamelink, M. (Eds.). (2019b). *Arbeidsmarkt in kaart: werkgevers editie 2*. Sociaal en Cultureel Planbureau.

van Hoorn, A. (2015). Sociale innovatie en de concurrentiekracht van sectoren. *ESB, 100*(4702), 42–45.

van Lieshout, P. (Ed.). (2016). *Sociale (on)zekerheid. De voorziene toekomst*. Amsterdam University Press.

van Luijk, F. (2011). *Waarom werken wij? De betekenis van werken 1983–2008/2009*. Vrije Universiteit Amsterdam.

van Willigen, M. (2000). Differential benefits of volunteering across the life course. *Journal of Gerontology, 55B*(5), s308–s318.

Vandaele, K. (2018). *Will trade unions survive in the platform economy? Emerging patterns of platform workers' collective voice and representation in Europe*. European Trade Union Institute.

Veldheer, V., Jonker, J., van Noije, L., & Vrooman, C. (Eds.). (2012). *Een beroep op de burger. Minder verzorgingsstaat, meer eigen verantwoordelijkheid?: Sociaal en Cultureel Rapport 2012*. Sociaal en Cultureel Planbureau.

Vermeer, H., & Groeneveld, M. (2017). Kwaliteit van babyopvang: een literatuurstudie. In R. Fukkink (Ed.), *De Nederlandse kinderopvang in wetenschappelijk perspectief* (pp. 39–86). Uitgeverij SWP.

Versantvoort, M., & van Echtelt, P. (2016). *Beperkt in functie. Trendrapportage ziekteverzuim, arbeidsongeschiktheid en arbeidsdeelname van mensen met gezondheidsbeperkingen*. Sociaal en Cultureel Planbureau.

Verweij, R., & Stulp, G. (2019, August 29). Eerst zekerheid, dan pas kinderen. *Sociale Vraagstukken*. Retrieved from https://www.socialevraagstukken.nl

Visser, J. (2002). The first part-time economy in the world: a model to be followed? *Journal of European Social Policy, 12*(1), 23–42.

VNO-NCW. (2015, December 16). WRR Heeft Gelijk: Robots Leveren Vooruitgang En Nieuwe Banen Op. *Forum*. Retrieved from https://www.vno-ncw.nl/forum

VNO-NCW. (2018, November 30). Meer bedrijven aan de slag met Duurzame Ontwikkelings- doelen. Retrieved from https://www.vno-ncw.nl/nieuws/meer-bedrijven-aan-de-slag-met-duurzame-ontwikkelingsdoelen

Vrooman, C. (2010). Een succesvolle gedaantewisseling? De hervorming van de sociale zekerheid. 1985–2010. *Tijdschrift voor Arbeidsvraagstukken, 26*(4), 358–377.

Vrooman, J. C. (2016). *Meedoen in onzekerheid. Verwachtingen over participatie en protectie*. Universiteit Utrecht.

Vrooman, C., Josten, E., & van Echtelt, P. (2017). Weinig scholing, weinig toekomst? Mechanismen van vraag en aanbod bij laagopgeleiden. *TPEdigitaal, 11*(1), 37–61.

Vrooman, C., Josten, E., Hoff, S., Putman, L., & Wildeboer Schut, J. M. (2018). *Als werk weinig opbrengt. Werkende armen in vijf Europese landen en twintig Nederlandse gemeenten*. Sociaal en Cultureel Planbureau.

Waldring, I. E. (2018). *The fine art of boundary sensitivity: Second-generation professionals engaging with social boundaries in the workplace*. Vrije Universiteit Amsterdam.

Warhurst, C., Mathieu, C., & Wright, S. (2017). Workplace innovation and the quality of working life in an age of urbanisation. In P. Oeij, D. Rus, & F. Pot (Eds.), *Workplace innovation: Theory, research and practice* (pp. 245–259). Springer.

Warr, P. (1987). *Work, Unemployment and Mental Health*. Clarendon Press.

Warr, P. B. (2007). *Work, happiness, and unhappiness*. Lawrence Erlbaum.

Warr, P., & Clapperton, G. (2010). *The joy of work? Jobs, happiness and you*. Routledge.

Weil, D. (2014). *The fissured workplace: why work became so bad for so many and what can be done to improve it*. Cambridge University Press.

Wennekers, A., Boelhouwer, J., van Campen, C., & Kullberg, J. (2019). *De sociale staat van Nederland 2019*. Sociaal en Cultureel Planbureau.

Went, R. (2015, January 30). Hoe meten we hoe blij we zijn?. *Follow the Money*. Retrieved from https://www.ftm.nl

Went, R. (2017). Naschrift: Globalisering heeft nieuwe regels nodig. *ESB, 102*(4749), 238–239.

Went, R. (2018). Bijsturen kan en gebeurt ook. *S&D, 75*(1), 36–44.

Went, R. (2019). Een mondiale beweging "voorbij het bbp". *ESB, 104*(4772S), 28–29.

Went, R., Kremer, M., & Knottnerus, A. (2015). *De robot de baas. De toekomst van werk in het tweede machinetijdperk* (WRR-verkenning No. 31). Amsterdam University Press.

Werff, S., van der Kroon, L., & Heyma, A. (2016). Flexibele werknemers leggen relatief groot beslag op sociale zekerheid. *ESB, 101*(4744), 779–781.

Wester, J. (2017, June 19). NRC checkt: Kosten van burn-out bedragen 60.000 euro. *NRC*. Retrieved from https://www.nrc.nl

WRR [The Netherlands Scientific Council for Government Policy]. (1981). *Vernieuwingen in het arbeidsbestel*. Staatsuitgeverij.

WRR [The Netherlands Scientific Council for Government Policy]. (1990). *Een werkend perspectief. Arbeidsparticipatie in de jaren '90*. Wetenschappelijke Raad voor het Regeringsbeleid.

WRR [The Netherlands Scientific Council for Government Policy]. (2004). *Bewijzen van goede dienstverlening*. Wetenschappelijke Raad voor het Regeringsbeleid.

WRR [The Netherlands Scientific Council for Government Policy]. (2007). *Investeren in werkzekerheid*. Amsterdam University Press.

WRR [The Netherlands Scientific Council for Government Policy]. (2013a). *Naar een lerende economie. Investeren in het verdienvermogen van Nederland*. Amsterdam University Press.

WRR [The Netherlands Scientific Council for Government Policy]. (2013b). *Toezien op publieke belangen. Naar een verruimd perspectief op rijkstoezicht*. Amsterdam University Press.

WRR [The Netherlands Scientific Council for Government Policy]. (2017). *Weten is nog geen doen. Een realistisch perspectief op redzaamheid*. Wetenschappelijke Raad voor het Regeringsbeleid.

Wielers, R., & Koster, F. (2011). Welvaart en arbeidsmotivatie: een internationale vergelijking. *Tijdschrift voor Arbeidsvraagstukken, 27*(1), 9–24.

Wielers, R., van der Meer, P., & Willems, M. (2018). Ongelijkheid en zelfrespect: het effect van inkomen en arbeidspositie. *Tijdschrift voor Arbeidsvraagstukken, 34*(2), 221–237.

Wiezer, N., Schelvis, R., van Zwieten, M., Kraan, K., van der Klauw, M., Houtman, I., et al. (2012). *Werkdruk*. TNO.

Wilkinson, R., & Pickett, K. (2009). *The spirit level: Why equality is better for everyone*. Penguin Books.

Wilthagen, T. (2019). *Een radicale ommezwaai van de arbeidsmarkt* (Participatielezing 2019) [PDF file]. Retrieved from https://www.movisie.nl/sites/movisie.nl/files/2019-03/190307%20 presentatie%20Ton%20Wilthagen.pdf

Woittiez, I., & Putnam, L. (2016). Op weg naar werk. *TPEdigitaal, 10*(1), 27–36.

Woittiez, I., Putman, L., Eggink, E., & Ras, M. (2014). *Zorg beter begrepen*. Sociaal en Cultureel Planbureau.

Woutersen, E. (2019). *Uitgebuit. Het verhaal van de Nederlandse werkvloer*. Atlas Contact.

Xavier, M., & Pot, F. (2012). *Doorgeven = aanpakken. Tussenstand van 10 jaar sociale innovatie*. NCSI.